Basic
Legal Writing
for
Paralegals

Basic
Legal Writing
for
Paralegals

Hope Viner Samborn
Loyola University Chicago

Andrea B. Yelin
Loyola University Chicago

PUBLISHERS

Library of Congress Catalog Card No. 96-077253

ISBN 0-7355-0619-1

5   6   7   8   9   0

MV-NY

 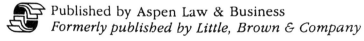

Published by Aspen Law & Business
Formerly published by Little, Brown & Company

Printed in the United States of America

To my loving and supportive family and friends: You have helped me to accomplish my goals and dreams by giving me your love, your energy, and your friendship. Thank you, all, especially my husband Randy, my children Eve and Sarah, and my cousins Marc, David, Becky, and Linda, who push me to do what I love to do — write.

HVS

In memory of my grandparents.

ABY

Summary of Contents

Table of Contents

---

4. Writing Fundamentals   43

Part II   59

5. Briefing Cases   61

6. The Legal Memorandum   79

9. The IRAC Method   127

13.   In-House and Objective Client Documents   229

List of Illustrations

Preface

The Role of the Paralegal in Legal Writing

Legal writing is one of the tasks paralegals must learn to perform efficiently and cost effectively for law firms and their clients. But to do so, paralegals must understand the legal system and legal writing techniques. Objective memos must be drafted to inform the attorney of all the relevant law, both for and against the client's position, so that the attorney can best handle the matter. Paralegals also brief cases to expedite the research process, as well as write persuasive documents and draft complaints and answers in litigation matters. Delegating the task of writing an objective memo to the paralegal is cost effective for the attorney and saves the client money.

The Purpose and Structure of this Text

Basic Legal Writing for Paralegals guides the student and the practicing paralegal through the writing process in a step-by-step manner using the objective memo as a teaching tool. The text also introduces persuasive writing and instruments and documents drafted by legal assistants. In addition, the book contains information about grammar and organization and serves as a reference manual for any legal assistant who has to produce a written document.

Objective writing is explored in great detail. Mastering objective writing requires developing the ability to articulate legal concepts and to draft documents in a manner reflecting legal analysis. Learning to perform legal analysis and to organize a legal discussion is the basis of objective writing. Much time must be spent to refine and to master these skills. Only after a foundation has been built on objective writing skills can other forms of legal writing be learned.

The book begins with an overview of the legal system and then discusses case briefing. Understanding how our legal system operates and knowing how to read and to brief legal opinions is an essential prerequisite to effective legal writing. You are guided through the concept of the objective memo and its purpose. The next chapter discusses the question presented and the conclusion or brief answer. The facts and drafting the statement of the facts are explored in a separate chapter where you will learn to identify legally significant facts. The IRAC method is then introduced. IRAC, an acronym for Issue, Rule, Application, and Conclusion, is the format for the discussion portion of the memo. Building on the skills that you have acquired, you are then introduced to the task of synthesizing cases and authorities. Synthesis requires you to distill the general legal concept and then to create a statement of the law using more than one case or statute. These chapters are very detailed because you are also being taught legal reasoning and legal analysis. After you master these skills, other forms of legal writing are easier to master. The rest of the text discusses writing documents, persuasive writing, and letter writing.

Basic Legal Writing for Paralegals is designed to be both a handbook and a textbook, and therefore helps you develop your writing skills now and in the future. You will learn to convey the results of your research in written documents, and to articulate legal concepts to convey information, to answer a question, or to craft a persuasive argument. These skills require attention to detail, keen analysis, and precision with language. Legal writing skills are developed through practice; often the best writing is done in revision.

You should view this book as a launching point in developing your legal writing skills. Refer to the guidelines and concepts in this book throughout your career as you hone your writing skills.

Acknowledgments

We would like to thank the special people who assisted us in creating this text and molding its contents.

Thank you to Jean Hellman, director of the Loyola University of Chicago Institute for Paralegal Students, for all of your encouragement and support. Jean has provided us both with an opportunity to teach, and led us to Little, Brown and Company.

We are also grateful for the help our students and colleagues provided us in shaping the exercises. Some students who deserve special thanks for their critiques and suggestions include Amy Berezinski, Nanette Boryc, Mara Castello, Patricia Cochran, Beverly Dombroski, Cheryl Morgan, Patricia Naqvi, Shay Robertson, Louise Tessitore, and Amy Widmer.

Thank you also to Carolyn O'Sullivan, Betsy Kenny, Lisa Wehrle, Joan Horan, Katie Byrne Butcher, and John Lyman of Little, Brown and Company for their time, their counsel, and their expertise. We will always be indebted to Carolyn for getting us started on this project and *The Legal Research and Writing Handbook,* our first book. We are sorry she was unable to complete this project with us. And although Lisa did not work directly with this book, we appreciate how much her major contribution to *The Legal Research and Writing Handbook* helped to shape the words of this book.

To the Loyola Law School Library, particularly Lev Preble and Bob Doyle, thank you.

Thanks to Susan Bodie for assistance with the typing.

Finally, thank you to both of our families. Randy, Eve, and Sarah, and the rest of my extended family, I will always be indebted to you for providing me with support, love, and the time to do this project.

Thanks to David, Rachel, and Henry, and to Andrea's parents, for all of your love and support.

Thanks to West Publishing Company for their kind permission to reprint a case and a statute.

We would also like to thank the reviewers listed below. Their careful review of the manuscript produced many valuable comments and suggestions. We greatly appreciate their efforts.

Laura Barnard	Lakeland Community College
Brenda L. Rice, J.D.	Johnson County Community College
Joy O'Donnell	Pima Community College
Eric Olson	Barry University

Holly L. Enterline	State Technical Institute at Memphis
Kay Y. Rute	Washburn University
Sy Littman	Platt College
Paul Klein	Duquesne University
Adelaide Lagnese	University of Maryland
Robin O. McNeely	McNeese State University

Basic
Legal Writing
for
Paralegals

Part I.

1. The Legal System

CHAPTER OVERVIEW

Before you begin to research and to write about a legal problem, you must know which legal system governs and how that system operates. This chapter discusses the organization of the United States federal government, which is divided into three separate branches: the legislative, the executive, and the judicial. It also provides a general explanation of how state governments are structured. Finally, the role of major governmental bodies is explored.

A. Introduction to the U.S. Legal System

How Is the Legal System Organized in the United States?

The United States consists of a multitiered system of government. The **federal government** and the **state governments** are the top two tiers. See Illustration 1-1.

Several lower-tier governmental bodies, including **city** and **county governments,** exercise authority over the citizens of the United States. For the most part, your research will concern either federal or state law. Therefore, this book focuses its discussion on the federal and state systems. The knowledge of these systems, the type of law they generate, and how to find legal standards for these systems later can be applied to any research you plan to do concerning other government bodies and the law they generate.

ILLUSTRATION 1-1.   *U.S. and State Government Systems*

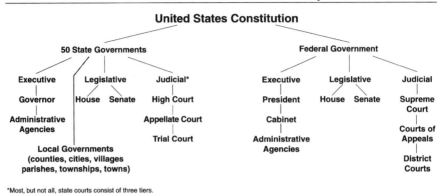

*Most, but not all, state courts consist of three tiers.

How Did the Federal and State Systems Originate?

Representatives of the states adopted a **constitution** for the United States that is the framework for the operation of this federal/state system of government. To that end, the U.S. Constitution creates three branches of government and defines their powers. The Constitution reserves for the states all of the remaining powers. In addition, the Constitution establishes the rules for the relationship between the federal and state governments. The U.S. Constitution is the supreme law of the United States. For example, Congress, the legislative body of the federal government, cannot enact a law that is contrary to the U.S. Constitution. The state legislatures similarly are prevented from adopting laws that violate provisions of the U.S. Constitution. You can think of the Constitution as an umbrella over all of the United States' governing bodies.

B. Components of the Federal System and Governing Law

What Bodies Comprise the U.S. Government, and What Body of Law Defines Their Relationship to Each Other?

The federal government consists of three branches of government: the legislative, the executive, and the judicial. The U.S. Constitution created each branch and defines the relationship between them. The Constitution establishes a system in which each branch of government can monitor the activities of the other branches to prevent abuses.

1. The Legislative Branch

What Government Bodies Are Part of the Legislative Branch, and What Do They Do?

The **legislative branch** of the federal government is called the **Congress**. It is comprised of two houses or chambers called the **Senate** and the **House of Representatives**. The Congress creates laws called **statutes**. Some statutes are new rules of law. Other statutes supersede or codify court-made law, commonly referred to as case law or the common law. The statutes and the U.S. Constitution comprise a body of law called **enacted law**.

How Is a Statute Created?

Anyone can propose that Congress adopt a new law, and either chamber can introduce a law for consideration. When a proposed law is introduced, it is called a **bill**. Before the bill can become a law, both chambers must approve it. If both houses approve the same version of the bill, it is sent to the President. The President can sign or veto the bill or withhold action on it. If the President signs the bill, it becomes law. If the President does not act within ten days and the legislative session is still in progress, the bill becomes law. If the President vetoes the bill, Congress may override the veto by a two-thirds majority vote of each house.

If the President fails to act on the bill within the ten days and the legislature is out of session, the bill does not become law. This action is called a **pocket veto**.

2. The Executive Branch

What Comprises the Executive Branch?

The **executive branch** of the government includes the President as well as some **federal administrative agencies**. See Illustration 1-2.

The President is the country's top executive. The President has the authority to control many administrative agencies.

What Are Administrative Agencies, and What Duties Do They Have?

Administrative agencies enforce many of the laws of the United States. These agencies are responsible for the daily regulation of activities controlled by federal law. For a listing of some of the many administrative agencies, see Illustration 1-2.

ILLUSTRATION 1-2. *The Government of the United States*

THE CONSTITUTION

LEGISLATIVE BRANCH

THE CONGRESS

Senate   House

Architect of the Capitol
United States Botanic Garden
General Accounting Office
Government Printing Office
Library of Congress
Office of Technology Assessment
Congressional Budget Office
Copyright Royalty Tribunal

EXECUTIVE BRANCH

THE PRESIDENT

Executive Office of the President

White House Office
Office of Management and Budget
Council of Economic Advisors
National Security Council
Office of the U.S. Trade
  Representative

National Critical Materials Council
Council on Environmental Quality
Office of Science and Technology
  Policy
Office of Administration
Office of National Drug Control Policy

THE VICE PRESIDENT

JUDICIAL BRANCH

The Supreme Court of the United States
United States Courts of Appeals
United States District Courts
United States Sentencing Commission
United States Court of International Trade
Territorial Courts
United States Court of Military Appeals
United States Court of Veterans Appeals
Administrative Office of the
  United States Courts
Federal Judicial Center
United States Tax Court

DEPARTMENT OF AGRICULTURE	**DEPARTMENT OF COMMERCE**	**DEPARTMENT OF DEFENSE**
DEPARTMENT OF THE INTERIOR	**DEPARTMENT OF JUSTICE**	**DEPARTMENT OF LABOR**

DEPARTMENT OF EDUCATION	**DEPARTMENT OF ENERGY**	**DEPARTMENT OF HEALTH AND HUMAN SERVICES**
DEPARTMENT OF STATE	**DEPARTMENT OF TRANSPORTATION**	**DEPARTMENT OF THE TREASURY**

DEPARTMENT OF HOUSING AND URBAN DEVELOPMENT

DEPARTMENT OF VETERANS AFFAIRS

INDEPENDENT ESTABLISHMENTS AND GOVERNMENT CORPORATIONS

ACTION
Administrative Conference of the U.S.
African Development Foundation
Central Intelligence Agency
Commission on Civil Rights
Commission on National and Community Service
Commodity Futures Trading Commission
Consumer Product Safety Commission
Defense Nuclear Facilities Safety Board
Environmental Protection Agency
Equal Employment Opportunity Commission
Export–Import Bank of the U.S.
Farm Credit Administration
Federal Communications Commission
Federal Deposit Insurance Corporation
Federal Election Commission

Federal Emergency Management Agency
Federal Housing Finance Board
Federal Labor Relations Authority
Federal Maritime Commission
Federal Mediation and Conciliation Service
Federal Mine Safety and Health Review Commission
Federal Reserve System
Federal Retirement Thrift Investment Board
Federal Trade Commission
General Services Administration
Inter–American Foundation
Interstate Commerce Commission
Merit Systems Protection Board
National Aeronautics and Space Administration
National Archives and Records Administration
National Capital Planning Commission

National Credit Union Administration
National Foundation on the Arts and the Humanities
National Labor Relations Board
National Mediation Board
National Railroad Passenger Corporation (Amtrak)
National Science Foundation
National Transportation Safety Board
Nuclear Regulatory Commission
Occupational Safety and Health Review Commission
Office of Government Ethics
Office of Personnel Management
Office of Special Counsel
Panama Canal Commission
Peace Corps
Pennsylvania Avenue Development Corporation
Pension Benefit Guaranty Corporation

Postal Rate Commission
Railroad Retirement Board
Resolution Trust Corporation
Securities and Exchange Commission
Selective Service System
Small Business Administration
Tennessee Valley Authority
Thrift Depositor Protection Oversight Board
Trade and Development Agency
U.S. Arms Control and Disarmament Agency
U.S. Information Agency
U.S. International Development
  Cooperation Agency
U.S. International Trade Commission
U.S. Postal Service

Are Administrative Agencies Created and Empowered by the U.S. Constitution?

No. Congress created the agencies and delegated some of its own power to them because it alone is unable to handle the day-to-day enforcement of the overwhelming number of federal laws. Agencies, however, have the staff and often the technical expertise to deal with the daily enforcement of Congress's enacted laws. To do this, agencies often make rules that explain in detail how individuals should act to comply with congressional mandates. In some cases, agencies hold hearings to enforce the law.

For example, Congress enacted the Consumer Product Safety Act and delegated its enforcement power to the U.S. Consumer Product Safety Commission. Congress charged the commission with the responsibility for the daily enforcement of that act. As part of the commission's duties, it adopts rules or regulations. It also has administrative hearings, which often result in decisions.

3. The Judicial Branch

What Is the Federal Court System, and What Are Its Duties?

The third branch of government is the judicial system. The judicial system includes three levels of courts that resolve disputes. See Illustration 1-3.

The entry-level court is the **trial court.** In the federal system, this court is called the **district court.** In that court, disputes are heard and decided by either a judge or a jury. This court also hears appeals from some administrative agencies and the federal bankruptcy courts. Some administrative agency decisions, however, are appealed directly to the **appellate courts.**

Who Can Bring an Action in Federal Court?

Litigants can present a case to the federal court if the issue concerns federal law or if the dispute is between parties of different states. Cases in which both the plaintiff, who is the party bringing the lawsuit, and the defendant are citizens of different states are called diversity cases. For cases that involve state law questions, the amount in dispute must exceed $50,000.

What Do the Trial Courts Do?

These courts decide disputes when a party (which can be a person, corporation, or other entity) brings an action against another party.

In such cases, the trial courts often are asked to interpret congressional enactments such as statutes, ordinances, charters, or executive branch-created laws including agency rules or decisions. When a court interprets a statute or regulation, it is overseeing the actions of other government branches. Courts often consult a body of law called the "common law" before rendering any decisions. **Common law** is court-created law found in the judicial opinions or cases; it is not found in the statutes.

What Happens When a Party Is Unhappy with a Trial Court Decision?

The federal trial courts' decisions can be appealed to one of the 13 **federal appeals courts** known as the U.S. Courts of Appeals. This is the second tier of courts in the federal system. See Illustration 1-3. The circuits are geographic, except for the Federal Circuit. See Illustration 1-4. These courts only decide issues of law posed in appeals of trial court decisions. These courts do not consider new factual evidence. An excellent source of information about the federal

ILLUSTRATION 1-3. *Federal Judicial System*

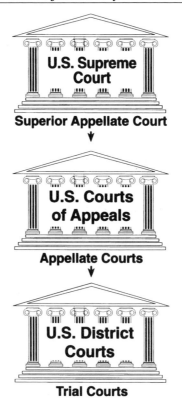

ILLUSTRATION 1-4. *Circuit Map of the U.S. Courts of Appeal*

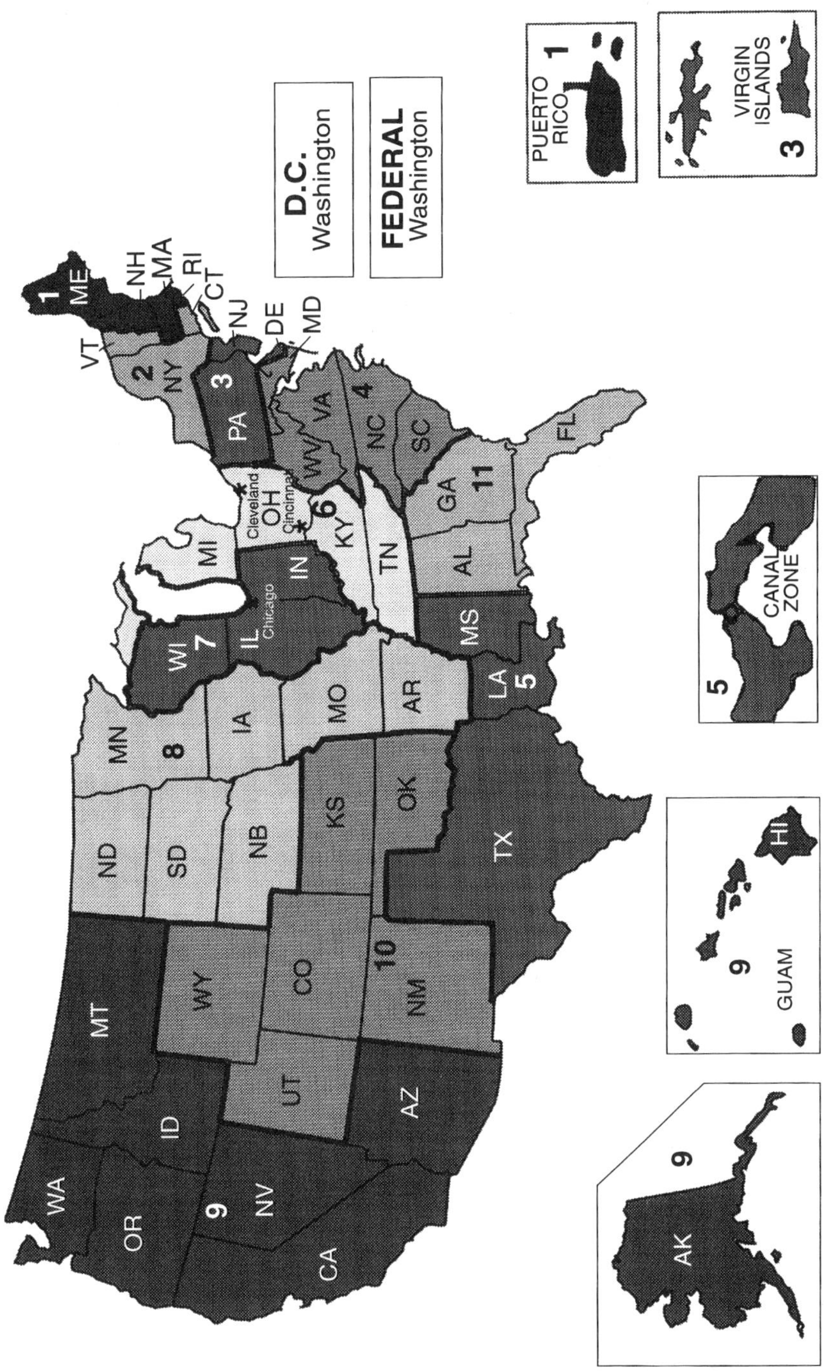

courts, their boundaries, and the names and phone numbers of the courts and their officials is *BNA's Directory of State and Federal Courts, Judges and Clerks,* published and regularly updated by the Bureau of National Affairs.

Can an Intermediate Federal Appellate Court Decision be Appealed to a Higher Court?

Yes, such a decision can be appealed to the U.S. Supreme Court.

What Is the U.S. Supreme Court, and What Does It Do?

The **U.S. Supreme Court** is the highest court in the United States. See Illustration 1-3. The U.S. Constitution establishes this court. Today nine justices, appointed by the President and confirmed by the U.S. Senate, sit on this tribunal. The U.S. Supreme Court has discretion to consider many issues. This discretion is called **certiorari.** If the court decides not to hear an issue, it denies certiorari; if the court decides to hear an issue, it grants certiorari. By law, this court alone has the authority to hear appeals of a state court of last resort decision when a substantial federal constitutional issue is presented. The U.S. Supreme Court also may hear a dispute between two states.

Can a Federal Court Decide an Issue of State Law?

Yes. A federal court can decide an issue of state law if the state issue is presented with a related federal issue or if the state question is raised in a dispute between parties of different states in a complete diversity action.

What Effect Does a Federal Decision Have on State Law?

A federal court decision generally cannot change state law. It may persuade the state courts to review state law, but its decision usually does not force any change in the law. Because states are separate sovereigns, usually only the state governing bodies can change state law. One exception to this rule does exist. The U.S. Supreme Court can determine whether state law violates the U.S. Constitution. If such a violation is found, the decision of the U.S. Supreme Court would invalidate state law.

C. Organization of State Government

Are Federal and State Agencies Part of One Governing Body?

No. The federal government is one sovereign or governing body. That means that the state cannot control the federal government agencies or change federal law. The state government is a separate governing body from the federal government. In general, the federal government branches cannot control the state government or change state law. However, the U.S. Constitution, the umbrella, can limit actions of the state government. The Constitution prohibits the states from making any laws that are contrary to its provisions.

Are the State Governments Organized Like the Federal Government?

Most state governments are organized in a manner similar to that of the federal government. State governments are governed by constitutions. That constitution defines the organization of the state's government and the relationship between the branches of government. The states have legislative, executive, and judicial branches.

The legislative branches operate in a manner similar to that of Congress. Some legislatures enact enabling laws that create administrative agencies and provide such agencies with the responsibility for the daily enforcement of state laws. The chief executive in each state is a governor.

Each state has a judicial system. However, not all state systems mirror the federal government's three-tier court system. Each state establishes which courts can hear different disputes. Some states have a three-tier system similar to that of the federal judicial branch. In some states, the intermediate appellate court is eliminated. The following systems do not include an intermediate appellate court: Delaware, District of Columbia, Maine, Mississippi, Montana, Nevada, New Hampshire, Rhode Island, South Dakota, Vermont, West Virginia, Wyoming, and Puerto Rico.

Are the Duties of the State Courts Similar to Those of Their Federal Counterparts?

In most state court systems, a trial court determines the facts and legal issues of a case. This court might include a family court and a municipal or small claims court. The jurisdiction of these courts is generally limited, sometimes according to the amount of money in dispute.

The next level generally is an appellate level court. However, as noted above, some states do not have this level. As in the federal court system, this court does not hear new facts or evidence. Instead, it decides whether the lower court erred in deciding substantive law or procedural issues. Finally, most states have another appellate level court, similar to the U.S. Supreme Court, which is the final arbiter of disputes.

Can State Courts Decide Issues of Federal Law?

Yes, state courts can decide issues of federal law.

If a State Court Decides an Issue of Federal Law, What Effect Does It Have?

A state court decision concerning federal law does not change the federal law. However, it may persuade federal governing bodies to change federal law. The state court decision's impact is limited to the case in which the federal issue was presented.

The federal government controls all issues of federal law. The state governments exercise authority over all issues of state law. These areas are not always well defined. In some areas, both the state and federal government exercise authority. For example, both the state and federal governments control how industries dispose of their wastes. Do not be discouraged if you have difficulty separating state and federal issues in some cases.

CHAPTER SUMMARY

In this chapter, you learned about the branches of the U.S. government and their functions, as well as the general structure of the state governments. The United States has three branches of government: the legislative, the executive, and the judicial. All of these branches were created by the U.S. Constitution, which guides their activities. In addition, administrative agencies enforce the laws created by the legislature.

The legislature, which consists of the House of Representatives and the Senate, creates laws called statutes. The executive branch enforces the laws of the United States, and the judicial branch resolves disputes and interprets the laws.

The judicial branch is comprised of a three-tier court system. The highest court is the U.S. Supreme Court; the middle courts are the U.S. Courts of Appeals; the trial or lowest courts are the U.S. District Courts. All three branches of government create law. Law created by these bodies is considered primary authority.

Key Terms

Appellate courts
Bill
Certiorari
City government
Common law
Congress
Constitution
County government
District court
Enacted law
Executive branch
Federal administrative agencies

Federal appeals court
Federal government
House of Representatives
Judicial branch
Legislative branch
Pocket veto
Senate
State government
Statutes
Supreme Court
Trial court
Veto

2. What Law Governs

CHAPTER OVERVIEW

In researching legal issues, you must have goals and understand the value of the legal authorities you will find. This chapter will explain the concept of legal authority and the determination of governing law, as well as discuss the value of various authorities and how authorities interrelate with each other. You will learn which authorities should determine the outcome of a case and which authorities will merely provide persuasive support for a case.

A. Determination of Governing Law

How Do You Determine What Law Governs Your Case?

To determine what law controls your case, you must determine the jurisdiction.

1. Jurisdiction

What Is Jurisdiction?

Jurisdiction is a complex concept. For purposes of determining what law governs, you can think of jurisdiction as the right of a court to interpret and apply the law to a particular case. When a court or a governing body has jurisdiction over a case or situation, it has the authority to control the case or outcome of the situation.

What Factors Determine What Jurisdiction Governs Your Case, and Should You Make That Determination?

A variety of factors can affect which jurisdiction governs a claim in a particular case, including where the dispute arose, the parties involved in the case, and the nature of the dispute. Sometimes making this determination is a complex task. Ask the assigning attorney to assist you in making this determination.

2. Hierarchy of Authority

After You Have Determined the Jurisdiction, How Do You Determine What Cases or Laws Control the Outcome of Your Research Issue?

First, determine which authority is most current. Second, consider the level of each authority. Then, determine the highest legal authority regarding a claim. To make this determination, you must consider the **hierarchy of authority.**

What Is the Hierarchy of Legal Authorities?

This is a system in which legal authorities such as court decisions, statutes, administrative rules and decisions, and constitutions are ranked according to the effect they have in controlling the law of a governing body.

How Does This Determination Work in Practice?

Determining the hierarchy of authorities is based in part on the nature of the case, the currency of an authority, and the structure of the court system. For example, if you find that the law that governs your case is a federal law and the case involves a question of federal constitutional law, the highest legal authority would be the U.S. Constitution because the Constitution is the supreme law of the United States.

In another case that does not involve a constitutional issue, a federal statute might be the highest authority. This would depend on whether a court had interpreted the statute. If a federal court had interpreted the statute's language and that language affected the issue involved in your case, you need to determine whether the court decision or the statute is more recent. The most current authority would be the highest authority.

Example

Your case involves a statute that was enacted on December 1, 1994. All of the court cases you have found that may have a bearing on this case were decided before December 1, 1994. Therefore, the statute — the most current authority — is the highest authority concerning this issue.

Courts often are asked to interpret statutes or enacted laws that are vague and ambiguous. The courts also must follow the law enacted by the Congress. The same principle is true in the state systems.

For some cases, you must consider the level of the court to determine the hierarchy of authority. For example, a decision of the highest court, the U.S. Supreme Court, would be at the top of the hierarchy of authorities of court decisions.

Do Decisions of the Federal Trial Courts, Appellate Courts, and the U.S. Supreme Court Carry the Same Weight?

No. The decisions of the courts are ranked according to a system that is called the legal hierarchy of authority.

Within the Federal System, How Does This Hierarchy Operate?

Except for the U.S. Supreme Court, all of the federal courts are within defined groups called **circuits.** Within each circuit is a group of district courts and one circuit court of appeals. The key to the relationship between the federal courts is that the district courts, which are the entry-level courts, must follow decisions of the U.S. Circuit Court of Appeals within its circuit. A district court does not have to follow decisions of appellate courts that are outside of its circuit. Two examples of how such a hierarchical ranking would work in practice follow.

The U.S. District Court for the Northern District of Illinois, which is in Chicago, falls in the Seventh Circuit and is outside of the Sixth Circuit. See Illustration 1-4. If the federal district court in Illinois was asked to determine whether federal law permitted a union to charge a fee to nonmembers for activities that benefit nonmembers, it would be bound to follow any U.S. Seventh Circuit Court of Appeals decision concerning this issue. This is because this appellate court is a higher court than the district court. But the

Illinois district court would not have to follow decisions of the
U.S. Sixth Circuit Court of Appeals in Cincinnati concerning the
above issue.

The U.S. District Court for the Northern District of Ohio,
based in Cleveland, falls within the Sixth Circuit. See Illustration
1-4. That district court must follow decisions of the Sixth Circuit
appellate court rather than the decisions of the Seventh Circuit
Court of Appeals in Chicago.

Can Decisions of Courts Concerning the Same Issue Differ Between Circuits?

Yes. Each circuit is independent of the other circuits. The appellate
courts are all on the same level. Therefore, the decisions of these courts
carry the same amount of weight in impacting federal law. Each appellate
court can make its decision independent of any decision concerning the
same issue rendered by another appellate court. Often, however, one
appellate court will be guided in its decision by the decision of another
appellate court.

If Two Appellate Courts Have Conflicting Decisions Concerning the Same Issue, How Can You as Researchers Decide What Law Governs?

In some cases, the U.S. Supreme Court will decide such issues. A
decision of the Supreme Court—the highest level of court—will be at
the top of the hierarchy of authority.

How Does the Hierarchy of Authority Work When You Have Both State and Federal Decisions Concerning an Issue?

The key is to determine which court has jurisdiction or the right to
hear the case. The court systems of the state and federal governments
operate in tandem. As explained above, the federal courts may decide
issues of both federal or state law. For example, a diversity case may
involve a negligence issue. This is a state law issue. The federal courts
must look to decisions of the highest court of the state to make a
determination of state law.[1] The federal court decision, however, does
not bind later state court decisions.

State courts also may decide issues of either federal or state law.
For instance, a plaintiff may bring an age discrimination case based on
both the state and federal age discrimination in employment statutes.
State courts will look to federal courts for guidance in deciding issues
of federal law. However, they are not bound to follow those decisions.

---

1. For a more complete discussion of this point, see Charles A. Wright, *The Law of Federal
Courts* (4th ed. 1983).

Does the Authority of the Federal and State
Governments Ever Conflict?

Yes. Although the federal and state governments are independent
governments, they sometimes regulate some of the same areas, such as
environmental pollution and securities. They operate in tandem. In some
cases, the federal government by congressional action will control an
area extensively, and a state will attempt to monitor the same area.
Who controls varies.

The federal courts sometimes are asked to decide who controls. For
example, if a case involves a section of the U.S. Constitution, the U.S.
Supreme Court is the final authority. In other cases, it depends on the
area being regulated.

B. Court Decisions

When the Highest Court of One State Decides an
Issue, Must the State Court in Another State Follow
That Decision?

No. Each group of state courts is a separate court system. State
courts of one state do not have to follow decisions made by courts of
other states. For example, New York courts do not have to follow
decisions of the Illinois Supreme Court. Often, however, state courts
will consider other court decisions for guidance in how to decide a
case. That is because decisions of other states are merely advisory or
persuasive decisions, not decisions that can impact the law of another
state.

1. Precedent

How Do You Understand a Court Decision and Its
Impact on a Case?

You already have learned that the courts generate decisions or cases
that are law. The basic rule of law decided by the court is the **holding.**
If the court is presented with more than one issue, the decision will
include more than one holding. The holding also is called the **precedent.**

Why Is Precedent Important?

Theoretically, the lower courts must follow decisions or precedents
of the higher courts in their jurisdiction. The theory is called **stare
decisis.** The idea behind it is that parties should be able to rely on what

the courts have done in the past. Doing so allows parties to predict how a court is likely to rule in their cases.

The doctrine of stare decisis makes your job as researchers important. You must determine what the courts have decided in the past in order to assist the attorneys in predicting what the court is likely to do, or likely to be persuaded to do, in your case. Sometimes a court will not follow precedent. Even though stare decisis and precedent are the controlling doctrines, courts decide cases based on the facts before them and the changes in society. This allows the law, through the holdings, to evolve and to meet contemporary needs.

2. Dicta

Does Every Statement Made in a Court Decision Have the Force of Law?

No. Often, a court will address an issue that is not directly presented by the parties. In such cases, a court will state what it would do if it was presented directly with the issue. When the court makes such a statement, it is called **dicta**. Dictum does not have the same force and effect as a holding. It is not authoritative, and lower courts are not bound to follow such statements.

If Dicta Is Not Binding, Why Is It Important?

You might use dicta when no court has ever been asked directly to decide the issue addressed in the dicta. The dicta explains how the court would decide the issue if it was directly presented to the court. Because of this, the dicta might help you to predict how a court might decide an issue. Dicta also can be used to persuade a court to decide an issue in a certain manner. Although dicta may be helpful, finding dicta is not the goal of your research.

C. Goal of Your Research

What Is the Goal of Your Research?

Your task is to find primary authority "on point" or "on all fours" with your case, in other words, cases that are similar in fact and in legal issue to your case and whose holding addresses an issue presented in your case.

1. Primary Authority

What Is Primary Authority?

Primary authority is law generated by a government body. Cases decided by any court are primary authority. Legislative enactments such as constitutions, statutes, ordinances, or charters are primary authorities. See Illustration 2-1. Administrative agency rules and decisions are primary authorities.

These authorities often are published chronologically. However, statutes are arranged by subject. Some sources of primary authorities will be more appropriate for your research than others. In some cases, primary authority is **mandatory** or **binding authority** because a government body must follow that authority when it makes future decisions.

How Do You Determine Whether a Case Is Mandatory or Binding Authority?

To determine whether a case is mandatory or binding, you must consider the rank of the authorities. Follow the steps below.

1. Determine the jurisdiction that applies to your case. Then, look to the hierarchy of the courts within that jurisdiction.
2. Note what court decided the case you are reviewing.
3. Determine whether this is a court within the jurisdiction that applies to your case.
4. If the court is within the appropriate jurisdiction, next you must determine the level of that court within the court system. Is it a trial court or an appellate court? Is it the highest court of the system? States often have rules that specify the effect of a court decision on other courts within the same system. In general, the lower courts in a system must follow the decisions of the highest

ILLUSTRATION 2-1. *Authorities and Finding Tools*

Primary Authorities	*Secondary Authorities*	*Finding Tools*
Court decisions	Encyclopedias	Digests
Statutes	American Law Reports	Citators
Agency rules and regulations	Periodicals and law reviews	Updaters
Constitutions	Dictionaries	Annotated statutes
Charters	Thesauri	
Ordinances	Model codes	
Adopted pattern jury instructions	Unadopted uniform laws	
	Treatises	
Court rules	Restatements of the Law	

court in the system. The rules concerning which courts must follow the decisions of the intermediate-tier courts vary by jurisdiction. Consult the rules for that jurisdiction.

Is All Primary Authority Mandatory or Binding?

No. Some primary authority is merely persuasive. An authority is only mandatory if it controls or shapes the law of a particular jurisdiction, for example, an opinion from a state appellate court or an applicable state statute.

When Is an Authority Merely Persuasive?

An authority is **persuasive** when it is made by a court outside of a particular jurisdiction. For example, decisions of one state court are not binding on courts of other states. Decisions of the Illinois Supreme Court are mandatory or binding on the lower courts in Illinois, but these decisions are merely persuasive primary authority in Michigan.

A decision will also be persuasive rather than mandatory if it is made by a court whose decisions according to the law do not bind other courts. For example, decisions of the federal trial courts do not have to be followed by other federal courts.

2. Secondary Authority

What Is Secondary Authority?

Another type of authority is **secondary authority.** Such authority is not generated by government bodies. Instead, secondary authority includes commentary of attorneys or other experts. Secondary authority is persuasive only, and it is never binding or mandatory. In general, an attorney would not base an argument to a court on a secondary authority.

Why Is Secondary Authority Important If You Would Not Use It in an Argument in Court?

Secondary sources are helpful in understanding an issue of law, in determining other issues, and in finding primary authorities. Sometimes secondary authorities help to interpret primary authority for you and the court. Secondary sources include treatises, Restatements of the Law, dictionaries, encyclopedias, legal periodicals, *American Law Reports,* books, and thesauri. See Illustration 2-1. Often these sources direct you to cases, statutes, and other primary authorities.

Do All Secondary Authorities Carry the Same Weight?

No. Some secondary authorities are more persuasive than others. Many restatements and treatises are authoritative and can be noted in court documents and legal reports called memoranda addressed to attorneys. However, most secondary authorities should not be noted in these reports.

3. Finding Tools

How Do You Find Primary and Secondary Authorities?

To find primary and secondary resources, often you will need to consult "finding tools," such as digests and citators. See Illustration 2-1. These finding tools are neither primary nor secondary authority. They should never be noted or cited in memoranda or court documents. Among the finding tools are **digests,** which are books containing case abstracts arranged according to publisher-assigned topics rather than in chronological order. **Annotated statutes** also include case abstracts written by the publishers. **Citators,** such as *Shepard's*®, provide you with listings of cases and some secondary authorities.*

Finally, many cases will be found in hybrid sources of authority such as looseleaf services, formbooks, and proof of facts.

What Is a Hybrid Source of Authority?

A **hybrid source of authority** contains primary authorities, secondary authorities, regulations, cases, and finding tools such as citators and digests.

Would You Consult Nonlegal Sources in Your Research?

Yes. You often must consult nonlegal sources, such as newspapers or corporate information statements. These sources are not authoritative. These should never be used to determine the law that governs a case. However, they can assist you in your work. These sources often provide insight into the purpose behind a court decision or the enactment of a law.

---

*Shepard's® is a registered trademark of Shepard's/McGraw-Hill, Inc.

CHAPTER SUMMARY

In this chapter, you learned that as a researcher you first seek primary authorities because these authorities carry more weight with the courts than secondary authorities. Primary authorities include court decisions, statutes, court rules, constitutions, and administrative rules and regulations.

Some primary authorities are binding. If an authority is binding, a court should follow that authority. Other authorities are merely persuasive. Such authorities provide guidance to the courts and often are followed by the decision-making tribunal.

Most state systems of government in the United States parallel the federal government structure: Most have three branches of government and administrative agencies. These state bodies also generate primary authorities.

As you are researching, you often will refer to secondary authorities. Secondary authorities generally provide you with information to understand primary authorities. Generally, secondary authorities are commentaries prepared by experts in a particular field. These authorities often include citations to primary authorities. Secondary authorities are persuasive only. Therefore, you would rely on a primary authority rather than a secondary authority. Secondary authorities include encyclopedias, treatises, and legal periodicals.

Finding tools are designed to assist you in your research, but they are not considered authorities. These tools provide you with citations to primary and secondary authorities. Finding tools include annotated statutes, digests, and citators.

Key Terms

Annotated statutes	Hybrid sources of authority
Binding authority	Jurisdiction
Circuits	Mandatory authority
Citators	Persuasive authority
Dicta	Precedent
Digests	Primary authority
Hierarchy of authority	Secondary authority
Holding	Stare decisis

EXERCISES

Court Systems

1. What is the highest court of your state?
2. Within your state's court system, what type of authority are decisions made by the highest court named in question 1?
   a. primary binding

defective product. Some of the material in the brief has been created for the purpose of the example.

ILLUSTRATION 3-1. *Sample Case Brief,* Olson Rug Co. v. Smarto

Olson Rug Co. v. Smarto

204 N.E.2d 838 (Ill. Ct. App. 1965)

FACTS

On March 16, 1962, Marty and Rose Smarto signed a contract with Olson Rug Company for the purchase of $450.62 worth of carpeting. They paid $120 as a down payment and agreed to pay the balance in monthly installments. The contract clearly stated that if the Smartos defaulted on payments, not only did the outstanding balance become immediately due, but Olson Rug had irrevocable authority to have an attorney represent them and seek to have a judgment confessed against the Smartos. Prior to signing the agreement, Olson Rug assured the Smartos that the color and nap of the carpet would withstand their intended use for it. Two weeks after installation of the carpet, the color faded and the nap lost its original shape. After two more weeks, the Smartos notified Olson Rug's agent and asked him to take the carpet back. He refused the request. The Smartos did not return the carpet, continued to use it, and stopped paying installments. Approximately one year later, Olson Rug sought a judgment by confession against the Smartos for the outstanding balance and court costs.

ISSUE

Did the buyers effectively reject a defective product when they continued to use the carpet for more than one year after discovering that the seller delivered a defective product?

HOLDING

A buyer, upon discovering goods to be defective shortly after delivery, should soon thereafter return or offer to return the goods to the seller. The Smartos neither returned the carpeting nor offered to return it. For that reason, the court held that the Smartos, through their more-than-one-year-long delay, waived their right to rescind the carpet purchase contract.

RATIONALE

The Smartos neither returned the carpeting nor offered to return the carpeting after discovering the defect.

ILLUSTRATION 3-1. *Continued*

DISPOSITION

The appellate court affirmed the circuit court's decision to deny the defendants' motion to open or vacate the judgment confessed against them.

All of the page numbers, indicating where the information is found within the text of the case, are included. This helps you when you are writing your memo and must include citation references to the case. You will not have to go back to the reporter and review the case again when your brief contains all of the page references and the complete Bluebook citation.

4. Example of the Research Process

Problem

Mrs. Jones bought a fur coat from John J. Furriers. The coat was labeled 100 percent raccoon. One day Mrs. Jones was smoking a cigarette and a hot ash fell on the coat while she was wearing it. The ash melted a hole in the coat. Mrs. Jones knew that fur burns, but acrylic melts.

How Would You Phrase the Issue If You Were Researching the Fur Labeling Problem?

ISSUE

Whether a furrier is liable to a consumer for mislabeling a product?

What Steps Would You Follow First?

First, perform background research using secondary sources to educate yourself about the area of law and to acquire a working vocabulary to use when you write. This helps you become familiar with the types of legal materials controlling the issue. For example, you are to write about acquiring a license to enter a neighbor's property. After educating yourself about the topic you realize a license is not a permit. The background research provides information indicating whether the topic (in our problem, fur labeling) is controlled by statutes, cases, or regulations, and whether federal or state law controls. You should develop a basic knowledge about the topic from your readings, which will help you use the appropriate terms more effectively.

Start with the descriptive word index of the relevant state statute and the descriptive word index of the *United States Code Annotated* (U.S.C.A.) to see if any federal statutes have been violated. For the fur labeling problem, the words to check might be "label," "fur," "product," and "mislabeling." For the fur labling problem, the annotated statutes would be checked to see if any relevant cases are cited discussing or analyzing the issue. Any relevant cases would be Shepardized, and the *Shepard's* citations would be updated by using the paperbound *Shepard's Supplements*. *Shepard's* indicates the validity of the cases and statutes and leads you to newer cases that discuss the same issue.

After determining that the relevant cases and statutes are valid, a thorough reading of the decisions is necessary. Gather all the information from your sources to cite them accurately in Bluebook format. You ` ould make a list of all of the cites that are valid. Add an additional ` ck next to the cite after you have read the full text of the opinion o. statute. This will save you time later if you expand your research. Yo. `an merely review your list of cites to see if it is valid and to see if yo. `ave read the full text of the authority.

`hat Sources Would You Consult, and Why?

1. You ` `onsult the *United States Code Annotated* or the *United States* `ervice* because fur labeling is regulated by the Federal Trade ` `ion. An annotated code provides recent case references as well ` `nces to administrative material (particularly the U.S.C.S., whic` `s references to administrative materials). Also, consumer frau` `ould be researched. Use the index to the U.S.C.A. and look up ` `licable research terms that you derived from the secondary sour`

2. You would consult ` `de of Federal Regulations* (C.F.R.) to see the particular agency rul` `ining to fur labeling and intentional mislabeling. Use the index to ` `F.R. to find the appropriate titles that discuss furs, fur labeling, la` `and labeling requirements. The research vocabulary that you ge` `are the words you look up in the index.

3. You would consult the *Americ` `*Reports* because this is a narrow, well-defined issue and the A.L. ` `have explored this issue thoroughly.

How Do You Incorporate Compu`                   `urces with Hardcopy Metho`

The principal difference between using hardc` sively and using the combination of computerized an` als is that instead of using indexes to the statutes, C.F.R. you construct a search query and search the materi` also search legal periodicals online with search queries. T` Shepardizing, is performed online as well.

Performing background research using secondary sour`

important for educating yourself in the area of law and for generating a research vocabulary to use later when constructing the research queries for LEXIS or WESTLAW. Secondary source research is still most efficiently and cost-effectively done with hardcopy sources.

Computerized legal research requires you to select precise words to retrieve documents that contain those words and that are on point. Using LEXIS and WESTLAW is most productive after you are versed in the subject and are aware of the words that judges, legislatures, and agencies use when writing about a legal topic. In turn, this process of selecting vocabulary words assists you when writing about the topic.

B. Process Writing

1. Preparing to Write

How Do You Complete the Research Process and Make the Transition to Writing?

Remember that what we plan as we prepare to write is as important as the final product. The more time you can put into the process, the better the product. Spend at least 50 percent of the time budgeted for writing in the pre-writing stage. However, time management is crucial with any assignment because time is money and knowing when to stop researching and when to begin writing is important. Therefore, when the project is assigned ask how much time you should spend on the project. What is the budget? A good clue as to when you have completed your research is when you do not retrieve any new information; the same sources keep appearing. Ask your law librarian or another paralegal to review, briefly, your research strategy and ask if there are any other avenues that he or she would have taken.

Take detailed notes and make careful citations to references for each source. Also, keep a complete list of all sources consulted, whether a statute, case, regulation, periodical article, or other source. Your list of sources consulted helps later on, when you may have to expand your research. You can then check the list to see if you already reviewed a source and to see if it was pertinent.

Shepardize any primary authority that you use in your memo. *Shepard's* ensures that the authority, whether it is a case, statute, or regulation, is still good or valid law. Never start to write using a source of authority without Shepardizing it first.

2. The Writing Process

Follow a method or format when preparing to write to make the actual drafting process easier. Focus on the mechanics and components of the writing process rather than the finished product. The method that follows is a checklist to ensure thoroughness and to give you confidence in your newly acquired skills. The fundamental components of process writing are assessing the document's purpose and intended audience, drafting a detailed outline before writing, revising your findings in the categories of purpose and audience, and outlining and revising your work.

3. Purpose

What Is the Purpose of the Document?

When you sit down to write, you must begin by asking yourself: What is the purpose of the document that I am preparing? Because a legal document has a variety of goals (to inform, persuade, or advise), you must determine the document's intent before writing. The purpose determines the posture and the format of your work product. If the document is to inform the attorney as to all available law on a particular issue, it is neutral in tone and takes the form of an objective memo. If your goal is to convince another party that your position is correct, then the document may be in the form of a memo for the assigning attorney, a memo for the court, a trial or an appellate brief, and the tone will be persuasive. Sometimes a persuasive document takes the form of a letter that requests an individual or entity to act in a certain way. Examples of persuasive letters are demand letters requesting payment owed, or eviction letters demanding that a tenant vacate the premises. See Chapter 12, Persuasive Writing. Sometimes you must advise a client as to an action that he or she must take. The document may then be in the form of a letter giving counsel but one that is written as simply as possible; a client is often a sophisticated individual who may not have a legal education. The purpose of the document determines its format and the rhetorical stance: objective, persuasive, or instructive.

4. Audience

To Whom Are You Speaking?

As you prepare to write, determine carefully who the reader is. Is the reader the assigning attorney? This is often the case when the project is the preparation of an office memo. The memo should be easy for the intended reader to understand; you should insert headings, if necessary, to guide the reader. If the document is intended for a court, then the reader will be a judge and opposing counsel, and your tone will be formal yet persuasive. Your assertions or points that you want to prove should be clear and straightforward. The document should always be prepared using language that the reader can comprehend; this is also required when drafting client letters and demand letters.

Your audience determines the voice of the document that you are preparing. Voice is how the document sounds. A good way to test the appropriateness of the voice of your document is to read it aloud. An informative document requires a neutral tone, whereas a persuasive document mandates an assertive tone. A document providing advice requires information, persuasion, as well as respectful recommendations for actions. Any document that you prepare in the workplace requires a level of formality, not casual writing, like corresponding with a favorite aunt.

Diction is another component of the process of tailoring a document for your audience. Diction is the selection of the appropriate word to express the purpose or idea. A general rule is to express all ideas as simply and concretely as possible. Try to avoid selecting esoteric, multisyllabic words. Also try to avoid legalese. Legalese is merely cumbersome and plodding. Attorneys think it is pretentious and lay people do not understand it.

5. Outline

How Do You Organize Your Ideas?

The next stage is to prepare an outline of whatever document you are writing. If it is an office memo, outline the issues and sub-issues of points that you want to articulate. Make sure that the outline flows logically. See if there are any gaps by reviewing your outline carefully. Organization is crucial to effective legal writing to ensure completeness. Having a complete outline also helps when you have to put your project down for a considerable period of time, or when you must work on more than one matter at a time and easily want to pick up where you left off.

Organize your research findings according to where they are pertinent in your outline. It is best to let your issues or assertions determine where the research should be placed rather than letting the sources determine the placement in the document. Never use your sources as your outline; rely on the issues.

6. Revision

How Do You Move Beyond the First Step?

Review all of the steps you have taken in the pre-writing stage. Ask yourself: Is the purpose of the document being prepared according to the assignment, and is it meeting the client's needs? Does the document clearly fulfill its goal of either informing, persuading, or advising? Do the language and format reflect the purpose?

Examine your intended audience. What language is appropriate for the intended reader? What level of sophistication is required? Ask yourself about voice (how it will sound), diction (word choice), and rhetoric (the way you use speech).

Review your outline. Check to see if the outline is well organized, logical, and flows smoothly. At this point, reexamine the issues or assertions that you want to include and make sure that the points are clearly discernible. Insert the appropriate research findings in the relevant place in the outline, as well as the necessary facts and the conclusions that you want to draw. Now you are ready to write.

7. Example of Process Writing Techniques

Ms. Partner calls you into her office and asks that you prepare a client letter to Mrs. Jones advising her as to a course of action that she can take to rectify the problem of her mislabeled fur coat. The facts of the problem are as follows:

> Mrs. Jones bought a fur coat from John J. Furriers. The coat was labeled 100 percent raccoon. One day Mrs. Jones was smoking a cigarette and a hot ash fell on the coat while she was wearing it. The ash melted a hole in the coat. Mrs. Jones knew that fur burns, but acrylic melts.

First, what is the purpose of the document? The document's goal is to advise Mrs. Jones as to a course of action against the seller, John J. Furriers. The partner specified the document's form, a letter.

Next, you must examine your audience. Who is your reader? Is Mrs. Jones an attorney? Probably not. You can ask the attorney making the assignment some background information about the client. This will help you tailor a document to the reader's precise needs. Mrs. Jones is a stock analyst. She is a sophisticated individual but she does not possess a legal education. The language used in the letter must be understandable to Mrs. Jones. The voice, how the letter sounds, should be instructive and advisory without being condescending. The diction, or word choice, should be simple; avoid legalese.

Now outline the points that you want to address in the letter. Begin by restating the facts as you know them. List the points.

1. The fur coat was mislabeled.
2. The seller misrepresented his product.
3. If the misrepresentation was intentional, there is the possibility of fraud.
4. Mrs. Jones would like to obtain a full refund for the coat that she purchased.
5. If a refund is not given in seven days, court action will proceed.

Insert your research findings, in general language, in the appropriate spot in the outline. In a client letter of this nature there is no need to cite to authority. Use the facts and advise Mrs. Jones as to how she should proceed with the matter. Always remember that an attorney must always review and sign any letter that you prepare that gives legal advise. Only an attorney may sign such a letter.

Revise all of your pre-writing steps by checking your purpose, audience, and outline once again. Now you are ready to write.

Checklist

I. When you receive the problem:
   a. Clarify the legal issues being researched.
   b. Determine the relevant jurisdiction.
   c. Determine the area of the law.
   d. Gather all of the facts.
   e. Draft a statement of the issue or question that you are researching.
II. Introductory research:
   a. Educate yourself in the area of the law.
   b. Scan a hornbook or textbook on the subject.
   c. Learn the relevant vocabulary.
   d. Note the major cases.
   e. Make an outline of the issues and sub-issues of your problem.
III. Targeted research:
   a. Use a legal encyclopedia or an annotated statute (use descriptive word index), helpful for matters involving state law, to find discussion of legal issue and relevant case and statute citations.
   b. Go to the digest for the relevant jurisdiction, and use the one good case method to find other cases.
   c. Shepardize, use WESTLAW's *Shepard's* Preview, QuickCite, and Insta-Cite, or LEXIS's LEXCITE and Auto-Cite, to find other cites and to validate your citations before relying on them as authority. Use *Shepard's* in the hardcopy format if the online version is too costly for the assignment's budget or if it is unavailable. Always remember to check the supplements to *Shepard's* to ensure that the references are up to date.
   d. Brief cases and relate them to one another (see Chapter 10, Synthesizing Cases).
   e. Review the outline of the issues and sub-issues that you drafted. Revise the outline to reflect your increased knowledge of the subject.
IV. Computerized research:
   a. Computerized research is particularly helpful when the facts

> are unique and the legal issue is narrow (for instance, whether malpractice occurred during the insertion of a chin implant), not broad (for instance, whether a breach of contract occurred).
>   b. It is best to be thorough and combine computerized and hardcopy methods.
> V. Create an audit trail of your research:
>   a. Take notes of sources and location, including page number.
>   b. Write citations to all sources in Bluebook format.
>   c. Note whether Shepardizing has been completed and date completed.
> VI. Process writing:
>   a. Purpose: Determine the purpose of the document. The document's goal is either to inform, to persuade, or to advise. Select the appropriate rhetorical stance and determine the format (office memo, court memo, brief, or letter).
>   b. Audience: Find out who the reader or readers will be. Determine the language that is most comprehensible to the particular reader. Select an appropriate voice for the purpose, format, and reader. Note your diction.
>   c. Outline: Outline the issues, assertions, or points that you want to include. Organize research findings according to the outline. Place facts in the appropriate spot and state conclusion.
>   d. Revise: Review the purpose and the audience of the intended document and check your outline for appropriateness. Revise your outline to reflect any new knowledge, legal or factual. Reread the outline to ensure that it is complete and flows logically.

CHAPTER SUMMARY

This chapter led you through the pre-writing process, from your receipt of the project to your completion of the research and the preparation for writing. Before writing, carefully analyze the document's purpose and audience. Refine the issue at the beginning; outline and revise all of your information. This chapter and your own experience will guide you through this process. Keep records of all sources consulted and make sure that your citations are accurate; these help when you are ready to write. Also, do not forget to Shepardize all necessary documents and to update all resources. The time that you spend in the pre-writing stage ensures a better work product that is produced more efficiently than one created by lunging into the writing process. Pre-writing takes planning, but with the methodology outlined in this chapter you will be equipped to write.

Key Terms

Audience	Outline
Background research	Purpose
Facts	Record keeping
Issues	Research vocabulary
Note taking	*West Law Finder*

EXERCISES

Hardcopy Research

Read the following fact pattern and answer the questions.

John Clark comes to your firm with a question regarding the tax status of his residence. He has just been ordained as a United Methodist minister and will be receiving a housing allowance from First United Methodist Church, where he will be an assistant pastor. He wants to know if this housing allowance can be excluded from income on his tax return even though the residence is his own.

1. How would you phrase this issue if you were researching this problem using hardcopy resources?
2. What would be your research strategy using hardcopy resources?
3. List three sources that you would consult. Why would you consult them?

Process Writing Exercise

1. The assignment partner requests that you draft a letter of your findings to Rev. Clark. List, in detail, the purpose, audience, and resulting outline of the letter.
2. How would the purpose, audience, and outline change if the assignment partner requests a memo concerning your research findings? Once again, how would the purpose, audience, and outline change if you are requested to prepare a court brief?

Hardcopy and Online Research Combined

Read the following fact pattern and answer the questions.

On November 29, 1993, Michael Jones purchased a used truck from Grimy's Auto and Truck Service. At the time of purchase, Grimy's stated that the engine was completely overhauled and consisted of rebuilt and reconditioned parts, all parts were guaranteed, and invoices for all new parts would be provided. On November 13, 1994, after using the truck for almost one year, Jones discovered that several engine parts were not rebuilt or reconditioned and other engine parts were defective, which caused the truck to break down. This resulted in lost wages and lost profits for Jones. Jones made repairs to the truck on November 13, 1994, December 13, 1994, and December 16, 1994. Jones did not attempt to return the truck and did not notify Grimy's that the truck was defective. The truck is currently disabled in Columbus, Ohio. Jones came to your firm because he wants to sue Grimy's for damages for breach of contract.

The issue that you will research is as follows: Is Jones entitled to receive damages for breach of contract because the truck does not conform to the terms of the agreement? Remember that Grimy's will assert that Jones continued to use the truck for more than a reasonable time and failed to return the truck or to notify Grimy's of its defects in a timely manner.

1. What would be your research strategy if you were using a combination of hardcopy and computerized resources?

2. How would you educate yourself on the relevant topic so that you could find primary sources?

3. List two primary sources and one secondary source that you would consult. Why would you consult these sources?

4. Use either LEXIS or WESTLAW and formulate a search query that you could use to find primary authority.

4. Writing Fundamentals

A. Clear Writing
B. Sentences
C. Paragraphs
D. Grammar Tips
E. Importance of Revision
F. Diction and Voice

CHAPTER OVERVIEW

This chapter stresses the fundamentals of good writing. Active and passive voice and other common grammar questions are discussed. You learn the importance of writing clearly and concisely and the value of rewriting your work.

A. Clear Writing

What Are the Goals in Writing?

The key to writing is **clarity.** Your readers must understand what you are trying to convey to them. Not only must you follow the proper format for your communication and thoroughly research the issues, they must be understandable and easy to read.

How Do You Make Your Writing Clear?

You must think about what you plan to write, outline it, write it using correct grammar and spelling, and, most important, rewrite it several times. As you rewrite your letters and memos, you will always find that you can eliminate unnecessary words and legalese. Use simple words even though you know more elaborate ones. Doing so makes your writing inviting rather than pompous.

Choose your words carefully. Select concrete words that allow the readers to visualize what you are saying. Read the following example:

> He harmed one of his body parts in the device at issue in this case.

It would be better to say:

> His arm was severed when the threshing machine stalled and he fell forward in front of the machine.

The second example is clearer because in it the reader knows what happened and to which body part it happened: The arm was severed. The second sentence also conveys that the device was a threshing machine and that it stalled, throwing the man forward.

Also use concrete verbs. Read the following examples:

> The parties entered into an agreement on September 1, 1995.
> There was an agreement entered into on September 1, 1995.
> The parties agreed to the terms on September 1, 1995.

The last example is the best because it is the simplest and uses the word "agreed" as a verb rather than as a noun. It is the easiest sentence of the three to understand and to visualize.

What Other Rules Should You Follow?

Avoid **legalese** or **legal speak.** What does this mean? Use plain English that your nonattorney clients would use. Consider your audience. Clear writing avoids using unnecessary legal words. For example, do not use the word "scienter" when you simply could say "intent." At the end of an affidavit, you often see the term "Further affiant sayeth not," which means that the person signing the affidavit has nothing further to say. Because that should be clear without the phrase "further affiant sayeth not," skip it and others like it that add nothing to your writing.

What Is Active Voice?

Active voice is when the subject of the sentence is doing the action of the verb. Active voice emphasizes the actor. Active voice is the preferred voice because it is clearer, more concise, and more lively.

What Is Passive Voice?

Passive voice is when the subject of the sentence is being acted upon. Although passive voice has its uses, it is generally wordier and not as strong as active voice.

Active voice:	Harold hit a home run.
	Donald danced the tango.
Passive voice:	The home run was hit by Harold.
	The tango was danced by Donald.

Often the word "by" is used in a passive voice sentence. When you see the word "by," consider rewriting the sentence.

Passive example:	Their initial quote for heat stamping equipment was rejected by Bailey.
Rewritten example:	Bailey rejected their initial quote for heat stamping equipment.

The second example is clearer and more concise.

In some passive voice constructions, the actor is unknown. For example:

Taxes were not deducted from her paychecks.
Walker received health and life insurance benefits.

In some cases, the person or thing performing the action does not need to be mentioned because it is unimportant. Passive voice is acceptable in this situation. If you believe it advantageous to change the emphasis of the sentence from the person doing the action to the action, use passive voice. For example, if your client was the defendant in an action and you did not want to emphasize an action of hers, you might write a sentence as follows:

The action stems from a contract dispute in which goods were rejected by the defendant.

This sentence in active voice would emphasize the defendant as follows:

The defendant rejected the goods, resulting in a contract dispute.

B. Sentences

What Is a Sentence, and How Should It Be Structured?

A **sentence** is a statement that conveys a single idea. It generally should be written in active voice and must include a subject and predicate. To avoid confusing your reader, do not place the subject too far from the verb.

The focus of your sentence should be the idea you wish to convey. Do not make your readers work too hard to understand your sentence. Be direct and to the point. Keep your sentences short, generally not more than 25 words in length. As with any rule, you may break this rule about sentence length, but be careful not to make your sentences too complex.

One common mistake in writing sentences is to use a sentence fragment or incomplete sentence.

Incomplete sentence:	The extent of the employer's control and supervision over the worker.
Complete sentence:	The court will consider the extent of the employer's control and supervision over the worker.

The first example is a sentence fragment. It is incomplete. The second sentence is a complete thought.

How Do You Use Commas Within a Sentence?

Commas tell a reader to pause. Use commas to separate a series of items. For example:

> Wally ran to the school, the store, the baseball field, and then home.

Be careful not to use commas to divide run-on sentences. These are sentences that contain two separate sentences.

Incorrect:	Tildy's role is merely advisory, although she might be called on to supply facts about the spill, her opinion probably would not form the basis of any final decision.
Correct:	Tildy's role is merely advisory. Although she might be called on to supply facts about the spill, her opinion probably would not form the basis of any final decision.

In the second example, the two sentences are correctly separated with a period. You also could use a semicolon. For some run-on sentences, you could divide the sentences with a comma and a conjunction. In the above example, that solution would not cure the problem completely because the second sentence is too long.

Commas also are used to set apart parenthetical phrases. In such a situation, commas should be used in pairs.

> The defendant, Larry Dwyer, filed an answer to the complaint.

The name "Larry Dwyer" is parenthetical because the meaning of the sentence would not be changed if the phrase was omitted. In contrast, read the following examples:

Judges who take bribes should be indicted.
Judges, who take bribes, should be indicted.

In these examples, the phrase "who take bribes" is not parenthetical. If it was omitted, the sentence would say that "judges should be indicted." The phrase "who take bribes" must be part of the sentence to convey the correct meaning. Therefore, it is not parenthetical, and the commas should be omitted.

Note: Commas and periods should always appear inside quotation marks. This rule is often mistakenly broken.

How Are Commas Used in Dates?

Commas separate a year from the date.

The plaintiff and the defendant agreed to the settlement on Nov. 15, 1995.

Commas also set off the date from a specific reference to a day of the week.

The judge decided the summary judgment motion on Monday, Nov. 7, 1995.

How Are Commas Used with Proper Names and Titles in a Sentence?

Commas separate a proper name from a title that follows it.

The plaintiff sued RAM Enterprises and Samuel Harris, company president.

When Should You Use Semicolons?

Semicolons are similar to commas because they tell a reader to pause and they break apart thoughts. Semicolons are used to separate two independent sentences.

Two sentences:	The paralegal's responsibilities are broad. They include summarization of depositions.
One sentence:	The paralegal's responsibilities are broad; they include summarization of depositions.

Semicolons also separate clauses of a compound sentence when an adverbial conjunction joins the two.

> The defendants presented a good case; however, they lost.

Semicolons are also used to separate phrases.

> The committee members were Robert Harris, vice president of Harris Enterprises; Karen Williams, owner of Walworth Products; Barbara Halley, an attorney; and Benjamin Marcus, an accountant.

When Should You Use Colons?

Colons are marks of introduction: what follow are explanations, conclusions, amplifications, lists or series, or quotations. A colon is always preceded by a main clause, one that can stand alone as a sentence. A main clause may or may not follow a colon.

> Help was on the way: Someone had called the police.

> Sandra had two assignments: a writing assignment and a book report.

> The mayor stepped to the podium: "I regretfully must submit my resignation."

Colons should appear only at the end of a main clause. They should never directly follow a verb or a preposition.

Incorrect:	The hours of the museum are: 10:00 A.M. to 6:00 P.M.
Correct:	The hours of the museum are 10:00 A.M. to 6:00 P.M.
Incorrect:	Maria loved many sports, such as: soccer, tennis, and softball.
Correct:	Maria loved many sports, such as soccer, tennis, and softball.

As with any punctuation mark, use colons only when they best serve your writing purpose. Do not overuse them.

When Should You Use Parentheses?

Parentheses tell the reader that the idea is an afterthought or is outside the main idea of a sentence. Use parentheses infrequently because they tend to break the flow of the sentence.

C. Paragraphs

What Is a Paragraph, and How Should It Be Structured?

A **paragraph** is a collection of statements that focus on the same general subject. The paragraph should have a unified purpose. To be effective, your paragraphs should have a thesis or topic sentence and transitions between sentences.

What Is a Thesis or Topic Sentence?

The **topic sentence** is generally the first sentence of a paragraph; it tells the reader the subject of the paragraph. This sentence also indicates that a new topic will be discussed. In legal writing, this sentence often introduces the issue or sub-issues that will be discussed within the paragraph.

How Do You Guide a Reader from One Paragraph to the Next?

You should use **transitions** to guide your reader from one paragraph to the next paragraph. Transitions tell the reader that the ideas follow from each other and are related. A transitional sentence ties two paragraphs together. Think of this sentence as a bridge. Whenever you start your new paragraph, think about how you will relate it to the previous paragraph.

D. Grammar Tips

This chapter reinforces grammar concepts and focuses on problem areas. However, it cannot address all points of grammar that students need to know. To learn more about important grammar points, consult the following books.

The Elements of Style, by William Strunk, Jr., and E. B. White
On Writing Well, by William Zinsser
The Careful Writer: A Modern Guide to English Usage, by Theodore Bernstein.

What Are Modifiers, and How Are They Used?

Modifiers provide a description about a subject, a verb, or an object in your sentence. If you misplace a modifier, you might confuse your reader or convey an incorrect message. A modifier should be placed in proximity to the subject, verb, or object it modifies.

Incorrect: Deadlocked for more than two days, the judge asked the jury to continue to deliberate.

Correct: The jury had been deadlocked for two days. Nonetheless, the judge asked the jury to continue to deliberate.

In the first example, the phrase "deadlocked for more than two days" incorrectly modifies the judge rather than the jury. This is a dangling modifier.

What Is Parallel Construction, and When Is It Used?

Parallel construction is when you make each of the phrases within your sentence follow the same grammatical pattern or number. A plural subject must have a plural verb. A singular subject must have a singular verb. You also must use parallel tenses when you are listing a series of activities. A parallel grammatical pattern makes your writing balanced.

Incorrect: The paralegal association set the following goals: recruitment of new members, educating the community, and improvement of paralegal work conditions.

Correct: The paralegal association set the following goals: recruitment of new members, education of the community, and improvement of paralegal work conditions.

In the correct example, the words "recruitment," "education," and "improvement" are parallel.
You also must use plural pronouns and verbs when the subjects are plural.

Incorrect: Software Developments Inc. sent Howard Grinwald, a company sales representative, and Mark Gaines, their plant manager, to Bailey's plant.

Correct: Software Developments Inc. sent Howard Grinwald, a company sales representative, and Mark Gaines, its plant manager, to Bailey's plant.

The second example is correct because Software Developments Inc. is a singular subject, therefore the pronoun before "plant manager" should be the singular possessive "its" rather than "their."

| Incorrect: | To assert the attorney-client privilege, the claimant must show that the statements were made in confidence and was made to an attorney for the purpose of obtaining legal advice. |
| Correct: | To assert the attorney-client privilege, the claimant must show that the statements were made in confidence and were made to an attorney for the purpose of obtaining legal advice. |

The second example is correct because the verbs must be plural when they have a plural noun. In this example, the word "statements" should have a plural verb.

If you have a singular subject, then each of the pronouns in the sentence that describes that subject should be singular.

| Incorrect: | To receive this protection in the corporate setting, an individual must show that they were a decision-making employee. |
| Correct: | To receive this protection in the corporate setting, an individual must show that he or she was a decision-making employee. |

Why Is Punctuation So Important?

The punctuation of a sentence, especially the placement of a comma, can change the meaning of that sentence.

What Rules of Grammar Are Tricky?

Subject and verb agreement, so essential to proper sentence construction, causes great confusion for many writers. The following are sample situations in which errors are most often made.

Collective nouns such as jury, court, committee, and group often pose a problem for writers. They take a singular verb because they are considered one unit. For example, jury is considered one unit as opposed to individual jurors.

| Incorrect: | The jury were to eat lunch at noon. |
| Correct: | The jury was to eat lunch at noon. |

Compound subjects also cause confusion. Subjects joined by the word "and" usually use a plural verb, regardless of whether any or all of the individual subjects are singular.

| Incorrect: | The attorney and the paralegal was available for the client. |

Correct: The attorney and the paralegal were available for the
                client.

When a compound subject is preceded by "each" or "every," the verb
is usually singular.

Incorrect: Each attorney and paralegal in the room have access
                to the library.

Correct: Each attorney and paralegal in the room has access
                to the library.

When a compound subject is jointed by "or" or "nor," it takes a singular
verb if each subject is singular. It takes a plural verb if each subject is
plural. If one subject is singular and the other is plural, the verb follows
the closest subject.

Subjects singular: An apple or an orange is my
                                favorite snack.

Subjects plural: Apples or oranges are my favorite
                                snacks.

Subjects singular and plural: Neither the mother nor the
                                children were happy.

To avoid awkwardness, place the plural noun closest to the verb so that
the verb is plural.

Awkward: Neither the dogs nor the cat was anywhere in sight.

Revised: Neither the cat nor the dogs were anywhere in sight.

Indefinite pronouns may also throw up roadblocks for writers. Indefinite pronouns are those that do not refer to a specific person or thing.
Some common indefinite pronouns are

all	nobody
any	none
anyone	nothing
each	one
either	some
everyone	something

Most indefinite pronouns refer to singular subjects and therefore take
a singular verb.

Incorrect: Everyone are free to go.
                Each of the stores were open on Sunday.

Correct: Everyone is free to go.
              Each of the stores was open on Sunday.

Some indefinite pronouns (all, any, none, some) may take either a singular or plural verb depending on the meaning of the word they refer to.

Singular: All of the library was quiet. (The library was quiet.)

Plural: All of the paralegals were researching the case. (The paralegals were researching the case.)

What Other Key Rules Should You Follow?

Do not start your paragraph or sentence with a citation. Instead, start with the rule summarizing the cited authority.

E. Importance of Revision

What Is the Final Step in the Process?

Rewriting is the final step in the writing process. Reread the material after you have reviewed your word choice and eliminated unnecessary words. As you reread the material, ask yourself the following questions:

1. Does the material make sense?
2. Is it logical?
3. Should the organization of a sentence be changed?
4. Does one sentence follow from the next?
5. Are there any gaps in the sentence?
6. Are there any gaps in the paragraph?
7. Does one paragraph flow into the other?
8. Should the paragraphs be rearranged?
9. Are there any punctuation errors?
10. Are any words misspelled?
11. Are there any typographical errors?
12. Are there any citation errors?

Why Is Rewriting Important?

Rewriting may seem like a tedious waste of time, but it is one of the most important steps in preparing a well-written document. Go through your manuscript word by word and decide whether each word conveys what you want your reader to know. Next, think about whether you can eliminate unnecessary words, a process called tightening or **editing.** Read it as if you were reading it for the first time. Look for verbs that have been made into nouns, a process referred to as **nominalization.** The following illustrates the use of such **gerunds:**

> The parties entered into an agreement on October 15, 1994, to make a change in the purchase price of the original contract from $1,500 to $2,000.

It is better to say:

> The parties agreed to increase the purchase price of the original contract from $1,500 to $2,000.

In the second sentence, "entered into an agreement" becomes "agreed" and "to make a change" becomes "increase." These changes eliminate the use of verbs as nouns.

When Should You Use Quotations?

Use quotations sparingly. Most often, you can paraphrase what a court decision or other authority states. Your words convey the concept more clearly to the reader. Direct quotations that are used to convey an idea often are cluttered with unnecessary words or do not effectively explain a concept in the context of your use of the quotation. An added bonus for you when you paraphrase a court decision or other authority is that you are forced to carefully analyze the language of the authority. This ensures that you understand the concepts presented.

When Are Single Quotation Marks Used?

These marks are used to define a quotation within a quotation.

> The client told the lawyer, "My boss said, 'You cannot be a good lawyer and be a good mother,' and then he fired me."

If you end a quotation with quoted words, you place a single quotation mark and follow it with a double quotation mark.

> The witness testified, "The robber said, 'give me all of your money.' "

When Are Double Quotation Marks Used?

These marks enclose direct quotations.

> The judge said, "The trial date will not be continued."

What Words Should Be Capitalized Within a Quotation?

The first word of the quotation should be capitalized if it is a complete sentence.

Where Should You Place a Comma or Period When You Use Quotation Marks?

Commas and periods always should be placed inside of quotation marks.

F. Diction and Voice

What Is Diction?

Diction means choice of words when writing. Selecting the appropriate words to express your idea precisely is a skill that is developed over time. When you are revising a document, you can read it over to make sure that the words that you selected to convey your ideas do precisely that. Sometimes you must use a dictionary or a thesaurus to assist you in selecting the best word.

Why Is Voice Important?

Voice is the tone of your document. In professional writing, the document's tone is formal and, accordingly, professional. Selecting language that is not colloquial and avoiding slang are ways to ensure that the tone of the document is correct for the law firm or corporate legal department environment. Avoid anything that personalizes the contents; this is achieved by never using the first person, "I." Conjunctions like "can't" are more casual than "cannot." If you are sensitive to the tone of your document, when revising, it will have the requisite formal voice.

CHAPTER SUMMARY

Think about what you want to say, outline it, and write it using good grammar and correct spelling. Then rewrite and edit your work.

Choose your words carefully. Select concrete verbs and avoid legalese. Most often, use active voice in which the subject of the sentence is doing the action of the verb.

Be certain that each phrase within your sentence is parallel. Match singular subjects with singular verbs.

Use quotations sparingly to effectively convey your messages.

Key Terms

Active voice	Modifiers
Clarity	Nominalization
Collective nouns	Paragraph
Colons	Parallel construction
Commas	Parentheses
Compound subjects	Passive voice
Concrete words	Rewriting
Diction	Semicolons
Editing	Sentence
Indefinite pronouns	Topic sentence
Legal speak	Transitions
Legalese	Voice

EXERCISES

Editing Exercise

1. Eliminate the unnecessary words from the following statement:

At the time when the parties entered into the agreement of purchase and sale it is important to note that neither of them had knowledge of contents of the dresser drawer. Because of the fact that previous to the contract the seller did not own the dresser and the seller's mother had not had many valuable pieces of jewelry despite having a large income, the seller had made the assumption that the dresser did not contain anything. Due to the fact that the seller had made a statement to the buyer of the fact that his mother did not own any jewelry in the buyer's thinking, he had no purpose for to make any further investigation or inspection of the drawers as he might otherwise have considered making. For these reasons, there was no provision in the contract for an upward modification in the payment to be made by the buyer to the seller in the event that the dresser drawer later proved to be filled with jewels.

Various Grammar Exercises

2. Which is the best sentence? Why?
   a. A modification to the contract occurred on July 8, 1995.
   b. There was a modification of the contract July 8, 1995.
   c. Harry and Morgan modified their contract on July 8, 1995.
3. Edit the following sentences.
   a. At a time when many law firms and corporations are elimi-

nating jobs for the purpose of elimination from the budget excess expenditures, paralegals may become more of an asset.

b. Because of the fact that paralegals' time is charged at lower rates, paralegals may be employed by law firms and corporations to perform tasks previously performed by lawyers.

c. With specificity, paralegals may be asked to perform legal research of case and statutory materials in the event that a client requests an answer to a problem of a legal nature and is concerned about saving money.

d. In the situation where a paralegal is well-trained, that paralegal can be asked by an attorney to perform legal research for the purpose of determining a response to the client's question.

e. With regard to ethical considerations, paralegals can perform legal research under the supervision of an attorney.

f. Subsequent to the research, however, the attorney must be the person who renders the legal opinions that need to be made, the reason being that a paralegal cannot provide legal advice.

g. It is important to note that some states are considering allowing paralegals to practice independently.

h. Try this schedule; shower, eat breakfast, drive to the train, go to work and come home.

i. There are only one hour and thirty-five minutes left to voir dire, the judge stated.

j. Among the defendants was Craig Fisher, David Michaels and Mitchell White.

k. The prosecutor will attempt to within the course of the trial persuade you that the defendant committed the crime.

l. The foreman, as well as half of the jury, were late for the afternoon court session.

m. Every one of the councilmen we have named to the commission want to serve.

n. The heart of a trial are the witnesses.

o. None of the players were willing to sign contracts.

p. The substance of Walter Mondale's speeches is more similar to Jimmy Carter.

q. The house was vacated by the tenants.

Part II.

ILLUSTRATION 5-2   *Continued*

cumstances of the relationship. The court considered the control exercised by the "employer" over the worker; the method of payment; who paid for the individual's benefits, such as life and health insurance; and who paid for the operation. In this case, the court found that King was an independent contractor because she was paid on commission; she paid for her own benefits; she supplied her own supplies; and she controlled her work. The court found that she set her own hours, selected the products she sold, and generated her own clients. Based upon these facts, the appellate court found that King should be considered an independent contractor rather than an employee.

DICTA

The 11-part test set by the *Spirides* court should be applied to determine whether an individual is an employee or an independent contractor.

DISPOSITION

The Court of Appeals affirmed the district court's judgment in granting summary judgment for the defendant.

Dogger, brought suit against Whole In One for sex discrimination. Their claims are based on a federal antidiscrimination statute commonly known as Title VII. You have been asked to research whether Whole In One is an employer and whether the women are employees under the definitions included in the federal law. During your research, you find the case of *King v. Miller*. Review Illustration 5-1.

To determine the issue, read the case. Ask yourself, "What did the parties ask the court to determine?" Sometimes, the court will note the issue directly in its opinion. Other times, you must ferret through the opinion to determine the issue. After you have read the *King* case, you should note that it involves a question of sex discrimination. However, your research is limited to the issues that concern the definitions of employer and employee. Therefore, the focus on your case brief should be issues that relate to your research problem.

Once you have read the *King* case, you will find that it addresses the question of whether an individual is an employee protected by Title VII. Now you are ready to draft the issue.

How Do You Draft a Statement of the Issue or Issues?

For the *King* case, you might start with this brief issue:

Is King an employee protected by Title VII or an independent contractor who is outside the protection of the federal law?

Now that the issue is presented in question format, you could leave the issue section here. However, the issue would be more meaningful for your research if you included more information about the legal issue the court focused on in making its determination. In its discussion, the *King* court focused on the amount of control that an employer must exercise before an individual is viewed as an employee rather than an independent contractor. You could incorporate the court's focus on control into the issue as follows:

> Is King, a worker subject to only minimal company control, an employee protected by Title VII or an independent contractor who is outside the protection of the federal law?

You also should include relevant facts in your issue statement. Again, this will make the issue more meaningful for your research. In this case, for example, you might add some facts about the company's method of payment and its lack of provisions for benefits:

> Is King, a worker subject to only minimal company control who was paid commissions rather than salary and benefits, an employee protected by Title VII or an independent contractor who is outside the protection of the federal law?

The final issue statement is the best because it incorporates the relevant facts that affect a court's decision concerning this issue and the rule of law that will be applied.

You might wonder why the issue did not focus on the appellate court's consideration of the district court's action in granting the motion for summary judgment in favor of the defendant. Students often phrase such an issue as follows:

> Did the district court err in granting summary judgment in favor of the defendant?

However, this issue focuses too heavily on the procedural question posed in the *King* case and does not include the applicable law or any of the legally significant facts. Your issue should concern the legal not procedural questions a court was asked to decide. As you learned above, the *King* case involved a motion for summary judgment.

To find the substantive legal issue, determine the legal question the parties asked the court to answer in the motion for summary judgment. In the *King* case, the parties asked the court to determine whether, as a matter of law, King was an independent contractor rather than an employee. This is the central legal issue. By focusing on this substantive issue rather than the procedural issue, your brief will be more useful to you in your research of the Whole In One case.

Some of you might wonder why you do not focus on the question of discrimination in your issue section. Remember the issue you were asked to answer with your research. You were asked to deal with the issues of the definition of employee and employer. You should tailor your brief to address these issues.

4. Holding

What Is a Holding, and How Do You Draft One?

The next section should be your **holding**. A holding often is called the rule of law. Essentially a holding is the court's answer to the issue or question presented. However, it is not a "yes," "no," or "maybe" answer to the issue. The holding should be a full sentence that responds directly to the issue posed and that incorporates both the legal standards and the significant legal facts on which the answer is based. Ideally, the holding should be a nugget you can use later in a summary of your research called a memorandum.

The process for drafting the holding is similar to the process for writing your issue statement. First, your holding should be a statement that answers the issue. If you selected the first issue statement considered in this discussion,

> Is King an employee protected by Title VII or an independent contractor who is outside the protection of the federal law?

then you might consider answering it as follows:

> King is an independent contractor rather than an employee and therefore is outside the protection of Title VII.

While this statement is simple and direct, similar to the first issue statement, it does not contain any relevant facts or incorporate any legal standards. This holding should be rewritten, incorporating the elements or legal standards that would be considered. Such a change would make the holding more meaningful in the context of this research.

The rewritten issue could read:

> Is King, a worker subject to only minimal company control, an independent contractor or an employee protected by Title VII?

Again you might want to include additional facts the court considered in determining that King was an independent contractor. For the holding, rewrite the final issue statement drafted above in the form of a statement.

> King, a worker subject to only minimal company control who was paid commissions rather than salary and benefits, was an independent contractor rather than an employee protected by Title VII.

The key to drafting a good issue statement, a holding, or any other type of writing is rewriting and editing. You must make your holding broad enough so that it could be useful for various research projects involving different fact patterns. However, you need to incorporate facts from the case at hand that make it unique and that limit the holding so that you can understand the facts that form the basis for the court's decision. Refine your statements and assess whether they are helpful in your research summary.

Also be careful to incorporate the facts and the underlying law into your holding statement as you did in your issue statement. A holding such as

> The district court did not err in granting summary judgment in favor of the defendant.

is not valuable for your research. It does not explain why the court found that the district court's decision was correct.

5. Facts

The next section of the brief should be the facts. Be certain to include the names of the parties, a notation concerning whether the party is a plaintiff, a defendant, an appellant or appellee, and some details about the party, such as whether it is a corporation or an individual. State the relevant rather than procedural facts in this section. Also explain why a party sought legal assistance.

What Are Relevant Facts?

Relevant facts are those facts that may have an effect on the legal issues decided in a particular action. To write this section, you must clearly understand the issues decided by the court. Decide which facts the court relied on to make its decision. Those are the facts that you should include in this section. The facts should be presented in a paragraph rather than in a list. Also mention any facts that will assist you in understanding the relationship between the parties and the dispute.

In the *King* case, the court relied on facts that explained the relationship between King and the Miller Co. For example, the court considered that King earned commissions and bonuses rather than a salary. That fact should be listed. Before you write your facts statement in paragraph format, make a rough outline of all of the facts that the court considered in making its decision. For the *King* case, your outline might look like this:

> King first worked as an "employee" agent
>   As an employee agent, was paid salary, company withheld taxes

King later was designated an "independent contract" agent, earned commission and bonuses but no salary

King signed an agreement that she was an independent contractor

Did not receive paid holidays, sick days, or vacation

Paid for her own health, life, and disability insurance

Miller supplied office space, furniture, file cabinets, forms, shared secretarial services, stamps, computers, and Miller stationery

Miller paid for insurance seminars and lunches at the seminars

Miller required that she attend weekly meetings, work in the office three and one half days per week and every third Saturday, check her mail and retrieve messages daily, and sell only Miller insurance

Miller restricted King's sales area

Miller did not regularly review King's work

King supplied her own personalized stationery, business cards, pens

King found her own customers, decided which products to sell, and set her own hours

The court listed additional facts, such as:

King had wanted to work for Miller because Miller had a good reputation

Before coming to Miller's office, King worked for three other insurance companies

King was a single, 30-year-old mother of two children

Before her experience in the insurance industry, she worked as a sales clerk at a local boutique

Note that for its decision the court did not consider any of the facts contained in the outline under additional facts. Therefore, they are not relevant facts and should not be included in your brief. After you have made your outline and determined which facts are relevant, you should draft your facts statement in a paragraph format. A list is not as helpful as a paragraph when you want to review the brief at a later date.

Your facts statement could be written in chronological order, in topical order, or using a combination of the two methods. Chronological order often works best when the case involves facts that need to be placed in order according to when they occurred. For example, in a personal injury action that results from a car accident, a chronological set of facts is best. Start with the first fact that occurred and work forward.

A chronological organization for the facts in the *King* case would read as follows:

In 1992, King started to work for Miller. King first worked for Miller as an employee agent. During that time, she received a salary and the company withheld income tax and Social Security payments. King later was promoted to contract agent. King was fired in 1993, and a man was hired to take her place.

A topical organization is the best choice for facts that have no temporal relationship. Instead, these facts are grouped by topic or legal claim. In this case, the topic is the legal question of whether King was an independent contractor. Therefore, you would group together all of the facts that relate to this question.

> As an independent contract agent, King earned a commission and bonuses, but did not receive a salary. She signed an agreement that stated that she was an independent contractor. As a contract agent, she did not receive paid holidays, sick days, or vacation days, and she paid for her own health, life, and disability insurance. King supplied her own personalized stationery, business cards, and pens. She found her own customers, decided which products to sell, and set her own hours.

> For its independent contract agents, Miller supplied office space, furniture, file cabinets, forms, shared secretarial services, stamps, computers, and Miller stationery. Miller also paid for required insurance seminars. Miller required that contract agents, such as King, attend weekly meetings, work in the office three and one half days per week and every third Saturday, check their mail and retrieve messages daily, and sell only Miller insurance. Miller also restricted King's sales area. Miller did not regularly review King's work.

In the *King* case, a combination of a chronological and topical organization works best. The *King* brief facts statement might read as follows:

> King first worked for Miller as an employee agent. During that time, she received a salary and the company withheld income tax and Social Security payments. King later was promoted to independent contract agent.

> As an independent contract agent, King earned a commission and bonuses, but did not receive a salary. She signed an agreement that stated that she was an independent contractor. As a contract agent, she did not receive paid holidays, sick days, or vacation days, and she paid for her own health, life, and disability insurance. King supplied her own personalized stationery, business cards, and pens. She found her own customers, decided which products to sell, and set her own hours.

> For its contract agents, Miller supplied office space, furniture, file cabinets, forms, shared secretarial services, stamps, computers, and Miller stationery. Miller also paid for required insurance seminars. Miller required that contract agents, such as King, attend weekly meetings, work in the office three and one half days per week and every third Saturday, check their mail and retrieve messages daily, and sell only Miller insurance. Miller also restricted King's sales area. Miller did not regularly review King's work.

The above facts statement begins with a chronological organization. It explains the beginning of the relationship between King and Miller. Next, it states all of the facts that pertain to King's benefits and her control of her work. The next paragraph explains what Miller provided for the independent contract agents and what Miller required of them. Following this facts section, you should include a reasoning or rationale section in a brief.

6. Rationale

What Should Be Included in the Reasoning or Rationale Section?

In the **rationale** or **reasoning** section, you should explain the court's thought process, relevant cases or statutes, and then apply the law to the facts of the case you are briefing. Essentially, you will explain the law the court relied on in making a decision. For example, the *King* court reviewed the definition of employee contained in Title VII and past case precedent, such as *Spirides v. Reinhardt*, 613 F.2d 826, 831 (D.C. Cir. 1979), and *Unger v. Consolidated Foods Corp.*, 657 F.2d 909, 915-916 n.8 (7th Cir. 1981) to determine that independent contractors are not protected by Title VII.

You also must review a decision for any tests a court considered in making its decision. In *King,* the court considered the economic realities test. Finally, note how the court applied the law to the facts of the particular case.

For the *King* case, you might include the following reasoning section in your brief:

> In order to determine whether an individual is an employee or an independent contractor, the employment relationship between the parties needs to be evaluated based on the economic realities and circumstances of the relationship. The court considered the control exercised by the "employer" over the worker; the method of payment; who paid for the individual's benefits, such as life and health insurance; and who paid for the operation. In this case, the court found that King was an independent contractor because she was paid on commission; she paid for her own benefits; she supplied her own supplies; and she controlled her work. The court found that she set her own hours, selected the products she sold, and generated her own clients. Based on these facts, the appellate court found that King should be considered an independent contractor rather than an employee.

In the reasoning section, you should include an application of the law to the facts of the case and a mini-conclusion that summarizes the court's decision. In the above example, the following section is the application of the court's reasoning to the facts of the case.

> In this case, the court found that King was an independent contractor because she was paid on commission; she paid for her own benefits; she supplied her own supplies; and she controlled her work. The court found that she set her own hours, selected the products she sold, and generated her own clients.

In the above example, the following statement is the mini-conclusion:

> Based on these facts, the appellate court found that King should be considered an independent contractor rather than an employee.

In some cases, you will find that a court bases its decision on reasons other than statutes or past cases. For example, a court might consider whether its decision would be fair under the circumstances. This type of analysis is called the court's consideration of policy, which sometimes is a question of what would benefit society, such as equal rights in an educational setting. Incorporate this policy into your reasoning section whenever it is useful for your research. After the reasoning or rationale discuss any dicta contained in the court's decision.

7. Dicta

What Is Dicta, and Why Would You Include It in a Case Brief?

If a court makes a statement concerning a question that it was not asked to answer, this statement is called **dicta**. Although dicta does not have any binding effect, it is often useful to predict how a court might decide a particular issue. Therefore, you want to include any dicta that might impact your case.

In the *King* case, the court stated that it was not asked to decide whether the district court should have considered all 11 factors before it rendered its decision. However, the court stated that the district court should have based its decision on all 11 factors. This statement by the court was dicta. It is helpful for your research problem because it states the factors that this circuit court might consider in determining whether an individual is an independent contractor rather than an employee.

The dicta section for the *King* case might read as follows:

> The 11-part test set by the *Spirides* court should be applied to determine whether an individual is an employee or an independent contractor.

ILLUSTRATION 5-3.   *Case Briefing Process*

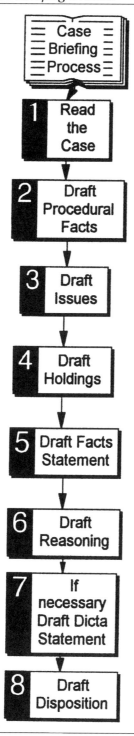

8. Disposition

The final section of your brief is the **disposition.** The disposition of a case is essentially the procedural result of the court's decision. For example, in the *King* case the court found that the district court's decision to grant summary judgment for the defendant was correct. Therefore the disposition section would state:

> The Court of Appeals affirmed the district court's judgment in granting summary judgment for the defendant.

Finally, remember to rewrite your brief, but do not spend too much time rewriting it. Use your own words rather than many quotes from the court opinions. Paraphrasing in your own words helps you analyze the case and better understand it when you review your brief in the future.

CHAPTER SUMMARY

A case brief is composed of several components, including an issue, a holding, the procedural facts, the relevant facts, the reasoning, and the case disposition. These briefs are designed to assist you and sometimes an attorney in understanding a case.

The brief's procedural facts statement should explain briefly how a case came before a court. The facts statement should include any relevant facts that affected the court's decision in the case.

The issue statement presents the questions posed by the parties. The holding is the rule of law established by the court. The reasoning explains how the court developed the rule of law and how it relates to the facts of the case. The disposition is the procedural result of the case.

Dicta often is included in a court decision. It is a statement made by a court concerning an issue other than one the court was asked to decide.

This chapter also provides you with your first exposure to legal writing. You learned the step-by-step process of drafting a case brief. Each component of a case brief relates to the other sections of the brief. For a review, see the flow chart.

Key Terms

Case brief	Issue presented
Case citation	Procedural facts
Dicta	Rationale
Disposition	Reasoning
Holding	Relevant facts
	Rule of law

EXERCISES

Issues

Review the following issues prepared for a case brief of the *King* case. List any problems you find. Which issue of the following five is best, and why?

Issue 1. Was the district court's decision that King was an independent contractor rather than an employee of the Miller Co. erroneous?

Issue 2. Whether King was an employee of Miller or an independent contractor for these reasons:

a. The control factor, in which agents are restricted in the selling of insurance as to whom or where. Agents also have mandatory requirements for working at designated times and dates. In addition, they are expected to attend weekly meetings and engage in daily office tasks.
b. The economic factor, in which agents are not allowed to sell products for anyone but Miller and that agents are "integral" to Miller's business.
c. As with employees, services, supplies, and education expenses are provided. Compensation is made in the form of commissions.
d. Work hours are based on flexibility for prime selling.
e. Performance evaluations and documents of rules of conduct are customary requirements of an employer-employee relationship.

Issue 3. Whether, in finding the plaintiff was not an employee under the Title VII definition, the trial court erred by:

a. failing to properly evaluate the nature of insurance sales;
b. and failing to evaluate and weigh the integral economic relationship between the defendant and the plaintiff;
c. and failing to discuss other evidence regarding the "control" criterion used to judge eligibility.

Issue 4. Whether the district court was clearly erroneous in determining that an insurance agent is an independent contractor rather than an employee when the individual is paid commissions and bonuses rather than a salary and her work is not supervised by the company.

Issue 5. Does an employer have to exercise control over a worker before that individual is considered an employee under Title VII?

Holdings

Review the holdings below that were drafted for a brief in the *King* case, list any problems you see with each, and note which is the best.

Holding 1. The court of appeals affirmed the lower court's decision that King is an independent contractor rather than an employee of the Miller Co.

Holding 2. Because the trial court did understand the law and its factual findings are not clearly erroneous, its decision is affirmed.

Holding 3. The district court's underlying factual findings are not clearly erroneous; therefore, the decision of the district court was affirmed.

Holding 4. Yes. An employer must exercise control over a worker before that individual is considered an employee under Title VII.

Briefing

Brief *Kalal v. Goldblatt Bros.*, 368 N.E.2d 671 (Ill. Ct. App. 1977).

6. The Legal Memorandum

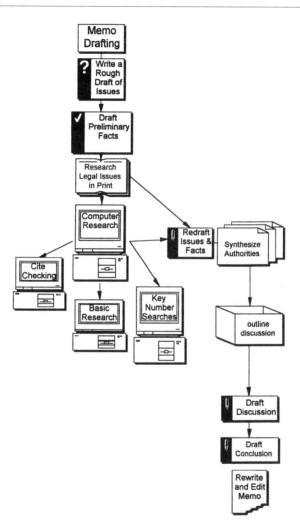

A. The Legal Memorandum
B. Audience
C. Organization of the Memorandum
    1. Heading
    2. Questions Presented
    3. Conclusion or Brief Answer
    4. Facts
    5. Discussion
D. Steps to Drafting a Memorandum

CHAPTER OVERVIEW

This chapter introduces you to the legal memorandum. You learn about your audience and how to write objectively. You are introduced to the components of the memorandum, such as the issues, conclusion or brief answer, facts, and discussion sections. The chapter concludes with a brief overview of the process of writing a memorandum.

A. The Legal Memorandum

What Is an Objective Legal Memorandum?

An **office memorandum**, often called a memo, explains in an objective rather than a persuasive or argumentative manner the current state of the law regarding an issue. It clarifies how that law applies to a client's transaction or legal dilemma. A memo should explain the current law—both favorable and unfavorable—and any legal theories pertaining to the issue.

Why Would You Draft a Legal Memorandum?

The balanced approach of a legal memo helps an attorney see the strengths and weaknesses of a transaction or dispute. Only in seeing all sides of an issue can an attorney determine how best to represent a client. If in writing a memo you advocate a single position or attempt to persuade an attorney, the attorney cannot make an informed decision about a dispute or transaction. This can be a very costly error in terms of money, time, client loyalty, and court favor.

A memo also assists an attorney in predicting how a court might decide a particular issue. A memo could be drafted to address an issue raised as a case progresses in court. You as a paralegal might research whether the law provides for the dismissal of an action; your research and memorandum might form the basis for such a motion to dismiss or for subsequent court documents. You might also write a memo to assist an attorney in drafting an appellate brief.

B. Audience

Who Reads a Memorandum?

Because you usually research a legal question to determine whether a client has a claim or should proceed with a transaction, you generally prepare your memo for an attorney following your research. Your memo also might be sent to the client. Your primary audience, then, is the attorney, and the secondary audience is the client.

Often memoranda are saved in **memo banks** accessible to all firm or corporation attorneys and paralegals, so other attorneys and paralegals might review your memo. These memo banks are a good place for you to start a research project because an attorney or a paralegal already may have researched the topic. These banks often save time and money for a client. After you review a memo from the memo bank, update the research.

C. Organization of the Memorandum

How Is a Memorandum Organized?

Different attorneys prefer different formats for a memorandum. Ask the assigning attorney if your firm or corporation has a particular style. Request a sample memo so that you can review the style he or she prefers or go to the memo bank to review a sample. The format discussed in this chapter is one commonly accepted style. See Sample Memo in Illustration 6-1.

ILLUSTRATION 6-1. *Sample Memorandum*

MEMORANDUM

To: Wallace Maine

From: Thomas Wall

Date: November 15, 1993

Re: Sex Discrimination Case against Whole In One No. C93 CIV 190 G12399990

QUESTIONS PRESENTED

1. Under Title VII, was Whole In One Golf Resort an employer when 14 people, including three full-time and 11 part-time workers, worked on any one day for 24 weeks and when 10 full-time employees were on the Whole In One payroll?

2. Under Title VII, was Walker an independent contractor rather than an employee when she worked exclusively for Whole In One, paid taxes quarterly rather than through deductions, and worked with limited company supervision?

ILLUSTRATION 6-1. *Continued*

3. Under Title VII, was Radiant an independent contractor rather than an employee when she worked with limited company supervision using company supplies and equipment and had taxes and medical deductions taken from her salary?

CONCLUSIONS

1. Whole In One was an employer. Under Title VII, an employer has at least 15 employees working for 20 or more weeks during the relevant year. Salaried employees are included in this number for each week they are on the payroll, while hourly workers are only counted on the days they actually work. In 1993, the year of the alleged discrimination, 14 workers, three full-time and 11 part-time people, worked for Whole In One on any day during the 24-week restaurant and golf season. However, 10 full-time workers were on the payroll. Because these part-time workers are only counted on the days that they work, the number of part-time individuals included in the count of employees is 11 for each day of the 24-week season. Because full-time workers, however, are counted for each day of a week that they are on the payroll, all 10 of the Whole In One full-time workers would be included in the count of employees. In total, Whole In One had 11 part-time workers and 10 full-time workers "working" for 20 or more weeks during the relevant year, bringing the total count of employees to 21. Therefore, Whole In One was an employer under Title VII.

2. Walker was an employee. The Seventh Circuit will weigh five factors to determine whether she was an independent contractor or an employee for this Title VII lawsuit. The primary focus will be on the company's control of Walker. Although Walker worked from home, set her own hours and had an impact on her commission pay, the company controlled her work by reviewing and revising it, restricting Walker's employment opportunities, and providing supplies for her. Therefore, the company exerted control over Walker and she would be considered an employee.

3. Radiant was probably an employee. To determine whether she was an employee or independent contractor for this Title VII lawsuit, the court will focus on five factors, primarily the amount of control the company exerted over Radiant's work. Whole In One provided Radiant with an office, supplies, a two-year contract, and additional training. Whole In One paid her regularly and deducted taxes from her salary. Although Whole In One did not actively supervise Radiant's work on a daily basis, she still worked in the company offices and was under the control of Whole In One. Therefore, the court probably will find that Radiant was an employee.

FACTS

Victoria Radiant and Karen Walker, two former Whole In One Enterprises workers, brought a federal sex discrimination lawsuit based

ILLUSTRATION 6-1. *Continued*

upon Title VII against our client, Whole In One Enterprises, owned by Nancy and Craig Black. The lawsuit, filed in the U.S. District Court for the Northern District of Illinois, stems from the dismissal of the two women by the Blacks during 1993.

The Blacks own Whole In One Enterprises, which operates a miniature golf course and restaurant in Glenview, Illinois. During the 24-week 1993 restaurant season, 10 people worked full-time and 14 people worked part-time for Whole In One. However, no more than 14 people worked on any one day. Of those 14 people, only three were full-time employees. The other full-time employees regularly took days off during the summer restaurant and golf season.

Among the full-time workers was Karen Walker who worked as a public relations director for Whole In One. Walker responded to an ad which said that "an employer" sought an individual to perform public relations work. Whole In One hired Walker without a contract and prohibited her from working for other firms. However, Walker worked from home and set her own hours. Whole In One required Walker to attend weekly staff meetings at the company offices where Whole In One would review and revise Walker's work. The company supplied Walker with paper, pencils, stamps, telephone service, and paid for her life and health insurance. Whole In One did not withhold taxes from Walker's commissions.

Victoria Radiant, who had a two-year employment contract with the company, provided marketing services to Whole In One from October of 1991 until she was fired in 1993. Although Radiant worked in the company office, Whole In One management rarely supervised her work. The company paid for her continued education, provided her with bonuses, and deducted taxes from her weekly salary.

Applicable Statute:

The term "employer" means a person engaged in an industry affecting commerce who has fifteen or more employees for each working day in each of 20 or more calendar weeks in the current or preceding calendar year. 42 U.S.C. § 2000e(b) (1988).

DISCUSSION

This memo first will address whether Walker and Radiant can successfully establish that Whole In One was an employer within the meaning of 42 U.S.C. § 2000e(b) (1988), commonly called Title VII. Next, the discussion will focus on whether Radiant can establish that she was an employee protected by Title VII. Finally, the memo will explore whether Walker was an employee protected by Title VII. If Whole In One was not an employer, then the Title VII claim will be dismissed. If the court finds that neither individual is an employee, the individual's claim will be barred.

ILLUSTRATION 6-1. *Continued*

I. Was Whole In One an Employer under Title VII?

Before a federal court can consider Walker's and Radiant's claims, the plaintiffs must establish that Whole In One was an employer under the definition established in Title VII. An employer is "a person engaged in a business affecting commerce who has fifteen or more employees for each working day in each of 20 or more calendar weeks in the current or preceding calendar year." 42 U.S.C. § 2000e(b). The focus of this discussion will be how to calculate whether 15 employees worked for Whole In One on each working day in each of 20 or more calendar weeks and how to determine which year's employment records are relevant. The Seventh Circuit has held that full-time employees are "working" each day of a week during a week for which they are on the payroll, but part-time workers are counted only on the days that they actually work. *Zimmerman v. North American Signal Co.*, 704 F.2d 347 (7th Cir. 1983). In 1993, the year of the alleged discrimination, 14 workers, three full-time and 11 part-time people, worked for the Whole In One on any day during the 24-week restaurant and golf season. In addition, 10 full-time workers were on the payroll. Based upon the counting method established in *Zimmerman*, these figures indicate that Whole In One had at least 15 employees working for each working day in each of 20 or more calendar weeks. Therefore, Whole In One was an employer under Title VII.

The central focus of this discussion will be how to calculate the number of employees. First, the relevant year must be determined. The statute states that the time to be considered is "twenty or more calendar weeks in the current or preceding year." 42 U.S.C. § 2000e(b). The current year of the discrimination was 1993. Since the statute specifies "or" the preceding year, 1992 also is relevant. However, in a persuasive decision a Tennessee district court held that the "current calendar year" is the year in which the alleged discrimination occurred. *Musser v. Mountain View Broadcasting, Inc.*, 578 F. Supp. 229 (E.D. Tenn. 1984). If the court follows *Musser*, the employment records from 1993 would be relevant because Whole In One fired Walker and Radiant in 1993.

The phrase "each working day" must be clarified. "Each working day" should be taken literally and must be a day on which an employer conducts normal, full operations on that day. *Zimmerman*, 704 F.2d at 353; *Wright v. Kosciusko Medical Clinic, Inc.*, 791 F. Supp. 1327, 1333 (N.D. Ind. 1992). Whole In One operated the golf course and restaurant seven days a week. Therefore, Whole In One must have 15 employees working on all seven days of a week to be considered an employer under Title VII.

The final issue is which individuals should be counted on each of the working days. The Seventh Circuit has determined that a salaried or full-time employee is counted as working for every day of the week that they are on the payroll, whether or not they were actually at work

ILLUSTRATION 6-1. *Continued*

on a particular day. *Zimmerman v. North American Signal Co.,* 704 F.2d 347 (7th Cir. 1983). However, part-time workers are counted only on the days that they actually work. *Id.; Wright,* 791 F. Supp. at 1327; *Norman v. Levy,* 767 F. Supp. 144 (N.D. Ill. 1991). In 1993, the year of the alleged discrimination, 14 workers, three full-time and 11 part-time people, worked for the Whole In One on any day during the 24-week restaurant and golf season. As these part-time workers are only counted on the days that they work, the number of part-time individuals included in the count of employees was 11 for each day of the 24-week season. Since full-time workers, however, are counted for each day of a week that they are on the payroll, all 10 of the Whole In One full-time workers should be included in the count of employees. In total, Whole In One had 11 part-time workers and 10 full-time workers "working" for 20 or more weeks during the relevant year, bringing the total count of employees to 21. Therefore, Whole In One was an employer under Title VII.

II. Are Walker and Radiant Employees or Independent Contractors?

If the plaintiffs can show that Whole In One was an employer, the court still must determine whether Walker and Radiant were employees entitled to Title VII protection or independent contractors. To determine whether an individual is an independent contractor or an employee, the "economic realities" of the relationship between an employer and his or her worker must be weighed. *Knight v. United Farm Bureau Mut. Ins. Co.,* 950 F.2d 377 (7th Cir. 1991); *Norman v. Levy,* 767 F. Supp. 144 (N.D. Ill. 1991); *Mitchell v. Tenney,* 650 F. Supp. 703 (N.D. Ill. 1986). The Seventh Circuit will weigh five factors to determine the economic reality of the relationship: 1) the amount of control and supervision the employer exerts over the worker; 2) the responsibility for the costs of the operation; 3) the worker's occupation and the skills required; 4) the method and form of compensation and benefits; and 5) the length of the job commitment. *Knight,* 950 F.2d at 378. Control is the most important factor. *Id.* Moreover, when an employer controls a worker in such a manner as to make that worker economically dependent upon the employer, the court is likely to find that an employment relationship exists. *Vakharia v. Swedish Covenant Hosp.,* 765 F. Supp. 461 (N.D. Ill. 1991).

The *Knight* case involved an insurance agent who was not allowed to sell insurance for any other company and who was required to attend weekly staff meetings in the office and work a specified number of hours in the office. *Knight,* 950 F.2d at 378. The insurance company provided Knight with supplies and paid for business expenses. *Id.* These agents were trained by the insurance company and were crucial to the company's continued operation. *Id.* Knight was paid on commission and did not have taxes deducted. *Id.* Knight also was free to leave the company and work elsewhere. *Id.* Based upon these facts, the *Knight* court failed to find that the agent was an employee.

Although Walker's work situation was factually similar in many ways to that of the plaintiff in *Knight,* the *Knight* case can be distinguished based upon the nature of the occupations. Knight worked in the insurance sales field. Most often, individuals who work in such positions are independent contractors rather than employees of a company. In addition, the Seventh Circuit indicated in the dicta of the *Knight* case that it might have found that Knight was an employee. *Id.* at 381.

In contrast to *Knight,* the U.S. District Court for the Northern District of Illinois found that control of an individual's livelihood could establish an employment relationship. *Vakharia v. Swedish Covenant Hosp.,* 765 F. Supp. 461 (N.D. Ill. 1991). The plaintiff in *Vakharia* was a physician who was dependent upon the hospital for business. *Id.* at 463. The district court found that this individual depended upon the hospital for patients and that when the hospital reduced the number of patients it assigned to the plaintiff, the plaintiff's livelihood was affected. *Id.* The court held that when an employer has this type of control over an individual's livelihood an employment relationship may be established.

The facts in our case are similar to the facts in the *Vakharia* case. In our case, Whole In One barred Walker from working for other companies and required that she attend weekly staff meetings at the company offices where Whole In One would review and revise Walker's work. Since Walker was barred from working for other individuals and was required to attend these meetings where Whole In One would revise her work, it seems that Walker could establish the central element of control necessary to prove an employment relationship. In addition, these facts show that Walker, like the plaintiff in *Vakharia,* was economically dependent upon her employer, Whole In One. Therefore, an employment relationship should be established.

However, the plaintiffs will be able to show more than control. They will be able to establish that Whole In One bore the cost of the operation of the business. Whole In One supplied Walker with paper, pencils, stamps, telephone service, and paid for her life and health insurance. These facts indicate that Whole In One was responsible for the cost of Walker's services to the company—a fact that would help to establish that Walker was an employee.

The factors which would mitigate the establishment of an employment relationship, however, are that Walker worked from home and set her own hours and Whole In One did not withhold taxes from Walker's commissions. Despite these factors, the court is likely to focus on the control Whole In One had over Walker and is likely to find that she was an employee rather than an independent contractor.

III. Was Radiant an Employee or an Independent Contractor?

Whether Radiant was an employee again turns on the amount of control Whole In One exerted over Radiant's work. The court will focus on the same factors established in *Knight* to determine whether an employment relationship exists. *Knight*, 950 F.2d at 378. Control will be the key factor the court will consider. *Id*. Radiant had a two-year employment contract with the company to provide marketing services. Whole In One also provided her with an office, supplies, and additional training. The company paid her regularly and deducted taxes from her salary. Based upon these facts, the company exerted control over Radiant. Therefore, the court is likely to find that Radiant was an employee of Whole In One.

1. Heading

In Illustration 6-1, the first part of the memo is the heading. A sample heading also is shown in Illustration 6-2. The first notation in the heading of either illustration is the word MEMORANDUM, placed in all capital letters at the top of the page. The next notations in both Illustrations 6-1 and 6-2 tell the reader who the memorandum is written to and from, the date, and the subject. The regarding line, indicated by the "Re:," varies depending on the firm's style. For example, some insurance clients ask that you include claim numbers in the regarding line. Some attorneys prefer court case numbers, and still others prefer clients' billing numbers and file numbers.

2. Questions Presented

The next portion of the memo seen in Illustration 6-1 is the questions presented section, sometimes called the issues section.

What Are the Issues or Questions Presented?

The terms **issues** or **questions presented** are synonymous. For our purpose, we will use the terms "question presented" or "questions pre-

ILLUSTRATION 6-2.   *Sample Memorandum Heading*

MEMORANDUM

To: Sarah E. Lillian

From: Kelsey Barrington

Date: July 8, 1994

Re: Negligence Action between Sack and Shop Grocery Store and Rebecca Harris

sented." The questions presented are the specific legal questions an attorney has asked you to research. The question presented is phrased in the form of a question concerning the legal issue posed and it includes a reference to the applicable law and some legally significant facts. See Illustration 6-3. The legal issue in Illustration 6-3 is whether the grocery store owner was negligent and whether he owed a duty to the patron. The legally significant facts are that the patron slipped on a banana peel that had been on the grocery store floor for two days. A detailed explanation of how to draft the questions presented will be provided in Chapter 7.

ILLUSTRATION 6-3.   *Question Presented*

Is a grocery store owner liable for injuries sustained by a store patron who slipped on a banana peel that had been on the grocery store floor for two days?

---

3. Conclusion or Brief Answer

What Is the Brief Answer or Conclusion?

You should follow the questions presented section with a **brief answer** or a **conclusion**. Brief answers and conclusions differ in format, although their purposes are similar. A brief answer is a short statement that directly answers the question presented or questions presented. See Illustration 6-4. Some attorneys prefer a brief answer immediately following the question or questions presented and a formal conclusion at the end of the memo. The brief answers should be presented in the same order as the questions they answer.

ILLUSTRATION 6-4.   *Brief Answer*

Probably yes. A grocery store owner probably will be liable based upon negligence for injuries sustained by a store patron who slipped on a banana peel that had been on the grocery store floor for two days.

What Is the Difference Between a Conclusion and a Brief Answer?

For other attorneys, a conclusion without a brief answer is sufficient. A conclusion is an in-depth answer to the question presented. There is no set length for a conclusion and it should be a succinct statement that summarizes the substance of the memo. See Illustration 6-5. As you can see in Illustration 6-5, the conclusion is more in-depth than the brief answer. However, note that both the conclusion and the brief answer include references to the legally significant facts—the failure to remove the banana peel from the grocery store floor. In the conclusion, you provide your opinion concerning the case. However, a paralegal should refrain from telling an attorney how to proceed. For example, do not say "I think that we will lose this case, so we should settle it." Instead, you should say that "This case is not likely to be won." Allow the attorney to determine whether the case should be settled. Drafting conclusions and brief answers will be explained in detail in Chapter 7.

ILLUSTRATION 6-5. *Conclusion*

A grocery store owner owes a patron a duty of reasonable care. The store owner is likely to be found to have breached that duty of reasonable care because he failed to remove a banana peel from the grocery store floor during the preceding two days. The injuries the patron sustained were directly caused by a slip on a banana peel. Therefore, the grocery store owner is likely to be found liable to the patron.

4. Facts

What Are the Facts?

Following the conclusion or brief answer, you should include a **facts statement** that explains the status of the case and all of the facts that might have a bearing on the outcome of a client's case. These facts are called **legally significant facts.** You should include facts that cast your client's dispute or transaction in a good light and those that shade it in a negative light. See Illustration 6-6.

ILLUSTRATION 6-6. *Facts Statement*

Our client, Sack and Shop Grocery Store, is being sued for negligence by Rebecca Harris.

Harris went to the store to purchase groceries on July 8, 1994. While she was in the produce section, she slipped on a banana peel that had been left on the floor by a grocery store employee. The employee had dropped it on the floor two days earlier and had failed to clean it up after a patron asked him to do so.

Harris sustained a broken arm and head injuries as a result of the slip and fall.

5. Discussion

What Is the Discussion?

Following the facts, you will include your **discussion** in which you will explain the current state of the applicable law, analyze the law, and apply the law to the legally significant facts noted in the facts statement. Any problems posed in the client's case and counterarguments should be presented here. This should not be an exhaustive review of the history of the law but should be a focused analysis of the current state of the law. The law should be applied to each of the legally significant facts.

Finally, following the discussion, you should include a conclusion if a brief answer rather than a conclusion has been used earlier.

D. Steps in Drafting a Memorandum

What Steps Should You Take in Drafting a Memorandum?

1. An attorney will assign a research problem to you. Discuss the problem thoroughly with the attorney. Be certain to ask the attorney questions to clarify the legal issues and the facts of a dispute or transaction. Ask for guidance concerning possible topics to research and resources to consult.

2. Immediately following your meeting, draft a preliminary statement of the legal issues and the relevant facts.

3. Begin your research. To develop an understanding of the issues and the general legal rules applicable to your problem, and to provide you with some search terms, read secondary authorities such as encyclopedias and *American Law Reports*. During your research, you often discover other issues that may be relevant, and you find that additional facts are important. If you are uncertain whether to pursue these additional issues, ask the attorney who assigned the case whether the issues are relevant.

4. If you have additional questions about the facts of a case, ask the attorney or the client for additional facts to assist you in determining what authorities are relevant to your research.

5. After you find relevant authorities, validate the authorities, and review the citators for more current, valuable authorities. If necessary, review these additional authorities.

6. Prepare case briefs of the relevant cases. (See Chapter 5 for a detailed discussion of case briefing.)

7. After you have completed your research, rewrite the questions presented.

8. Rewrite the facts and then draft the brief answers or conclusions (or both).

9. Next, outline the discussion section. (See Chapter 11 for a discussion of outlining and organizing the memorandum.) While you are preparing your outline, you should synthesize the legal authorities. (This process is explained in Chapter 10.) You should formulate your discussion and paragraphs in a special format called IRAC, which is an abbreviation for the formula Issue, Rule, Application, and Conclusion. (This format is discussed thoroughly in Chapter 9.) You can now begin to write your memorandum.

Checklist for Drafting a Memorandum

1. Discuss the case with the attorney
   a. Discuss the legal issues presented
   b. Discuss the known facts
   c. Determine whether additional facts should be investigated
   d. Determine what law governs
   e. Check the memo bank to determine firm's style and to learn whether the issue has been researched previously
2. Draft a preliminary statement of the facts
3. Draft a preliminary statement of the legal issues or questions presented
4. Research the legal issue or issues
   a. If you find additional relevant issues, discuss them with the attorney
   b. Determine whether additional facts should be considered in light of the new issues; ask the attorney or client about additional facts
   c. Research the new issues, if necessary
5. Rewrite the issues or questions presented after your research has allowed you to focus them better
6. Draft a brief answer or a conclusion (or both)
7. Rewrite the facts statement of the memo
8. Draft an outline of the discussion section of the memo; organize the discussion
9. Draft the discussion section
10. Reevaluate the facts and rewrite the facts statement to include only legally significant facts
11. Rewrite the conclusion

What Are Some Hints for Researching and Drafting a Memorandum?

You should be careful to guide your reader through each section of your memo and from issue to issue. To do this, introduce the legal issues in the facts section and again in the discussion section. Also, use headings and transitions to guide your reader into the new sections.

Your memo should be clearly written, accurate, concise, and thorough. Use everyday language rather than legalese. Write the memo as if the reader is unfamiliar with the law but do not be condescending. Your memo should not trace the legal history of the law. Instead it should be a statement of the current state of the law.

When you approach a legal rule, start with the rule rather than the citation for the authority. Doing so makes your discussion stronger.

Be certain that your discussion supports your conclusions. Incorporate the relevant facts into your discussion.

CHAPTER SUMMARY

The legal memorandum is composed of issues, conclusions and brief answers, facts, and a discussion section. These are written for attorneys and clients. Memoranda are designed to assist them in determining the current state of the law regarding a legal issue and how that law applies to the facts presented in a particular case.

In the next few chapters, you learn about each one of the components of a memorandum, the questions presented, the facts, the conclusions, the brief answers, and the discussion.

Key Terms

Brief answer	Issues
Conclusion	Legally significant facts
Discussion	Memo banks
Facts statement	Office memorandum
Heading	Questions presented

EXERCISES

True or False

1. A memorandum should be persuasive in its style.
2. A memorandum should present only facts that are favorable to your client's position.

3. A memorandum should inform the attorney and the client about the favorable authorities and known facts as well as the authorities and facts that pose problems for a client's case.

4. Your memorandum will never be read by a client.

5. You should include descriptive words in the facts section that slant the facts in favor of your client's position.

7. Questions Presented and Conclusions or Brief Answers

A. Questions Presented or Issues
   1. First Draft
   2. Research the Issues and Revise It
   3. Specificity and Precision
B. Brief Answers and Conclusions

CHAPTER OVERVIEW

Chapter 6 introduced you to the legal memorandum and its components. This chapter explains the reasons for drafting questions presented, issues, brief answers, and conclusions and teaches you how to draft these items.

A. Questions Presented or Issues

What Are the Questions Presented or Issues?

The **questions presented** or issues are the problems you must research to answer the attorney's or client's questions. These questions provide a preview to the reader about the applicable legal standards and the relevant facts.

Who Reads the Questions Presented Statement?

The questions presented statement often is the first portion of a memorandum an attorney reviews. Many attorneys focus on these questions and the conclusions or brief answers. Some attorneys read these questions and answers without reading the entire memorandum. Therefore, your questions presented statement must be easy to understand and allow the reader to quickly grasp the legal questions that the memo will address.

How Do You Draft and Refine the Questions Presented?

1. First Draft

The first draft of the questions presented should be done following the receipt of the initial research assignment from the attorney. Draft a simple statement that explains the questions you were asked to research. For example, an attorney provides you with the following facts:

> While driving a car Ronnie Randall struck Janice Kahn's son at 5 P.M. on August 29, 1993. It was bright and clear. No skid marks appeared on the dry street following the accident.
>
> Janice Kahn was working in her garden about five feet from the accident scene at the time of the accident. Her son was playing a game in the street before Randall's car struck him. Kahn saw the car strike her son. When she first looked up from her garden, she thought her 11-year-old son was dead. He was covered with blood and had several broken bones. However, Kahn's son was conscious after the accident.
>
> Immediately after the accident, Randall, who had a blood alcohol level of .11, was cited for drunk driving and driving with a suspended driver's license. Police charged him with drunk driving and suspended his license two weeks earlier after the car he was driving struck another child at the same spot. Randall has a drinking history.
>
> Following the accident, several witnesses said Randall was upset and wobbled as he walked. One witness said that Randall intentionally turned the steering wheel to hit Kahn's son. Kahn stated that Randall often swerved down her street to get her attention.
>
> Rhonda Albert, Kahn's neighbor, said she heard Randall say he would get even with Kahn after Kahn broke off a 10-year relationship with him. During Kahn and Randall's 10-year relationship, Randall was close to Kahn's son. He took him to ball games, including one in April, and attended the son's baseball games. Randall knew that Kahn's son was the most important person in her life.
>
> Since the accident, Kahn vomits daily and has nightmares about the accident. Dr. Susan Faigen, Kahn's internist, states that the vomiting and nightmares are the result of the accident.

The attorney wants you to research whether Janice Kahn has a claim against Ronnie Randall for intentional infliction of emotional distress. Your first draft of the question presented might be:

> Does Janice Kahn have a valid claim for intentional infliction of emotional distress against Ronnie Randall?

This question presented is too vague. To make your question more understandable in the context of Kahn's case, you must incorporate legally significant facts—facts that will have an impact on a jury's or judge's decision concerning Kahn's claim. You might rewrite the question presented with the facts as follows:

> Does Janice Kahn have a valid claim for intentional infliction of emotional distress against Ronnie Randall when Kahn saw Randall strike her 11-year-old child with his car?

By incorporating some **legally significant facts,** you have drafted a question presented that places the issue in perspective for the reader and that clearly identifies the parties in the action. This question presented allows the reader to understand the legal issue in the context of the factual circumstances surrounding the claim.

2. Research the Issue and Revise It

Now you are ready to research the issue. After you complete your research, you determine what law applies to a claim for intentional infliction of emotional distress. Once you determine the legal standard, you rewrite the question presented to incorporate that standard and only the legally significant facts. Your rewrite should frame the questions presented around the applicable legal standard and should present the applicable legal standard in the context of the facts that will affect the determination of a claim.

In the case of Janice Kahn, you learn from a decision of the highest court in your state that intentional infliction of emotional distress is "an act done by a person which is extreme and outrageous, done with intent to cause another to suffer severe emotional distress, and which results in distress and emotional injury to another. The emotional injury must manifest itself with a physical problem." If you rewrite the question presented above to incorporate the legal standard and legally significant facts, it might read as follows:

> Does Janice Kahn have a valid claim for intentional infliction of emotional distress against Ronnie Randall after Kahn saw Randall turn his car to strike Kahn's 11-year-old child in front of her causing her to suffer from anxiety, headaches, and vomiting?

This question presented incorporates legally significant facts and provides these facts in the context of the legal standard. Randall's intention is one of the legal factors or elements in determining whether Kahn has a claim for intentional infliction of emotional distress. The question presented notes the legally significant fact that Randall turned his car to strike the child. Although you should mention legally significant facts and the legal standard, keep the issue short enough for the reader to understand.

3. Specificity and Precision

The facts should be **specific** and your characterization of the parties and the issues should be **precise**. For example, one of the issues posed in the sample memo in Chapter 6's Illustration 6-1 involves the question of whether an individual is an independent contractor or an employee. You could pose the question presented as follows:

> Under Title VII, was Walker an employee when she worked exclusively for Whole In One, paid taxes quarterly rather than through deductions, and worked with limited company supervision?

This question presented is not precise because it does not characterize the legal issue presented completely. The legal issue is whether Walker is an independent contractor rather than an employee. Therefore, the question presented could be refined as follows:

> Under Title VII, was Walker an independent contractor rather than an employee when she worked exclusively for Whole In One, paid taxes quarterly rather than through deductions, and worked with limited company supervision?

You must only ask a question in the questions presented statement, not provide an answer. You will answer the question presented in the brief answer or conclusion section.

If you have more than one issue or question presented, place them in a logical order and make that order consistent throughout the memo. The first question presented, then, should be answered first in the conclusion or brief answer statement and should be the first issue discussed in the discussion. See Illustration 6-1 in Chapter 6.

B. Brief Answers and Conclusions

What Are Brief Answers?

Brief answers are the answers to the question or questions presented. A brief answer is a short statement. Some attorneys prefer a brief answer that is later accompanied by a formal conclusion at the end of the memorandum. The brief answer allows an attorney to read a memo in a hurry and determine the legal issues. It is a quick answer to the questions presented. Brief answers should be presented in the same order as the questions presented. See Illustration 7-1. The brief answer should include a brief statement of the applicable law and some relevant facts. A brief answer for the question presented above could be presented as follows:

> Yes. Kahn can bring a successful action for intentional infliction of emotional distress against Ronnie Randall because she saw Randall turn his car to strike her 11-year-old son causing her to suffer severe anxiety, headaches, and vomiting.

ILLUSTRATION 7-1. *Sample Memorandum: Questions Presented and Conclusions*

QUESTIONS PRESENTED

1. Under Title VII, was Whole In One an employer when 14 people, including three full-time and 11 part-time workers, worked on any one day for 24 weeks and when 10 full-time employees were on the Whole In One payroll?

2. Under Title VII, was Walker an independent contractor rather than an employee when she worked exclusively for Whole In One, paid taxes quarterly rather than through deductions, and worked with limited company supervision?

3. Under Title VII, was Radiant an independent contractor rather than an employee when she worked with limited company supervision using company supplies and equipment and had taxes and medical deductions taken from her salary?

CONCLUSIONS

1. Whole In One was an employer. Under Title VII, an employer has at least 15 employees working for 20 or more weeks during the relevant year. Salaried employees are included in this number for each week they are on the payroll, while hourly workers are only counted on the days they actually work. In 1993, the year of the alleged discrimination, 14 workers, three full-time and 11 part-time people, worked for Whole In One on any day during the 24-week restaurant and golf season. However, 10 full-time workers were on the payroll. As these part-time workers are only counted on the days that they work, the number of part-time individuals included in the count of employees is 11 for each day of the 24-week season. Since full-time workers, however, are counted for each day of a week that they are on the payroll, all 10 of the Whole In One full-time workers would be included in the count of employees. In total, Whole In One had 11 part-time workers and 10 full-time workers "working" for 20 or more weeks during the relevant year, bringing the total count of employees to 21. Therefore, Whole In One was an employer under Title VII.

ILLUSTRATION 7-1. *Continued*

2. Walker was an employee. The Seventh Circuit will weigh five factors to determine whether she was an independent contractor or an employee for this Title VII lawsuit. The primary focus will be on the company's control of Walker. Although Walker worked from home, set her own hours, and had an impact on her commission pay, the company controlled her work by reviewing and revising it, restricting Walker's employment opportunities, and providing supplies for her. Therefore, the company exerted control over Walker, and she would be considered an employee.

3. Radiant was probably an employee. To determine whether she was an employee or independent contractor for the purpose of this Title VII lawsuit, the court will focus on five factors, primarily the amount of control the company exerted over Radiant's work. Whole In One provided Radiant with an office, supplies, a two-year contract, and additional training. Whole In One paid her regularly and deducted taxes from her salary. Although Whole In One did not actively supervise Radiant's work on a daily basis, she still worked in the company offices and was under the control of Whole In One. Therefore, the court probably will find that Radiant was an employee.

What Is a Conclusion?

A **conclusion** also is an answer to the question presented and a summary of the discussion section. For some attorneys, a conclusion without a brief answer is sufficient. However, other attorneys prefer both a brief answer and a conclusion.

A conclusion does not have a set length, but it is generally longer than a brief answer. It is not a detailed or in-depth discussion of the legal issue presented in the case. It is a succinct summary of the substance of the memo. The conclusion should include legally significant facts and the applicable legal standard. In the conclusion, you must answer the question presented and provide your best prediction concerning the outcome of the case. It is acceptable to use terms such as "likely" or "probably" when you think that the outcome of an action is uncertain.

How and When Do You Draft a Conclusion?

Before you draft your conclusion, review the questions presented and your preliminary facts statement. (A detailed explanation of the facts statement is presented in Chapter 8.)

Next, write the conclusion as an answer to the question presented and incorporate some of the relevant facts contained in the facts section of the memo. Refine the conclusion so that the reader understands the legal standard and the applicable facts. Conclusions often work well when drafted in an IRAC formula: Issue, Rule, Application, and Conclusion. (For a thorough discussion of the IRAC formula, see Chapter 9.)

For the facts and the question presented in the *Kahn* case, the following conclusion might be prepared:

> The central question is whether Janice Kahn has a valid claim for intentional infliction of emotional distress against Ronnie Randall? To successfully prove a claim for intentional infliction of emotional distress Kahn must show that the act that caused the distress was extreme and outrageous and done with intent. In this case, Kahn saw Randall turn his car to strike her 11-year-old child. Seeing this accident caused Kahn to suffer from anxiety, headaches, and vomiting daily. Several witnesses can testify that Randall said that he intended to harm Kahn, and Kahn states that Randall turned the car to strike her son. Two factors, however, might show that Randall lacked intent: the statement that he made to the police that he did not intend to hit the child and the fact that his blood alcohol level was .11 possibly preventing him from formulating the needed intent. Kahn probably has a claim for intentional emotional distress.

This conclusion provides a summary of the writer's prediction of the outcome of the case after the legal standards are applied to the legally significant facts:

> Janice Kahn probably has a valid claim for intentional infliction of emotional distress against Ronnie Randall.

Facts such as that Kahn saw Randall turn the car to strike her son and that witnesses can testify concerning what Randall said he intended to do are relevant to the questions of whether the act was extreme and outrageous. The legal standard provides that the act must be extreme and outrageous before an individual can be liable for intentional infliction of emotional distress. In addition, the extreme and outrageous act must be done with intent. Randall's intent also is discussed in the conclusion.

Now read the questions presented in Illustration 7-1. For the question presented in Illustration 7-1, the issue is whether Whole In One is an employer under Title VII. The legal standards that determine whether Whole In One is an employer center on the definition of employer under Title VII and case law.

Now read the conclusion. It answers the question presented. In the second and third sentences, the conclusion provides the legal standard for determining this issue. These sentences refer to the definition of employer contained in the Title VII statute, which states that an employer "is a person engaged in a business affecting commerce who has fifteen or more employees for each working day in each of 20 or more calendar weeks in the current or preceding calendar year." 42 U.S.C. § 2000e(b). The next sentence concerning salaried employees and part-time employees is based on a synthesis of the applicable cases. Next, the relevant facts of this case are discussed and applied to the legal standards. Finally, the writer presents a single sentence summarizing how the issue is likely to be resolved based on the application of the legal standards to the facts presented.

Many students include an authority, such as a statute or case, in the conclusion. Most often, however, your analysis of a claim requires that you synthesize a number of authorities to determine the applicable law. It would be misleading, therefore, to include only one authority in your conclusion. You might include an authority if it is the sole authority governing a claim.

When you have multiple questions presented, the conclusion section should answer the questions in the same order as they were presented. See Illustration 7-1.

CHAPTER SUMMARY

In this chapter, you learned how to draft questions presented, issues, brief answers, and conclusions. Questions presented or issues should incorporate legally significant facts and the rule of law. Legally significant facts are facts that will affect a decision concerning an issue of law.

Legally significant facts and the current rule of law also should be included in the conclusions or brief answers that answer the questions presented or issues.

Some attorneys prefer both a brief answer and a conclusion, while others only require a conclusion.

The process of writing the questions presented, issues, brief answers, and conclusions requires that you rewrite these components of a memorandum several times. The questions presented or issues should be drafted before you perform your research. They should be rewritten after you complete your research. The conclusions or brief answers also should be rewritten in light of the facts presented in a case.

In the next chapter, you learn how to draft facts statements for your memoranda.

Key Terms

Brief answers	Precise
Conclusions	Questions presented
Issues	Specific
Legally significant facts	

EXERCISES

Questions Presented Exercises

Draft questions presented for memos in the following cases.
1. You work as a paralegal for the country prosecutor's office in

Houcktown County. One of the assistant prosecutors asks you to research whether Bonnie Bill has committed aggravated burglary under
the Houcktown Rev. Code § 2911. The attorney has provided you with
the following facts:

> Merriweather Halsey and Bonnie Bill were at the Masonic
> Temple for a fundraiser to fight AIDS. During the fundraiser Bill
> told a drunken Halsey that she intended to steal the $8,000 fund-
> raiser proceeds from the Masonic Temple after the fundraiser and
> that she intended to steal a pearl necklace from Alice McKinley.
>
> Bill, who had helped organize the fundraiser, watched as the
> chairperson of the fundraiser opened the safe and placed the money
> in it. She memorized the combination and decided that she would
> use it later to steal the money.
>
> After the fundraiser, Bill walked home to get a credit card and
> a crow bar to open the door if she needed it. Bill went to the
> Masonic Temple after the fundraiser, wearing a disguise, showed
> the guard her invitation, and told him that she lost her mother's
> diamond brooch inside. Although the guard did not remember her,
> he allowed her to go into the temple. She wandered around the
> building for about an hour with the brooch inside her purse.
>
> When the guard decided to eat his supper and call home, Bill
> went to the safe. She opened it and pulled out all the money, except
> for $1,000.
>
> Bill told the guard she found the brooch and then she left. She
> went to Alice McKinley's home, climbed into the house through
> an open ground-floor window, took the pearl necklace she had
> seen Alice wearing earlier, and then left.

The relevant statute is as follows:

§ 2911 Aggravated Burglary

(A) A person is guilty of aggravated burglary when the person,
by force or deception, trespasses in any house, building, outbuilding,
watercraft, aircraft, railroad car, truck, trailer, tent vehicle or shelter
with the purpose of committing a theft; and

(1) inflicts or attempts or threatens to inflict physical harm to
another; or

(2) the person has a deadly weapon, which is any instrument,
device, or thing capable of inflicting death or designed or specially
adapted for use as a weapon; or

(3) the person has a dangerous ordinance such as any automatic
or sawed off firearm, zip gun or ballistic knife, explosive or incendi-
ary device; or

(4) the structure is the permanent or temporary dwelling of a
person.

2. An assistant county prosecutor wants you to research whether
Merriweather Halsey committed aggravated burglary based on the following facts:

Merriweather Halsey considered borrowing money from a friend who worked at the local bulb factory. She wandered into the factory around 4:00 A.M., after an AIDS fundraiser. The guard had stepped away from the door for a break. She headed toward her friend's work station, but she stumbled into an open office where the petty cash was kept. She fell over a secretary's desk. Her leg caught the desk and pulled open a drawer that contained $500. She thought about taking the money but she passed out before she took it. She woke up the next morning at about 6:00 A.M. when a secretary found her and summoned the security guard.

Halsey then fell onto the security guard causing him to crash his head into a planter. The guard cut his head and later required six stitches. Halsey thought the security guard was a robber so she grabbed a letter opener off a nearby desk and told the security guard to back off. The security guard took the letter opener. Halsey's mind was still fuzzy from the alcohol but she decided to pull a squirt gun out of her pocket to scare the robber.

Draft a question presented for this problem based upon the aggravated burglary statute noted in question 1.

Conclusions Exercises

3. Review the conclusions 2 and 3 for Illustration 7-1. Analyze the conclusions. What is the applicable law? What are the relevant facts? Which statement summarizes the likely result of this action when the relevant facts are applied to the law?

4. Draft conclusions for a Bonnie Bill and Merriweather Halsey memo.

8. Facts

CHAPTER OVERVIEW

This chapter explains the purpose of a facts statement and how to draft one. To do this, you need to learn how to determine which facts are legally significant. We will also discuss the difference between a fact and a legal conclusion, and we will demonstrate the different organizational structures for the facts section.

A. Facts Statement

What Is a Facts Statement?

The **facts statement** is a summary of the information that is relevant to the determination of whether a legal claim exists or whether a defense to such a claim can be made. It is also a summary of the status of a pending case.

When Is a Facts Statement Used and Why Is It Important?

A fact statement is an integral part of the office memorandum. Often, an attorney reads this statement to refresh his or her memory about the facts of the case before meeting with a client or a judge. The facts detailed in a memorandum also provide a reference point for your research and the framework for the application of the law.

What Is a Fact?

A **fact** may be a thing that is known with certainty. It can be an event. It can be an observation. The answer is not clear cut. Some facts are "pure" facts, which means there is no dispute about them. For example, an individual's birth is a pure fact. Facts in the court document, such as a complaint or an answer, are "asserted" facts, which means the individual is claiming they occurred. Some information can be objectively tested. That is a fact. For the purpose of the facts statement, note all of this information as facts.

What Facts Should You Include in a Facts Statement?

All facts that might have an impact on the issues presented in a particular case must be included in the memo. These facts are called "legally significant" facts. A good rule is that if you plan to include a fact in your discussion of the law, it should be mentioned in the facts statement. Do not omit any legally significant facts even if you think that an attorney should remember them from client meetings. Attorneys are responsible for multiple cases and these statements often are used to refresh their recollection. If a fact is not legally significant, you generally would exclude it. However, if the fact explains how a dispute or transaction arose, or explains the relationship between the parties, then that fact should be noted. Such a procedural fact would assist the reader in understanding the status of a case.

What Are Legally Significant Facts?

Legally significant facts are those facts that may affect how a court would decide a particular legal issue. To determine which facts are legally significant, you must understand the legal issue or issues presented in your case. For example, you are asked to research the factors a court will consider when it decides whether Sack and Shop grocery store was liable to Rebecca Harris, a patron, for a slip-and-fall accident that occurred in the store. You determine that the action is based on negligence. A **legal claim** is comprised of components called elements that must be proven before a claim is successful. For this problem, you learn that negligence is the breach of a duty of reasonable care that results in an injury to another person. The legal elements of negligence are as follows:

- Existence of a duty
- Breach of that duty
- Injury caused by the breach of the duty

Legally significant facts are those facts that might prove or disprove any of those elements. In this case, the legally significant facts and the legal element that they might prove or disprove would include:

- The slip and fall occurred in the store. (**injury, breach**)
- Rebecca Harris slipped on a banana peel that had been left on the store floor for two days. (**injury, breach**)
- Rebecca Harris suffered injuries as a result of the fall. (**injury**)
- Rebecca Harris shopped daily at the store. (**duty**)
- Rebecca Harris went to the store to make a purchase. (**duty**)

A fact that is not necessarily legally significant is:

- Rebecca Harris's shopping list included bananas, cherries, and strawberries.

This fact does not prove or disprove any of the elements.

Should You Include Only Facts That Support Your Client's Case?

Facts statements provide facts that are advantageous for your clients, and those facts that are unfavorable to them. Remember that this is an objective memo. The facts should be presented in a neutral manner, devoid of emotion. Compare the following two examples.

Example

Our client, Janice Kahn, seeks to sue Ronnie Randall for intentional infliction of emotional distress following a car accident in which Randall brutally struck Kahn's only child while the precious child was playing t-ball in the street with his friends. This brutal act was done in the presence of Mrs. Kahn, a caring mother, who was gardening while watching her child play. As a result of the incident, Kahn was devastated and emotionally distraught.

Example

Our client, Janice Kahn, seeks to sue Ronnie Randall for intentional infliction of emotional distress following a car accident in which Randall struck Kahn's child while the child was playing t-ball in the street with his friends. After Randall struck the child, he backed up and struck the boy again, running over his head with the rear tire. Mrs. Kahn was gardening nearby while watching her child play.

The first example contains several adjectives that slant the statement in favor of Kahn. The statement "Randall brutally struck Kahn's only child" characterizes the action as brutal. This is not a statement of fact. The adjective "brutal" should not be included in a facts statement. The second example is devoid of these **emotional adjectives.** Instead of using the word brutal, the second example details the underlying acts that constitute a brutal strike:

> After Randall struck the child, he backed up and struck the boy again, running over his head with the rear tire.

The second example allows readers to draw their own conclusions. The facts statement should not be slanted. Facts such as that Kahn was "a caring mother," or that the child was "precious," should not be incorporated into a facts statement. You should mention only facts, not legal conclusions or definitions of the law.

What Is the Difference Between a Fact and a Legal Conclusion?

A fact is a piece of information that might explain to the reader what occurred in a particular case. In contrast, a **legal conclusion** is an opinion about the legal significance of a fact. Read the following facts statement:

> Our client, Janice Kahn, seeks to sue Ronnie Randall for intentional infliction of emotional distress following a car accident in which Randall maliciously struck Kahn's only child while the child was playing t-ball in the street with his friends. This malicious and intentional act was done in the presence of Mrs. Kahn, a caring mother, who was gardening while watching her child play.

The statements that the act was "malicious" and "intentional" are legal conclusions because the writer makes assumptions about the state of mind of the actor. The term "malicious" is a legal element of many claims; it describes a wicked state of mind. "Intentional" also describes a legal element. You should exclude such characterizations from your facts statements. Instead, describe the acts a person committed that could be considered malicious, or statements that could indicate that an act was intentional. For example,

> Randall struck Kahn's only child after he told a neighbor that he intended to hit the child with his car while the child was playing t-ball. Randall struck the child with his car while the car was traveling at 25 miles an hour.

The information about Randall's comments to the neighbor, coupled with the speed at which he struck the child, could indicate that Randall struck the child maliciously and intentionally. The proper place to discuss whether an act is either malicious or intentional is in the discussion section of the memo. A definition of the law also is not a statement of fact and should be noted only in the memo discussion.

Where Do You Find the Information to Include in the Facts Statement?

Most often, information from a client interview is the basis for your facts statement. See Illustration 8-7. During a court dispute, information for the facts statement can also be found in witness statements, complaints, answers, or discovery materials, such as depositions and interrogatories. For these facts, note the source of the information. For transactions, information might be contained in various business records or contracts.

B. Organizing the Facts Statement

How Do You Organize a Facts Statement?

A facts statement can be organized in several ways: chronologically, by claim or defense, by party, or according to a combination of these three methods.

1. Chronological Organization

A **chronological organization** is based on the order of events. You start with the event that occurred first and end with the event that occurred last. You can also write the statement in **reverse chronological order,** beginning with the last event and ending with the first. For some claims, such as those stemming from an accident, a contract dispute, or a criminal case, chronological organization works well because these concerns often are ordered by time.

ILLUSTRATION 8-1. *Chronological Organization*

Dr. James Panhandle is suing our client, Hospitality Resorts International, Inc., for negligence stemming from injuries he sustained when he slipped and fell on July 8, 1989, at the Hospitality Resort of Mexico. The doctor seeks $1 million in damages.

On the day of the accident, children were playing in the pool at 8:00 A.M. The children splashed water out of the pool and onto the marble floor near the pool. The floor had not been mopped at any time during the day.

At 8:00 P.M., Dr. Panhandle was walking slowly out of the hotel coffee shop that was adjacent to the pool. He slipped on the wet marble floor next to the pool.

The doctor hit his head on the marble floor, causing him to crack his skull and to bleed.

The statement in Illustration 8-1 first introduces the claim. In the succeeding paragraphs, the events are detailed in chronological order from start to finish. Illustration 8-2 starts with the last event and ends with the information about the beginning of the day.

ILLUSTRATION 8-2. *Reverse Chronological Order*

Dr. James Panhandle is suing our client, Hospitality Resorts International, Inc., for negligence stemming from injuries he sustained when he slipped and fell on July 8, 1989, at the Hospitality Resort of Mexico. The doctor seeks $1 million in damages.

The doctor hit his head on the marble floor, causing him to crack his skull and to bleed.

At 8:00 P.M., Dr. Panhandle was walking slowly out of the hotel coffee shop that was adjacent to the pool. He slipped on the wet marble floor next to the pool.

On the day of the accident, children were playing in the pool at 8:00 A.M. The children splashed water out of the pool and onto the marble floor near the pool. The floor had not been mopped at any time during the day.

---

2. Organization by Claim or Defense

Facts statements also can be **organized by claim or defense.** In statements of this kind, legally significant facts that relate to a claim or a defense are grouped together. See Illustration 8-3. This method is useful when the issue does not concern events that can be organized by time sequence, and the information involves individuals who are not parties to the action.

ILLUSTRATION 8-3.   *Organization by Claim or Defense*

> Our clients, the Black Hawks, want to know whether the attorney-client privilege can be asserted by a former company president, Debbie Irl, and a current employee, Meredith Tildy, head of the cleaning staff. These questions arose while the plaintiff's attorney was deposing these individuals on July 8, 1993, as part of the discovery in a personal injury lawsuit stemming from a slip and fall at the stadium.
>
> Irl, president of the Hawks at the time of the accident, left the organization in June 1992. During her tenure with the organization, she was a decision maker and she drafted the cleaning policy for the stadium. Irl had spoken with the Hawks' attorney, Ace Rudd, about the accident on July 10, 1992. Irl is not named as a party in the lawsuit and is merely a witness. During the deposition, the plaintiff's attorney asked Irl about her conversation with Rudd. Irl asserted the attorney-client privilege.
>
> Meredith Tildy, the current head of the Hawks' cleaning staff, knew about the accident. Beer had been spilled the night before the accident. A patron told the staff to mop up the beer when it happened. Tildy knew that the cleaning staff had failed to clean up the beer. In her position, Tildy schedules the staff and decides whether the stadium should be cleaned completely each night. On July 10, 1992, Tildy spoke with Rudd, the company attorney, about the accident. The plaintiff's attorney asked Tildy about her conversation with Rudd. Based upon Rudd's advice, Tildy asserted the attorney-client privilege.

In Illustration 8-3's sample facts statement, the details are organized by claim. The first paragraph introduces the claims — the assertion of attorney-client privilege by Irl and Tildy. The next paragraph includes the facts that are legally significant to Irl's claim of attorney-client privilege. The final paragraph focuses on the facts that are legally significant to Tildy, and Tildy's assertion of the attorney-client privilege. Because neither Irl nor Tildy is a party, this organization works well.

3. Organization by Party

Another way to organize the facts is to **organize by party**, grouping the facts according to the party the facts describe. This method is useful when multiple parties are involved in a dispute. See Illustration 8-4, which involves a dispute between three parties: a company and two individuals. The memo focuses on whether Whole In One is an employer under Title VII, and whether two individuals are employees or independent contractors.

ILLUSTRATION 8-4. *Organization by Party*

Victoria Radiant and Karen Walker, two former Whole In One Enterprises workers, brought a federal sex discrimination lawsuit, based upon Title VII, against our client, Whole In One Enterprises, owned by Nancy and Craig Black. The lawsuit, filed in the U.S. District Court for the Northern District of Illinois, stems from the dismissal of the two women by the Blacks during 1993.

The Blacks own Whole In One Enterprises, which operates a miniature golf course and restaurant in Glenview, Illinois. During the 24-week 1993 restaurant season, 10 people worked full-time and 14 people worked part-time for Whole In One. However, no more than 14 people worked on any one day. Of those 14 people, only 3 were full-time employees. The other full-time employees regularly took days off during the summer restaurant and golf season.

Among the full-time workers was Karen Walker, who worked as a public relations director for Whole In One. Walker responded to an ad that said that "an employer" sought an individual to perform public relations work. Whole In One hired Walker without a contract and told her she was prohibited from working for other firms. However, Walker worked from home and set her own hours. Whole In One required Walker to attend weekly staff meetings at the company offices where Whole In One would review and revise Walker's work. The company supplied Walker with paper, pencils, stamps, telephone service, and paid for her life and health insurance. Whole In One did not withhold taxes from Walker's commissions.

Victoria Radiant, who had a two-year employment contract with the company, provided marketing services to Whole In One from October of 1991 until she was fired in 1993. Although Radiant worked in the company office, Whole In One management rarely supervised her work. The company paid for her continued education, provided her with bonuses, and deducted taxes from her weekly salary.

The first paragraph in Illustration 8-4 introduces the claim. The next paragraph describes one of the parties, Whole In One. The next paragraph describes another party, Walker. The final paragraph tells the reader about Radiant, the third party in the action.

4. Combination of Chronological and Claim or Party Organization

Some facts statements do not lend themselves to one type of organization. Some facts should be arranged by the order of the events and others do not fit neatly into this arrangement. Therefore, you might group facts in chronological order and by party or claim. See Illustration 8-5.

ILLUSTRATION 8-5.   *Chronological and Claim Organization*

While driving a car, Ronnie Randall struck Janice Kahn's son at 5:00 P.M. on August 29, 1993. It was bright and clear. No skid marks appeared on the dry street following the accident. Janice Kahn was working in her garden about five feet from the accident scene at the time of the accident. Her son was playing a game in the street before Randall's car struck him. Kahn did not see the car strike her 11-year-old son. When she first looked up from her garden, she thought her son was dead. He was covered with blood and had several broken bones. However, Kahn's son was conscious after the accident.

Immediately after the accident, Randall, who had a blood-alcohol level of .11, was cited for drunk driving and driving with a suspended driver's license. Police had charged him with drunk driving and suspended his license two weeks earlier after the car he was driving struck another child at the same spot. Randall has a history of alcohol abuse.

Following the accident, several witnesses said Randall was upset and wobbled as he walked. One witness said that Randall intentionally turned the steering wheel to hit Kahn's son. Kahn stated that Randall often swerved down her street to get her attention.

Rhonda Albert, Kahn's neighbor, said she heard Randall say he would get even with Kahn after Kahn broke off a 10-year relationship with him.

During Kahn and Randall's 10-year relationship, Randall was close to Kahn's son. He took him to ball games, including one in April, and attended the son's baseball games. Randall knew that Kahn's son was the most important person in her life.

Since the accident, Kahn vomits daily and has nightmares about the accident. Dr. Susan Faigen, Kahn's internist, states that the vomiting and nightmares are the result of the accident.

The facts statement in Illustration 8-5 concerns the question of whether Janice Kahn can successfully pursue a claim against Ronnie Randall for intentional infliction of emotional distress after Randall struck Kahn's 11-year-old son with Randall's car. The accident itself is best described in a chronological manner because the events can be explained in a sequential order. However, the witness statements and other "facts" that relate to whether Randall intentionally struck the child and whether Randall intended to cause emotional distress when he struck the child should be organized by issue or claim.

In some instances, your organization should be structured by the sequence of the events and by the parties. See Illustration 8-6.

ILLUSTRATION 8-6. *Chronological and Party Organization*

Merriweather Halsey and Bonnie Bill were at the Masonic Temple for a fundraiser to fight AIDS. During the fundraiser Bill told a drunken Halsey that she intended to steal the $8,000 fundraiser proceeds from the Masonic Temple after the fundraiser and that she intended to steal a pearl necklace from Alice McKinley.

Bill, who had helped organize the fundraiser, watched as the chairperson of the fundraiser opened the safe and placed the money in it. She memorized the combination and decided that she would use it later to steal the money.

After the fundraiser, Bill walked home to get a credit card and a crow bar to open the door if she needed it. Bill went to the Masonic Temple after the fundraiser, wearing a disguise, showed the guard her invitation, and told him that she had lost her mother's diamond brooch inside. Although the guard did not remember her, he allowed her to go into the temple. She wandered around the building for about an hour with the brooch inside her purse.

When the guard decided to eat his supper and call home, Bill went to the safe. She opened it and pulled out all the money, except for $1,000.

Bill told the guard she had found the brooch and then she left. She went to Alice McKinley's home, climbed into the house through an open ground-floor window, and took the pearl necklace she had seen Alice wearing earlier, and then left.

Merriweather Halsey considered borrowing money from a friend who worked at a local bulb factory. She wandered into the factory around 4:00 A.M., after the fundraiser. The guard had stepped away from the door for a break. She headed toward her friend's work station, but she stumbled into an open office where the petty cash was kept. She fell over a secretary's desk. Her leg caught the desk and pulled open a drawer that contained $500. She thought about taking the money but she passed out before she

ILLUSTRATION 8-6. *Continued*

took it. She woke up the next morning at about 6:00 A.M. when a secretary found her and summoned the security guard.

Halsey then fell into the security guard causing him to crash his head into a planter. The guard cut his head and later required six stitches. Halsey thought the security guard was a robber so she grabbed a letter opener off a nearby desk and told the security guard to back off. The security guard took the letter opener. Halsey's mind was still fuzzy from the alcohol but she decided to pull a squirt gun out of her pocket to scare the robber.

The question is whether Bill or Halsey can be convicted of aggravated burglary under Houcktown County law.

In Illustration 8-6, the first paragraph introduces both parties, Bonnie Bill and Merriweather Halsey. The facts statement details most of the night's events in chronological order. However, the parties, Bill and Halsey, leave the fundraiser separately. At this point, the organization changes from chronological to one focusing on each party. First, facts that are legally significant to Bill's escapades are explained. These are noted in chronological order from start to finish. After the facts concerning Bill's adventure, the facts related to Halsey's acts at the bulb factory are detailed. These facts also are explained in chronological order. The final paragraph tells the reader the issues that will be considered in the memo.

C. Writing the Facts Statement

How Do You Begin to Draft a Facts Statement?

1. List of Facts and Preliminary Statement

After you meet with an attorney to discuss your research assignment, make a list of the facts and draft a preliminary facts statement. Illustration 8-7 shows an excerpt from a client interview. Following the interview is a list of the facts and a preliminary facts statement, Illustration 8-8, that includes all of the facts provided in the interview.

ILLUSTRATION 8-7. *Excerpt from a Client Interview*

Attorney: What can I do for you today Mr. Grocer of Sack and Shop?
Grocer: Rebecca Harris, one of my regular customers, is suing me for $1 million.

ILLUSTRATION 8-7. *Continued*

Attorney: What happened?
Grocer: Ms. Harris came to the store to purchase cherries, strawberries, and bananas. When she was turning the corner in the produce section, she slipped on a banana peel.
Attorney: How long had the banana peel been on the floor?
Grocer: Two days.
Attorney: Did you or any of your employees know about the banana peel on the floor?
Grocer: Yes. One of the patrons told the head of the produce department to clean up the banana peel two days before Ms. Harris fell.
Attorney: Why wasn't it picked up?
Grocer: The produce department head was in a hurry to leave and forgot to do it. The next day, he was very busy and he kicked the banana peel into a corner. Apparently it was knocked out of the corner and to the middle of the floor where Ms. Harris slipped on it.
Attorney: Were there any witnesses?
Grocer: I saw her slip.
Attorney: What was Ms. Harris doing when she slipped?
Grocer: She was walking to the green peppers.
Attorney: What day did the incident occur?
Grocer: July 8, 1994. The same day another accident occurred in the produce section that involved a piece of cut cantaloupe.
Attorney: Was Ms. Harris injured?
Grocer: She claims in the court papers that she hurt her head and broke her arm.
Attorney: Was anyone injured in the second accident?
Grocer: Yes. A man slipped on the cantaloupe and broke his finger.

List of Facts:

Client: Sack and Shop grocery store
Plaintiff: Rebecca Harris
Slip and Fall at grocery store on July 8, 1994
Plaintiff slipped on a banana peel, which had been left on the store floor for two days.
Harris was walking to the green peppers.
Another accident happened in the same section when a man slipped on a cantaloupe and broke his finger.
A patron told the store employee to clean up the banana peel two days earlier.
The employee kicked it into a corner.
Somehow the peel got to the middle of the floor again.
Harris came to the store to purchase cherries, strawberries, and bananas.

ILLUSTRATION 8-8.   *Sample Preliminary Facts Statement Based on the Client Interview*

Our client, Sack and Shop grocery store, is being sued for negligence by Rebecca Harris.

Harris went to the store to purchase cherries, strawberries, and bananas on July 8, 1994.

While Harris was in the produce section, she slipped on a banana peel that had been left on the floor by a grocery store employee. The employee dropped it on the floor two days earlier and had failed to clean it up after a patron asked him to do so. The employee had kicked the peel into the corner two days before the accident. Somehow the peel found its way to the middle of the floor on the date of the accident.

Harris sustained a broken arm and head injuries as a result of the slip and fall. Another man was injured in the produce department that same day when he slipped and fell on some cantaloupe.

---

2. Research the Issue

After you prepare your list and preliminary facts statement, the next step is to research the legal issue or issues and to determine the applicable law.

3. Revise to Include Only Legally Significant Facts

Revise your list so that it includes only the legally significant facts, the facts that will have a bearing on the applicable law. See Illustration 8-9. To draft this list, you must determine the legal elements necessary to establish a claim. In the case of negligence, you would learn that negligence is the breach of a duty of reasonable care that results in injuries to another person. The elements then would be:

- duty of reasonable care
- breach of the duty
- a link between the breach of the duty and the resulting injuries
- injuries

You should review the facts and determine which facts may affect whether the plaintiff can establish one of these elements or whether the defendant would be able to disprove one of the elements—in other words, the legally significant facts. In this case, you should include all of the facts listed in Illustration 8-9. In that illustration, the element of the legal theory is noted in bold face next to the legally significant fact. The fact that Harris was purchasing cherries, strawberries, and bananas is not legally significant. Similarly, the fact that another patron was injured in the produce section that day did not affect whether Harris was injured and therefore is not legally significant.

ILLUSTRATION 8-9. *List of Legally Significant Facts*

- The slip and fall occurred in the store on July 8, 1994. (**breach and duty**)
- Rebecca Harris slipped on a banana peel that had been left on the store floor for two days. (**breach and duty**)
- The store employee dropped the banana peel on the floor two days earlier. (**breach and duty**)
- A store employee knew about the banana peel on the floor two days before the accident. (**breach and duty**)
- The employee kicked the peel into the corner after a patron told him to clean it up. (**breach and duty**)
- Rebecca Harris suffered injuries as a result of the fall. (**link and injuries**)

4. Organize the Facts

After you have made your list of facts, decide how to organize them. After you select your organizational method, group the legally significant facts together in the organizational style you have selected.

5. Rewrite the Facts Statement

The facts contained in Illustration 8-9 led themselves to a chronological organization because they can be ordered by time. Illustration 8-10 is a rewritten facts statement that includes only the legally significant facts. Finally, remember to introduce the legal issue or issues presented in the facts statement as shown in the first paragraph of Illustration 8-10.

ILLUSTRATION 8-10. *Sample Facts Statement for Slip-and-Fall Case*

Rebecca Harris, a store patron, is suing our client, Sack and Shop grocery store, for negligence.

While Harris was in the produce department, on July 8, 1994, she slipped on a banana peel that had been left on the floor by a grocery store employee. The employee dropped it on the floor two days earlier and had failed to clean it up after a patron asked him

ILLUSTRATION 8-10. *Continued*

to do so. When he was told to pick up the peel, the employee kicked the peel into the corner.

Harris sustained a broken arm and head injuries as a result of the slip and fall.

CHAPTER SUMMARY

A facts statement is designed to refresh an attorney's memory about a case, or to educate a new attorney about the case. It is a statement of all facts that are legally significant (facts that might affect the outcome of a legal issue). Facts that are not legally significant should be omitted from a facts statement.

Facts statements can be organized in chronological or reverse chronological order, by claim or defense, by party, or any combination of these three.

To draft your statement, make a list of the facts, plan your organization, and then write the statement. Next, research the legal issue and then rewrite your facts statement because the legally significant facts may have changed based on your research.

In the next chapter, you will learn how to organize the IRAC methodology.

Key Terms

Chronological organization	Legal conclusion
Emotional adjectives	Legally significant facts
Fact	Organization by claim or defense
Facts statement	Organization by party
Legal claim	Reverse chronological order

EXERCISES

Drafting a List of Relevant Facts

1. Review the following Uniform Commercial Code Section and read the list of facts that follows. Make a list of the legally significant facts based upon the statute. Next to each fact, list the relevant portion of the statute.

§ 2-315

Implied Warranty of Fitness for a Particular Purpose

Where the seller at the time of contracting has reason to know any particular purpose for which the goods are required and that buyer is relying on the seller's skill or judgment to select or furnish suitable goods, there is unless excluded or modified under the next section an implied warranty that the goods be fit for such purpose.

FACTS

Your client is Sue A. Buyer. She lives at 3225 Wilmette Avenue, Glenview, Illinois. The defendants are Lee R. Merchant, owner of Mowers R Us, in Glenview, Illinois, and Manny U. Facture, the owner of a manufacturing concern that is not incorporated called Mowers, of Rosemont, Illinois. Ms. Buyer went to the defendant's store, Mowers R Us, to purchase a lawnmower for her new home. She was a first-time homeowner and was unfamiliar with lawnmowers. She had never operated a lawnmower because her brothers had always mowed the lawn when she was a child.

When she went to Mowers R Us, she asked to speak with the owner. She told Mr. Merchant: "I don't know anything about these mowers and I need to talk with an expert." Mr. Merchant said, "I'm the owner and you couldn't find a better expert anywhere in the Chicagoland area. I have been in the business of selling mowers for more than 40 years. I only sell mowers and the equipment to clean and repair them. Are you familiar with the type of lawnmower you would like?"

"No, I don't know anything about lawnmowers. I just know that I have to have a lawnmower that will mulch my grass clippings because I cannot bag the clippings. The village of Glenview does not permit me to bag the clippings, so the clippings must remain on my lawn."

"You're absolutely correct. You must have a mulching mower," Mr. Merchant said. "That type of mower will grind the grass clippings and you will not notice them on your grass. I have the perfect mower for you. It is a used model that will fit into your price range, only $200. It's a good brand, a Roro, and will mulch the grass as well as any of the new mowers. This one is true blue. You can purchase a separate mulching blade, which will easily attach to it for an additional $50," he added.

"Do you think that I need the mulching blade?" Ms. Buyer asked. "I've never used a lawnmower so I don't know what to expect and you appear to be the expert."

"I think that you could do without the mulching blade unless you want the grass ground up very fine."

"I think that I would like it ground up fine. I'll defer to your judgment. If you think a mulching blade is necessary, then I'll buy that with the mower. Do you think that this is the best mower for mulching or should I go with a new one?"

"Absolutely the used one is best; I told you: it's a true value. It will mulch with the best of them."

"If you think it can do the job, I'll trust your judgment," said Ms. Buyer. "I'll take the mower and the mulching blade. Can you install the mulching blade? I don't know anything about the installation."

"Sure, we can install any blade for another $30."

Ms. Buyer purchased the mower and the blade. She used the mower after Mr. Merchant installed the new mulching blade. It barely cut the grass and certainly didn't mulch the clippings into fine pieces as Mr. Merchant had claimed.

She brought the mower back to Mr. Merchant. He said that he had made no warranties about the mower. He showed her the language on the receipt that said that he did not expressly warranty anything.

Ms. Buyer brought the mower to a Roro dealer. The owners of the Roro dealership, Abe Saul and Lou T. Wright, said that the mower Ms. Buyer had purchased from Mowers R Us was not a mulching mower. It was a mower built before mulching was popular. Therefore, it would not perform the mulching task. It was designed merely to cut the grass. "Any merchant who has been in business even for one year should have known that mowers built before 1970 were not designed for mulching," Mr. Wright said. He showed Ms. Buyer where the manufacturing date appeared on the mower. "Manufactured in August 1969," it said on the plate with the serial number. "Also, mulching blades cannot be placed on these old mowers. Any mower dealer should know that too," Mr. Wright added. "However, this mower isn't bad. It can cut the grass without mulching it."

Ms. Buyer brought an action against Mr. Merchant and Mr. Facture in the Lucas County Ohio Common Pleas Court in Toledo, Ohio.

Objective Writing

2. Write three different discussions about your high school career. One discussion should present the experience in a negative manner. The second should attempt to persuade the reader that the experience was positive. Finally, write about your experience in a neutral manner, without any emotion. Compare the three discussions.

Drafting a Facts Statement

3. Draft a facts statement for our client, Ronnie Randall. Janice Kahn, the plaintiff, brought an action against Randall for intentional infliction of emotional distress. You should prepare your facts statement based up this excerpt from a deposition transcript, witness statements, and a police report. The facts statement will be included in a memo that discusses the issue of intentional infliction of emotional distress. For the purpose of this memo, intentional infliction of emotional distress is defined as follows:

> An act by a person that is extreme and outrageous conduct, done with intent to cause another to suffer severe emotional distress, and which results in distress and emotional injury to another. The emotional injury must manifest itself with a physical problem.

Below is a portion of Janice Kahn's deposition transcript.

Q. What were you doing when the accident occurred?
A. Working in my garden. I planted tomatoes, green peppers, carrots, and broccoli.
Q. Where is your garden located on your property?
A. In the front, near the street. It is next to a brick wall. I can't see the garden from my house.
Q. What direction were you facing in your garden?
A.   North.
Q. Does that direction face the street?
A. No.
Q. What do you usually do in your garden when you work?
A. Weed it.
Q. What were you doing in your garden when the accident occurred?
A. Weeding it.
Q. Where is the street in relation to your garden?
A. About five feet.
Q. Where do your children generally play?
A. In the backyard.
Q. Where were your children playing on the day of the accident?
A. They were playing t-ball in the front yard.
Q. Were you watching your children at the time of the accident?
A. Yes. I could see them.
Q. Did you see the accident occur?
A. Sort of.
Q. Did you or did you not see the accident?
A. I saw my son, who is 11 years old, on the ground covered with blood, and blood all over the front of the Cadillac.
Q. Did you actually see the driver strike your son?
A. No. But I know Ronnie hit him. I saw my son next to Ronnie's car. I heard him swerve.
Q. Did you know the driver?
A. Yes.
Q. How did you know him?
A. We met at a state fair. We dated for 10 years. I broke up with him two weeks before the accident.
Q. Did he know your son?
A. He knew my son was the most important person to me and he tried to kill him to pay me back for dumping him.
Q. Are you accusing the driver of intentionally striking your son?
A. Yes. He wanted to get back at me so he hit my boy.
Q. What happened to your son on the day of the accident?
A. He sustained head injuries and several broken bones. He can't play t-ball for the rest of the season and we had to cancel our vacation to the Dells because he's been hurting so much.
Q. Was he conscious when you first saw him after the accident?
A. He was awake but I thought he was dead at first. He had blood everywhere. I knew the driver, Ronnie, was drunk when he hit him. He wasn't even looking where he was going. He always swerves down our street to get my attention.
Q. Did your son speak to you right after the accident?

A. Barely. I told him that Ronnie was speeding and trying to run him down
    on purpose. I was horrified to see the blood and the broken bones.
    I couldn't move and I was so angry at Ronnie because I knew he
    did this on purpose.

Q. Did you go to the doctor after this accident?

A. I went by ambulance with my son to the doctor. His doctor looked me
    over and said I was suffering from shock. Since then, I haven't been
    able to sleep or eat. I have nightmares about the accident. I throw
    up every day.

Q. Have you seen a doctor for your complaints?

A. Yes. She said that they are related to the accident. I just keep thinking
    back to that day when the neighbor told me that Ronnie intentionally
    turned the wheel to hit my boy.

Q. Was your son able to move after the accident?

A. Slightly. He looked just like our neighbor's son did after Ronnie hit him
    with his car two weeks ago at the same curve.

Police Report, State of Illinois

Ronnie Randall, the driver of a 1993 Cadillac, was cited for driving
while under the influence of alcohol and/or drugs, reckless driving, and
driving with a suspended license. I will ask the prosecutor to consider
either reckless assault charges or vehicular homicide, depending upon the
condition of the boy. I tested Randall for alcohol intoxication. His blood/
alcohol level was .11. Randall struck another boy, Tommy Albert, at the
same site two weeks earlier. He was cited for reckless driving for that
accident and drunk driving. As I arrested Randall, he said that he was
daydreaming during the accident and that he did not mean to hit the
child. There were no skid marks. The street was dry.

The little boy's mother, Janice Kahn, was working in her garden
about five feet from the accident scene at the time of the accident. Her
son, Billy Kahn, was playing a game in the street.

Witness Statement

Two days before the accident, Rhonda Albert, a neighbor of Janice
Kahn, heard Randall say that he planned to get even with Kahn after
Kahn broke off her 10-year relationship with Randall. Albert saw the
car strike Kahn's son. According to Albert, after the car struck the boy,
Randall got out of his car and said "Oh my God. I didn't mean to hit
him. Is he OK?" Albert could smell alcohol on Randall's breath.

Witness Statement

Rebecca Mark saw the driver, Ronnie Randall, turn the car toward
Kahn's son.

Review of Facts Statements

4. Now that you have reviewed the facts for the *Janice Kahn* case
and have drafted a statement of your own, read the following statements
of facts. Determine which facts statement is best. List any errors you
find in any of the statements.

A. The plaintiff, a single mother, and the defendant, her ex-boyfriend, are involved in a lawsuit. The plaintiff alleges in her deposition that the defendant was driving recklessly and intentionally struck her son with his car. The defendant's motive was to pay her back for ending their relationship. He tried to kill her son for this reason. As a result of the accident, the plaintiff went into shock and suffers from insomnia, loss of appetite, nightmares, and vomiting.

B. The plaintiff was working in her tomato garden located in the front of the property about five feet from the street. She could see the children playing in the front yard. She did not see the driver, Ronnie Randall, hit her son with his Cadillac, but did see blood on the front of the Cadillac and on her son who was on the ground.

The plaintiff dated Randall for ten years and had just ended their relationship. She states that Ronnie hit her son to pay her back for ending their relationship. Two weeks before, Ronnie had hit a neighbor's son at the same curve.

The plaintiff states that her son was covered with blood, able to move slightly. He suffered head trauma and broken bones.

The plaintiff is suffering from shock after seeing her son. She remembers a neighbor telling her that Ronnie intentionally turned the wheel to hit her son.

The plaintiff is unable to eat or sleep, has nightmares, and vomits daily.

C. Janice Kahn is bringing an action against Ronnie Randall for the intentional infliction of emotional distress. Her son was recently hit by Ronnie Randall's car on the street in front of the Kahn home. At the time of the injury, Kahn was working in the front yard near her son. Her son went into the street and Randall hit him. At the time of the accident, Randall was legally drunk, and driving with a suspended license.

Randall had previously told Kahn's neighbor, a Ms. Albert, that he was going to get even with Ms. Kahn over the break-up of their 10-year relationship. He also told Ms. Albert that he knew that Ms. Kahn's son was very important to her.

Since the accident, Kahn has been unable to eat or sleep properly. She vomits daily and often has nightmares about her son's injury. She has stated that Mr. Randall often drives by her home in an erratic fashion, and on another occasion hit a neighbor's child. Kahn feels that Randall hit her son intentionally. Kahn did not see the injury take place, but was at her son's side immediately after the injury. Kahn also says that Randall never slowed down until after he hit her son.

D. On August 12, 1993, Janice Kahn filed a lawsuit against Ronnie Randall for intentional infliction of emotional distress stemming from an accident involving Kahn's 11-year-old son.

On July 8, 1993, Janice Kahn was weeding her tomato garden while her children played t-ball a few feet away from her in the street. As she worked, Kahn heard a car swerve. She looked up to see her son, covered in blood, lying on the ground in front of a Cadillac, driven by Ronnie Randall.

Two neighbors witnessed the accident. Rebecca Mark saw the driver, Ronnie Randall, turn the car toward Kahn's son. Rhonda Albert also saw the car strike Kahn's son. According to Albert, after the car struck the boy, Randall got out of his car and said "Oh my God. I didn't mean to hit him. Is he OK?"

Albert could smell alcohol on Randall's breath. Police tested his blood/alcohol level and found that it was .11. Police cited Randall for drunk driving, speeding, and reckless driving.

After police arrived, an ambulance took Kahn and her son to the hospital where he was treated for head injuries and broken bones. The doctor who treated Kahn's son told Kahn that she should be treated for shock. Since the accident, Kahn has been unable to sleep because of nightmares about the accident. She vomits daily. Her doctor said that the vomiting and nightmares are the result of the accident.

The driver of the car involved in the accident was Kahn's former boyfriend. They had dated for ten years, however, Kahn broke off the relationship about two weeks before the accident. Kahn stated in her deposition that she believes that Randall intentionally struck her son to pay her back for ending the relationship.

Also, two days before the accident Albert heard Randall say that he planned to get even with Kahn after Kahn broke off her 10-year relationship. However, the police report stated that Randall said that he was daydreaming during the accident and that he did not mean to hit the child. Since the break-up, Kahn has seen Randall often swerve down the street in front of her home. Two weeks before the accident, Randall hit Rhonda Albert's son with his Cadillac at the same curve.

9. The IRAC Method

A. Purpose of IRAC
B. IRAC Components
    1. Issues
    2. Rules
    3. Application of the Law to the Problem's Facts
    4. Conclusion

CHAPTER OVERVIEW

The IRAC chapter focuses on the writing style used for the discussion portion of the memo.

A. Purpose of IRAC

What Is IRAC?

IRAC stands for Issue, Rule, Application, Conclusion. IRAC is the architectural blueprint for the legal discussion. It gives legal writing continuity and clarity and organizes the contents of the discussion. IRAC provides legal support and analysis for the issues posed by the problem and guides the writer toward a well-supported conclusion.

IRAC benefits both the writer and the reader because the components are essentially a checklist designed to ensure that the discussion is analytically well thought out and that it contains the necessary legal authority. IRAC is very important because it lets the reader see the particular legal point being addressed, the relevant legal rule, the application of the law to the facts, and the conclusion. IRAC is formula writing in the same way that formula movie romances, westerns, and thrillers are. The predictability of the IRAC format enables the reader to obtain the information quickly.

B. IRAC Components

What Does an IRAC Paragraph Look Like?

This fact pattern forms the basis of the IRAC paragraph example.

> On August 7, 1992, Ms. Howard went to Rough & Tough Pawn Shop in Chicago to obtain a loan using a diamond ring as collateral. Rough & Tough loaned Ms. Howard $800, and she agreed to pay $75 per month for a total of 13½ months. Ms. Howard knew that she would have to pay off the balance of $1,025 in 12 months because at that time Rough & Tough would have the right to sell the ring. On September 11, 1992, Ms. Howard received a postcard from Rough & Tough stating that it was selling the shop and all of its assets to Able Pawn. Mr. Sam Able would assume the business of Rough & Tough including all pawned items and outstanding loans. On the bottom of the postcard was a notice stating: "If you want your item, please pick it up by September 29, 1992, and pay off your note by September 29, 1992." Because Ms. Howard did not have the money to pay off the note, she decided to pay Able Pawn the $75 per month once the loan was transferred in the sale. In October 1992, Able Pawn was robbed and all the jewelry, including Ms. Howard's ring, was stolen. Able Pawn had a security alarm system and a guard dog to protect the property, but the robbers were able to circumvent these obstacles.

We will work through the following sample IRAC paragraph, based on the Howard fact pattern, and its components to illustrate how to draft an IRAC paragraph.

> (I) Whether a bailment for the mutual benefit of Rough & Tough and Howard existed? (R) A pawn is a form of bailment, made for the mutual benefit of bailee and bailor, arising when goods are delivered to another as a pawn for security to him on money borrowed by the bailor. *Jacobs v. Grossman*, 141 N.E. 714, 715 (Ill. Ct. App. 1923). In *Jacobs*, the court found that a bailment for mutual benefit did arise because the plaintiff pawned a ring as collateral for a $70 loan given to him by the defendant. *Id.* (A) In our problem, Howard pawned her ring as collateral to secure a $800 loan given to her by Rough & Tough. (C) Therefore, Howard and Rough & Tough probably created a bailment for mutual benefit.

Note that the first sentence of the IRAC paragraph is a **statement of the issue** that will be examined in the paragraph. The issue is narrowly defined and focused on one of the analytical elements of the problem. The **rule of law,** the next component of the paragraph, provides the legal basis for the analysis of the issue. Then, it is appropriate to discuss some of the **facts** of the cited case if these facts help explain how the legal rule can be applied to your facts. Notice that everything that comes from an opinion is given citation credit.

The most important component of the IRAC paragraph is the **application** portion. The application is where you use the facts of your problem to demonstrate, but not to conclude, why the legal rule should apply to the issue posed. This is the legal analysis. After you let the facts speak for themselves by demonstrating how the legal rule applies to the scenario at hand, then you draw a **conclusion.** The conclusion answers the issue posed. The issue is the question being examined in the discussion, and the conclusion is the answer.

This example illustrates how the conclusion responds directly to the issue:

Issue:	Whether a bailment for the mutual benefit of Rough & Tough and Howard existed?
Conclusion:	Therefore, Howard and Rough & Tough probably created a bailment for mutual benefit.

1. Issues

What Are the Issues?

The question presented is the overall legal **issue** that will be resolved in the memo. A **sub-issue** in the IRAC paragraph is a point or query that must be addressed to substantiate one legal element of the problem. When analyzing and writing about a legal problem objectively, it is often important to address sub-issues in the order that they must be resolved to support legal analysis. For example, the general rule for arson in Illinois is the malicious burning of the dwelling house of another. The question presented for a memo on arson would be:

> Whether Mr. Smith committed arson by intentionally burning down his brother's factory?

The sub-issues addressed in the IRAC paragraphs would be:

> Whether there was a malicious burning?
> Whether the factory is a dwelling house?
> Whether the factory of Mr. Smith's brother constitutes the property of another person?

The sub-issues form the **topic sentences** of the IRAC paragraphs. They provide the analytical steps that you must take in your thought process and your legal reasoning to resolve the overall issue posed by the problem, the question presented. The topic sentences in the IRAC paragraph introduce the legal element in question that needs to be resolved to complete the steps necessary to thoroughly examine the problem and to determine a response to the question presented.

What Is the Difference Between the Question Presented and the Issues in the IRAC Paragraphs?

The question presented is the overall problem that must be resolved in the objective memo. The question presented for the Howard fact pattern is:

> Whether Ms. Howard has a claim against Rough & Tough or against Able Pawn Shop for the value of her ring?

The sub-issues are determined by the legal elements or tests involved in the problem. The elements are discussed individually along with the relevant legal rule. There is a certain logical order when presenting the elements. Let the legal rules guide you in establishing the order of the sub-issues. Notice that each issue centers on a single step of the legal analysis necessary to fully examine the question presented.

The sub-issues that form the topic sentences of the IRAC paragraphs in a memo addressing Ms. Howard's problem would be as follows:

> The first issue is what type of relationship does a pawner and a pawnee have?
> What property rights do Ms. Howard and Rough & Tough Pawn have when they enter into a mutual bailment?
> Whether Rough & Tough Pawn can transfer its interest in Ms. Howard's property to Able Pawn?
> Whether Rough & Tough Pawn received the proper consent for the transfer of the ring from Ms. Howard?
> Whether Rough & Tough is liable for the loss of Ms. Howard's property after transferring its interest to Able Pawn?
> Whether Able Pawn is liable for the theft of Ms. Howard's property while it was in its possession?

All of these queries are really elements that must be addressed, step by step, to resolve the question presented.

Each of the sub-issues will be a topic sentence of the IRAC paragraph highlighting the analytical focus of the legal discussion in that paragraph. Each issue is a step in the thought process required to thoroughly prove all of the underlying elements necessary to address the question presented.

Notice how one issue statement logically leads into the next. A good test to see if your discussion is well organized is to write down all of your issue statements from your IRAC paragraphs. If the issue statements flow logically, one to the next, then the organization of your discussion will be logical.

To analyze the problem thoroughly, a number of issues must be examined in the discussion. To make the analysis logical, the issues must be examined in a certain order.

2. Rules

The **legal holding** or **rule,** or synthesized compilation of the pertinent legal rules, follows the issue at the beginning of the IRAC paragraph. For an in-depth discussion of the process of synthesizing authority, see Chapter 10.

What Is a Rule of Law?

A rule of law is the court's holding or a synthesis of various courts' holdings on the same point. A rule also can be a statute and the legal elements laid out by the statute. A synthesis of a statute and a case applying or interpreting the statute also constitutes a rule.

In our IRAC example, note that the first sentence is the issue, and the second sentence is the legal rule.

Issue:	Whether a bailment for the mutual benefit of Rough & Tough and Howard existed?
Rule, followed by pinpoint citation:	A pawn is a form of bailment, made for the mutual benefit of the bailee and the bailor, arising when goods are delivered to another as a pawn for security to him on money borrowed by the bailor. *Jacobs v. Grossman,* 141 N.E. 714, 715 (Ill. Ct. App. 1923).

When organizing the discussion, first discern what issues are to be addressed and then find the pertinent mandatory authority that addresses the issues raised. Do not write the discussion around the authority, but make the authority address the issues. To demonstrate clearly how the authority supports or addresses the issues raised, discuss the pertinent facts of the cited case after you state the case's holding or legal rule. This is particularly helpful when the holding is very broad. You must demonstrate that the cited case truly supports the premise discussed in the IRAC paragraph.

Why Is Citation Important?

Citation is an essential component of the rule portion of the IRAC paragraph. You must always give proper credit in Bluebook format to any statement made that is not wholly your own. Any legal principle or authority must be attributed to its source. Proper attribution of authority tells the reader where you obtained the legal principle that supports the discussion. Most important, the cite tells the reader whether the authority is primary mandatory authority, primary persuasive, or secondary authority. A cite also provides information without including the information in the discussion's text. For example, you could write a holding as follows:

> The state of Kimberly Supreme Court held in 1983 that individuals have a right to privacy. *Jones v. City of Moose*, 121 Kim. 12, 13 (1983).

A much more effective version of the same holding to include in the rule portion of the IRAC paragraph is:

> Individuals have a right to privacy. *Jones v. City of Moose*, 121 Kim. 12, 13 (1983).

The citation itself provides the information about the court, its jurisdiction and level, and the year. The text need not repeat this information. Citations are valuable sources of information about the legal authority presented in the rule component of the IRAC paragraph.

3. Application of the Law to the Problem's Facts

How Do You Use the Legally Significant Facts?

Think of the legal rule as a test or a series of elements requiring certain facts to be used to support the outcome of the test. The facts used are legally significant facts because they bear legal significance as to the outcome of an issue. Our arson example mentioned at the beginning of the chapter illustrates this point.

THE ARSON HYPOTHETICAL

John Smith lived in Arkville. John Smith's brother, Richard Smith, lived in Barkville Estates. Richard Smith owned a factory in downtown Barkville. John Smith was consumed by a jealous rage over his brother Richard's success and intentionally and maliciously burned down the factory in Barkville. The question to be examined is whether John Smith committed arson by intentionally and maliciously burning down his brother's factory?

The general rule for arson is the malicious burning of a dwelling house of another. This general rule would be the legal authority used in the rule portion of the IRAC paragraph.

An IRAC paragraph on this topic would be as follows:

Issue:	Whether John Smith committed arson by burning down his brother's factory?
Rule:	Arson is the malicious burning of a dwelling house of another. 9 Stat. §§ 21, 23 (1976).
Application:	John Smith burned down the factory of his brother, Richard Smith. John Smith's actions were intentional and malicious. Richard resides in Barkville Estates.
Conclusion:	John Smith did not commit arson because he burned down his brother's factory, not his brother's residence or dwelling house.

The **application** lays a factual foundation on which the conclusion can be based. The facts are selected because each fact illustrates a legal point related to your rule of law: the malicious act, the intentional burning down of a building, the use of the building—whether it serves as a residence or dwelling house or whether it serves another purpose. The rule indicates which facts you should examine. Once you lay the factual foundation by using the problem's facts to illustrate how the law should apply, you draw a conclusion.

4. Conclusion

What Purpose Does the Conclusion Serve?

The **conclusion** resolves the issue posed at the beginning of the IRAC sequence. The conclusion should reflect directly the issue posed. If you remove the rule and the application portions of the IRAC paragraph, the issue and the conclusion should read as if they are a question and an answer. The conclusion generally restates the issue and includes the basis for the answer. The arson example with John Smith illustrates the role of the conclusion.

Issue:	Whether John Smith committed arson by burning down his brother's factory?
Conclusion:	John Smith did not commit arson because he burned down his brother's factory, not his residence or dwelling house.

Notice how the conclusion responds directly to the issue posed. The conclusion focuses directly on the question raised at the beginning of the IRAC sequence. Each element of the discussion is resolved before addressing the next element or issue. Always test to see if your conclusion is focused on the issue raised by reading the issue at the beginning of the IRAC sequence and then reading the conclusion. If the issue and the conclusion read like a question and a reasoned answer that responds directly to the question posed, then you have adequately resolved the issue raised.

CHAPTER SUMMARY

IRAC—standing for Issue, Rule, Application, Conclusion—provides the structure for the legal discussion. The IRAC structure provides a checklist for you to make sure that you have included all of the necessary components in the discussion and supported every premise with legal authority. Because it follows a predictable pattern, IRAC permits the reader to obtain information quickly. Mastering the IRAC format requires practice, which involves rereading and revising your work. Once you feel comfortable with the IRAC format, you should be confident that the discussion portions of your memos are logically ordered and analytically complete.

Key Terms

Application	Legal holding
Citation	Rule
Conclusion	Sub-issue
IRAC	Topic sentence
Issue	

EXERCISES

1. Diagram the IRAC components of each paragraph in the discussion section. Note where the writing digresses from the IRAC format.

Discussion

To be successful in a claim against Rough & Tough or Able Pawn, Ms. Howard would have to prove that Rough & Tough was liable for the loss of her ring. First, for an action against Rough & Tough, she would have to show that they had no right to transfer her pawned property without her written consent. Illinois Pawnbrokers Act, 205 ILCS 510/7 (1992). If pledged property was transferred without written consent of the property owner, the pawnbroker can be held responsible for loss or theft of pawned property because the property was in his safekeeping and was transferred illegally. *Jacobs v. Grossman,* 141 N.E. 714, 716 (Ill. Ct. App. 1923). Rough & Tough did not get a written consent for the transfer of Ms. Howard's property. In their defense they could claim that written correspondence without the written consent would be enough to inform the pawner of the transfer of her property. Second, for an action against Able Pawn, Ms. Howard would have to show negligence in its care of her pawned ring. Illinois courts have ruled that in bailment for mutual benefit, the ordinary care or diligence that one would give to their own property would be adequate to avoid negligence. *Id.* at 715; *Bielunski v. Tousignant,* 149 N.E.2d 801, 803 (Ill. Ct. App. 1958). She would have to prove that a security system and a guard dog would not be ordinary care and diligence. In his defense Mr. Able could argue that it was sufficient to be considered ordinary care and diligence. For a claim against Village Jewelers to be successful, Ms. Howard would have to establish that she held good title to her property because a thief cannot convey good title to stolen property. *Hobson's Truck Sales, Inc. v. Carroll Trucking, Inc.,* 276 N.E. 89, 92 (Ill. Ct. App. 1971). Village Jewelers, who purchased the ring from the robbers, could not have good title to Ms. Howard's ring. Ms. Howard probably could have a successful claim against Rough & Tough and Village Jewelers. She probably would not be able to prove Able Pawn negligent in the care of her ring.

Whether a pawnbroker has the right to transfer pawned property or interest in that property without written consent of the pawner? Pawned property cannot be transferred within a year from the pawner's default without written consent of the pawner. Illinois Pawnbrokers Act, 205 ILCS 510/7. One Illinois court ruled that a pawnbroker had no right to transfer plaintiff's pledged diamond ring to another pawnbroker within a year of the plaintiff's default of her loan, without written consent of the pawner. *Jacobs,* 141 N.E. at 716. In our situation, Rough & Tough sold their shop and assets to Sam Able within two months of Ms. Howard's pawning her grandmother's engagement ring. Because the sale occurred within a year of Ms. Howard's transaction with Rough & Tough, they had a legal obligation under the Illinois statute to require a written consent for the transfer of her property. Also, the statute states that the time period for requirement of written consent for transfer of pledged property is established from the time of the pawner's default. 205 ILCS 510/7. Our client has not defaulted, and she deserves at least all of the rights offered by the statute to a pawner who is in default. Rough & Tough did send Ms. Howard a postcard notifying her that they had sold all the pawned items and outstanding loans, including her ring, but they did not get her written consent for the sale of her property. Rough & Tough did not have the right to transfer Ms. Howard's ring without her written consent, and the sale of her property was probably not a legal sale.

Whether a postcard sent to a pawner by a pawnbroker would be sufficient notice for the transfer of pawned property? Personal pawned property cannot be sold by a pawnee within one year from the time the pawner has defaulted in the interest payment unless the pawner has given written consent. Illinois Pawnbrokers Act, 205 ILCS 510/7. The statute uses a definite and clear term: "written consent." Ms. Howard did not default, and she would have at least all of the rights of a pawner that did default. Therefore, the pawnbroker was required to receive her written consent before transferring her property. A postcard with written notice of a sale of pawned property is not a written consent by the pawner and would probably not be sufficient notice to constitute a legal sale.

2. Diagram the IRAC components of each paragraph in the discussion section. Note where the writing digresses from the IRAC format.

Facts

The Blacks came to us with the following problem and want to know what type of damages they are entitled to.

Mr. and Mrs. Black wanted to have a chair and a loveseat made to match the living room in their new home. The Blacks searched for weeks at various local furniture retailers for a furniture style and fabric that they liked but were unsuccessful. Finally, the Blacks went to a fabric sale at Fabric Retailers and found the upholstery fabric of their dreams. The Blacks purchased 50 yards of the fabric to make sure that they would have enough for any project. Mr. Black called all of the furniture retailers around to inquire as to whether customers can have furniture covered in their own material. Finally, Comfy Furniture said that they permit customers to bring in their own material to cover upholstered furniture ordered from Comfy's. The Blacks hurried over to Comfy with the 50 yards of fabric and placed an order for a chair and a loveseat using their own fabric. The price agreed on was the base price of $500 for the chair and $800 for the loveseat. Mr. Blaine, of Comfy Furniture, was their salesperson. Mr. Blaine said that the fabric was ideal for the styles selected because it required no matching. He added that there was plenty of yardage because 30 yards is adequate for jobs of this nature. The fabric was a small paisley print, with the right side having a lovely sheen and vibrant coloration. The Blacks placed the order on July 7, 1993, because they were planning a family reunion for Thanksgiving and felt that that date would give them plenty of time to completely decorate their living room. The new pieces would provide plenty of seating for the family reunion. The Blacks indicated to Mr. Blaine that they needed the furniture for the reunion. Mr. Blaine asserted that the furniture would be ready by September 15. The Blacks gave Comfy Furniture a deposit of $1,000. The loveseat and the chair were delivered to the Black home on September 10, but the furniture was upholstered with the fabric inside out with the reverse side showing. The Blacks were devastated.

Issues

Whether the Blacks are entitled to damages from Comfy Furniture for incorrectly upholstering their furniture?

Whether the Blacks are entitled to damages from Comfy Furniture for the expense of decorating their living room to match the furniture they did not receive in the agreed on condition?

Discussion

Are the Blacks entitled to special damages from Comfy Furniture for the cost of the redecoration of their living room? An Illinois Appellate Court decided that the nonbreaching party should be put back in the position that they were in when the contract was formed. *Kalal v. Goldblatt Bros., Inc.*, 368 N.E.2d 671, 673 (Ill. Ct. App. 1977). The Blacks stated their intention at the beginning concerning the fabric, the redecoration of the living room, and the family reunion. This fact was a part of their original position. The living room was redecorated. The furniture was delivered; however, the fabric was incorrect. Therefore, the Blacks have a right to recover consequential damages for the cost of the redecoration of their living room because the end result was not achieved: correctly upholstered furniture, newly redecorated living room to match, and a new living room look for the reunion. The conditions of the original contract were not met, and there was a breach of contract as embodied by the incorrectly upholstered furniture.

Under contract law, what damages are the Blacks entitled to pursue? Damages for breach of contract should place the plaintiff in a position he would have been in had the contract been performed. *Kalal*, 368 N.E.2d at 671. The plaintiffs in *Kalal* received a sofa that had been reupholstered in the wrong fabric after numerous delays, during which they had chosen three different fabrics in succession. *Id.* The court held that the defect could be remedied by the cost of reupholstering the sofa in the proper fabric. *Id.* at 674. The Black's sofa and loveseat were improperly upholstered. Comfy Furniture upholstered their furniture with the reverse side of the fabric showing. Therefore, they were entitled to damages equal to the cost of upholstering their furniture correctly. However, the Blacks' situation is distinguished from *Kalal* in that their furniture was delivered before the date set in the contract, and it can be argued by Comfy that there was time to remedy the defect before their target date of Thanksgiving.

Are the Blacks entitled to compensation for the loss of use of their furniture? The question of compensation for loss of use of the furniture was considered by both parties in *Kalal* to be appropriate since the plaintiffs in the case were without their furniture for several months while waiting for it to be reupholstered. *Id.* The Blacks have been similarly inconvenienced in that they, too, have been without the use of their new furniture. Thus, they are entitled to compensation for the loss of use of the furniture. However, it can be argued by Comfy Furniture that the furniture in the *Kalal* case was used and had been removed from the home for the purpose of reupholstering it. *Id.* In the present case, the furniture was new and had never been in the Blacks' home, and Comfy may argue that the Blacks did not actually suffer loss of use of the new furniture.

Are the Blacks entitled to damages for the expense of decorating their living room to match the furniture they did not receive in the agreed on condition? The redecorating of the living room in *Kalal* was not in the contemplation of either party at the time the contract was executed. *Kalal,* 368 N.E.2d at 671. Subsequently, the court held that the only damages that were recoverable for breach of contract are limited to those which were reasonably foreseeable and were within the contemplation of the parties at the time the contract was executed. *Id.* at 674. By the express terms of the Uniform Commercial Code, the court cannot follow tort theories to award damages. The legislative history of the U.C.C. indicates that contractual disputes should apply to the findings of the court. *Moorman Mfg. Co. v. National Tank Co.,* 435 N.E.2d 443, 453 (Ill. 1982). The Blacks only told Mr. Blaine that they need the furniture to be completed in time for a family reunion. Comfy knew that the Blacks were under a time constraint for the delivery, but apparently there was no communication regarding the redecorating of the living room. With regard to Comfy Furniture, the redecorating of the Blacks' living room was an unforeseeable event and consequently they would not be held responsible for the expense. Because the fact that the redecorating of the living room was unforeseeable, it was not included within the terms of the contract. Therefore, Comfy only breached the express terms of the contract. The Blacks probably will not be awarded compensatory damages.

Application Exercises

3. Label the components of the discussion that follows to indicate Issue, Rule, Application, and Conclusion, and where each component begins. The discussion is based on these facts:

> Drake Industries has been leasing warehouse space at 2700 North Bosworth Avenue, in Chicago, Illinois, from the owner of the building, Michael Martin. Drake began leasing space from Martin beginning January 1, 1969, at $700 per month until the lease expired on December 31, 1980.
>
> Martin offered a new lease to Drake on November 25, 1980, to be signed and returned by December 31, 1980. The new lease began January 1, 1981, and expired on December 31, 1994, and the rent increased to $850 per month, payable on the first of each month. Drake never signed or returned the new lease, but did pay the increased rent amount during the term of the unsigned lease ending December 31, 1994. Since then, Drake has continued paying $850 on the first day of each month. On August 15, 1995, Martin

requested that Drake surrender the premises. Drake came to your firm to find out what type of tenancy he has and whether Martin gave Drake the proper notice to quit the premises.

Is Drake Industries a holdover tenant? A holdover tenancy is created when a landlord elects to treat a tenant, after the expiration of his or her lease, as a tenant for another term upon the same provisions contained in the original lease. *Bismarck Hotel Co. v. Sutherland,* 92 Ill. App. 3d 167, 415 N.E.2d 517 (1980). In *Bismarck,* defendant Sutherland's written lease expired. Bismarck presented her with a new lease that included a rent increase. She began to pay the increase but did not sign the new lease. Sutherland could not be a holdover tenant since the terms of the old lease were not extended to the terms of the new, unsigned lease. Drake Industries was offered a new lease in 1980 that included a rent increase. Since the terms were different from the original lease, Drake could not be considered a holdover tenant.

It is the intention of the landlord, not the tenant, that determines whether the tenant is to be treated as a holdover. *Sheraton-Chicago Corp. v. Lewis,* 8 Ill. App. 3d 309, 290 N.E.2d 685 (1972). When a landlord creates a new lease and presents it to the tenant, it is clear that it was his intention that a new tenancy was created. *Holt v. Chicago Hair Goods Co.,* 328 Ill. App. 671, 66 N.E.2d 727 (1946). Martin presented Drake with a new lease to sign in November 1980, with new terms beginning January 1, 1981. It was never his intention to hold over the same lease from 1969. Therefore, Drake was not a holdover tenant and has never been one. 735 ILCS 5/9-202 (West 1993) could not apply to Drake. Martin could not demand double rental fees from Drake when it remained in possession of 2700 North Bosworth after the written lease expired on December 31, 1980.

Is Drake Industries a year-to-year tenant? When the payment of rent is annual, there arises a tenancy from year-to-year, even if the agreement provides for a payment of one-twelfth of the annual rental each month. *Seaver Amusement Co. v. Saxe et al.,* 210 Ill. App. 289 (1918). The terms of the 1969 written lease would have to have said "$8,400 a year rent, payable in monthly installments of $700" for it to have been considered a year-to-year lease. Since the terms of the 1969 lease only provided for monthly payments and not a yearly rental rate, Drake was not a year-to-year tenant. 735 ILCS 5/9-205 (1993) does not apply at all to Drake. Martin would not be required to tender 60 days' notice in writing to terminate the tenancy.

Is Drake Industries a month-to-month tenant? A month-to-month tenancy is created when a tenant remains in possession of the premises after a lease expires under different terms of tenancy. 92 Ill. App. 3d at 168; 415 N.E.2d at 517. By paying Bismarck's increased rental amount, different terms of the tenancy were established, so Sutherland's tenancy was considered month-to-month by the court. Drake remained at 2700 North Bosworth after its lease expired in 1980, but began paying the increased rent to Martin under the new terms of the unsigned lease.

This established different terms of tenancy, so Drake has been a month-to-month tenant since 1980.

What type of tenancy is created under an oral lease? When a tenant goes into possession of real estate under an oral leasing agreement for a term over one year at monthly rental, the agreement is voidable under the Statute of Frauds. The most that the tenant in possession can claim is that the leasing is from month to month and that the landlord can terminate the tenancy by providing 30 days' notice in writing to the tenant. *Creighton v. Sanders,* 89 Ill. 543 (1878). Charles Creighton had an oral agreement to lease a house from Patrick Sanders for a five-year term. When Creighton ceased paying rent, Sanders gave him a written notice to quit the premises. Creighton maintained that he had a five-year lease, but the most the court allowed was that he was a month-to-month tenant, based on the parol lease. When Drake never signed or returned the new lease in 1980, he entered into a parol lease agreement with Martin. Martin cannot hold Drake to any terms of that lease because the tenancy was for a duration of 12 years, well over the one-year limit under the Statute of Frauds. The most Martin can claim is that Drake is a month-to-month tenant.

What type of notice is necessary to vacate the premises? Under 735 ILCS 5/9-207 (1993), notice to terminate a month-to-month tenancy must be given in writing 30 days before termination before any action for forcible entry and detainer can be maintained. Drake said that on August 15, 1995, Martin "requested" that Drake surrender the premises. An oral request may not be sufficient and Drake may maintain that proper notice has not been made and it need not surrender the premises by September 15, 1995. A forcible entry and detainer action could not be entered and maintained and Drake need not surrender the premises until proper notice has been given.

Drafting Exercises

4. Write an IRAC paragraph based in the following facts, issue, and cases. The fact pattern is:

> Ms. Jones was waiting to get off the commuter train in the train's vestibule. The commuter train pulled into the station and Ms. Jones descended the stairs to disembark from the train. The conductors exit the train first to watch the passengers exit the train, and then signal to close the doors and for the train to start rolling. Ms. Jones was carrying her briefcase, which had a long strap. As Ms. Jones exited the train, the briefcase strap was behind her. The train doors shut with Ms. Jones on the platform but with the briefcase strap still inside the door. The train dragged Ms. Jones about 10 feet and she suffered a broken shoulder. The issue you have to consider is whether the conductor's negligence in signaling for the train to start was the proximate cause of Ms. Jones's broken shoulder.

The issue upon which you should focus your case synthesis is whether the conductor's failure to see that Ms. Jones's briefcase strap was inside the door as he signaled for the train to start moving is the proximate cause of her injury, a broken shoulder.

Cases:

Smith v. Atlantic City Railroad

12 Nowhere 2d 5 (1994)

Mr. John Smith was injured on the Atlantic City Railroad when the train lurched with great violence as it rounded a curve on the track. The train was overcrowded. Smith was injured without fault on his part. The motorman drove the overcrowded car too fast around the curve, as to cause it to lurch severely. When a passenger train is overcrowded and the employees operating the train know of such condition, it is their duty to exercise additional care commensurate with the dangers. The motorman knew of the over-crowded conditions and failed to exercise additional care when rounding the curve. When the train lurched as it rounded the curve, Mr. Smith was injured because he fell onto another passenger. The motorman's failure to exercise the requisite care was the proximate cause of Mr. Smith's injuries.

Blue v. Boardwalk Railroad

15 Nowhere 2d 9 (1980)

Mr. Robert Blue was blinded by a sudden gust of steam and fell underneath the train he was in the process of boarding; Mr. Blue's arm was severed by the train as the train started to leave the station. Regular inspection of couplings is a required duty of conductors; therefore, failure to inspect the couplings for leaks is a negligent act on the part of the defendant. Since a person of ordinary prudence could have foreseen that escaping steam would result from leaks in the uninspected couplings, Railroad's oversight of uninspected couplings was the proximate cause of Mr. Blue's injury. The consequence of the escaping steam, because of the railroad's failure to inspect the couplings, resulted in a foreseeable injury to a passenger or person waiting on the platform.

5. Write an IRAC paragraph based on the following facts, issue, and statutes. The fact pattern is:

Ms. Jones was waiting to get off the commuter train in the train's vestibule. The commuter train pulled into the station and Ms. Jones descended the stairs to disembark from the train. The conductors exit the train first to watch the passengers exit the train, and then signal to close the doors and for the train to start rolling. Ms. Jones was carrying her briefcase, which had a long strap. As Ms. Jones exited the train, the briefcase strap was behind her. The train doors shut with Ms. Jones on the platform but with the briefcase strap still inside the door. The train dragged Ms. Jones about 10 feet and she suffered a broken shoulder. The issue you have to consider is whether the conductor's negligence in signaling for the train to start was the proximate cause of Ms. Jones's broken shoulder.

The issue that you should focus your case synthesis on is whether the conductor's failure to see that Ms. Jones's briefcase strap was inside the door as he signaled for the train to start moving is the proximate cause of her injury, a broken shoulder.

Statutes:

Chapter 131

Nowhere Revised Code § 12 (1991)

An operator of a common carrier must perform regular inspections of all components of the common carrier. Failure to do so constitutes negligence. The failure to perform inspections and the resulting negligence will be considered the proximate cause of all injuries occurring aboard a common carrier.

Chapter 131

Nowhere Revised Code § 14 (1991)

It is the duty of an operator of a common carrier to exercise additional care when dangers are foreseeable.

6. Write an IRAC paragraph using the following information. You need not include all of the information. The issue is whether the plaintiff can show that his attorney's failure to attend hearings was excusable neglect. A number of the text blocks below contain statements of rules. Other text blocks include legally significant facts. In some paragraphs, conclusions have been drawn for you. Combine the rules where necessary and form an IRAC paragraph for the issue:

Fed. R. Civ. P. 60(b) provides for relief from judgment if plaintiffs can show that a mistake was made or that there was excusable neglect on the part of their attorney.

Rule 60(b) is an extraordinary remedy, granted in only exceptional cases. *Harold Washington Party v. Cook Cty. Illinois Democratic Party,* 984 F.2d 875 (7th Cir. 1993).

In this case, the plaintiff's attorney, Mark Adly, missed four court-set status hearings. He failed to appear. He failed to answer motions. Court status hearings are routinely held every three months.

Adly claims he did not have any notice of the hearings. Adly knew status proceedings normally were held. He attended depositions in this matter. Court records show that he was sent notices of the hearings to the address Adly says is correct.

"Excusable neglect may warrant relief under Rule 60(b)." *Zuelzke Tool & Eng. v. Anderson Die Casting,* 925 F.2d 226 (7th Cir. 1991). In this case, the defendant relied upon a third party who told them to refrain from further action because efforts were being made to have the defendant removed as defendant. *Id.* at 228. Anderson did not answer any complaints or file any pleadings. *Id.* The lack of response led the court to enter a default judgment against the company. *Id.* at 229. The district court refused the motion to vacate, saying that the defendant had voluntarily chosen not to control its fate in the litigation. *Id.*

7. Review the following paragraph. Note the issue, the rule, the application of law to facts, and the conclusion.

An important factor in determining whether a funeral home is a nuisance is the suitability of its location. "Funeral homes are generally located on the edge of purely residential but not predominantly residential areas." *Bauman v. Piser Undertakers Co.,* 34 Ill. App. 2d 145, 148, 180 N.E.2d 705, 708 (1962). A carefully run funeral home may be located on a property zoned for business at the edge of a residential neighborhood. *Id.* The funeral home in this case is located in a predominantly rural area. It is outside of the boundary lines of the Up and Coming Acres subdivision. It is a lawful business located on a parcel zoned for business. The funeral home is in a suitable location.

10. Synthesizing Cases and Authorities

A. Synthesis
B. Types of Synthesis
C. Step-by-Step Process to Synthesizing Legal Rules
D. Examples of Case Synthesis

CHAPTER OVERVIEW

Synthesis is the bringing together of various legal authorities into a unified cohesive statement of the law. The process of synthesizing authority requires finding a common theme or thread that relates to the various legal rules and tying the holdings to that unified theme. Discussing related decisions and statutes separately in a memo makes your points sound more like a list than an integrated, well thought-out whole. Synthesis adds analytical insight to your legal documents and makes reading them easier.

A. Synthesis

What Is the Process of Synthesizing Legal Rules?

Enacted law that emanates from more than one statute section must be synthesized together under a common legal principle to add cohesiveness and to add your analytical viewpoint to the memo. We synthesize cases and enacted law because memos and opinion letters are organized by legal issue and not by cited references. Frequently, more than one source of primary authority addresses a particular legal issue. The synthesis of related legal principles enables you to compare and to contrast the legal rules easily as well as to demonstrate how factual applications differ and to show how legal rules expand or contract. Often enacted law and case law are synthesized together because the case law applies the statute or interprets the extent to which the statute can be applied.

Why Do We Synthesize Legal Authority?

The legal issues form the framework for the memo discussion. The synthesized authority groups the legal holdings together to address the issues raised.

The following example demonstrates how one case defines an easement in gross and then another case explains how an easement in gross is retained. Both cases discuss easements in gross, yet one expands on the other. The facts on which the example is based are as follows:

> Robert and Jan Murray live in Evanston and are building an addition to their house on Ashland. There is eight feet between their house and their neighbor's, Mrs. Brown's, house. The properties are adjoining. A driveway does not separate the houses, and they cannot be accessed by an alley. The Murrays' contractors and construction workers must enter Mrs. Brown's property to work on the addition. Mrs. Brown is not very pleased that workers are entering her property. The Murrays came to our office wondering whether they should purchase an easement from Mrs. Brown, their neighbor.

Example

Whether the Murrays should purchase an easement in gross from Mrs. Brown? An easement in gross, sometimes called a personal easement, is a right in the land of another, without being appurtenant to or exercised with the occupancy of the land. *Willoughby v. Lawrence*, 116 Ill. 11, 4 N.E. 356 (1886). It belongs to the easement holder independent of his ownership or possession of any tract of land and does not benefit the possessor of any tract of land in his use of it. *Schnabel v. County of DuPage*, 101 Ill. App. 3d 553, 428 N.E.2d 671 (1981). The Murrays are building an addition to their house. They want to have a right to use the adjoining land to perform the construction of their addition. They do not need an easement, which would be appurtenant to the estate. The interest that the Murrays have in Mrs. Brown's land is personal and would not benefit either tract of land. Therefore, the Murrays can purchase an easement in gross from Mrs. Brown that would permit the workers to enter the Brown property.

B. Types of Synthesis

What Are the Types of Synthesis?

As we discussed previously, synthesizing primary authority requires finding a common theme that is used to unify all of the sources related to the issue. The common legal theme can be developed by classifying the applicable precedent into categories. There are four basic ways to combine and to analyze legal rules to render a coherent distillation of the law:

1. **Primary authority** can be grouped by rule of law found in the text of the decision or in the statute or constitution.
2. Synthesis can be focused around the **reasoning** that a judge uses as the basis of the synthesis.
3. The various **facts** from different cases can form the foundation of the synthesis.
4. The **causes of action** are the last category of case synthesis.

C. Step-by-Step Process to Synthesizing Legal Rules

How Do You Synthesize Legal Rules?

The most effective synthesis of legal rules follows conscientious case briefing and careful reading of enacted law. Case briefing requires conforming a decision into set categories: citation, procedure, issue, facts, holding, rationale, disposition. (See Chapter 5, Briefing Cases.) The following steps take you through the synthesizing process.

1. *Brief decisions*. Once you have carefully and meticulously briefed all of the decisions that you plan to use in your memo you can establish categories of legal precedence to make comparing and contrasting decisions easier. It is far simpler to compare and to contrast seven holdings from briefed decisions than to flip through photocopies of authority.

2. *Outline the problem*. The next step is to formulate the analytical outline of your letter or memo and to pinpoint the issues and sub-issues that must be addressed to fully explore the memo topic.

3. *Relate research to legal issues raised*. Organize the primary authority by relating the research findings to the issues raised by the problem. Remember: legal writing is never organized around your sources of authority but around the issues raised by the problem. After pinpointing the legal issues that will be explored, decide on the general rule relating to that point of law.

4. *Under each issue, organize your primary sources by hierarchy of authority*. Enacted law comes before common law, constitutions come before statutes, newer case decisions interpreting statutes come before common law cases, higher court holdings come before lower court holdings, and newer case holdings are more relevant than older holdings on the same point of law from the same court.

5. *Compare and contrast holdings and statutes*. Using the case briefs that you prepared and the notes you made from the plain reading of the enacted law, compare and contrast the holdings and statutory texts.

6. Formulate a statement of the law. Your statement should incorporate all of the primary sources that will be used under the sub-issue heading. Ask yourself: What are the similarities and differences between the various cases and statutes? How do the facts differ? What do the documents have in common?

7. Correct Bluebook citation. Remember that you must attribute the authority for any legal statement, even if it is a clause, using proper Bluebook citation.

D. Examples of Case Synthesis

A problem and two fictitious legal decisions are provided below on which case synthesis is performed.

Problem

Mr. and Mrs. Black wanted to have a chair and a loveseat made to match the living room in their new home. The Blacks searched for weeks at various local furniture retailers for a furniture style and fabric that they liked but were unsuccessful. Finally, the Blacks went to a fabric sale at Fabric Retailers and found the upholstery fabric of their dreams. The Blacks purchased 50 yards of the fabric of their dreams to make sure that they would have enough for any project. Mr. Black called all of the furniture retailers around to inquire as to whether customers can have furniture covered in their own material. Finally, Comfy Furniture said that they permit customers to bring in their own material to cover upholstered furniture ordered from Comfy. The Blacks hurried over to Comfy with the 50 yards of fabric and placed an order for a chair and a loveseat using their own fabric. The price agreed on was the base price of $500 for the chair and $800 for the loveseat. Mr. Blaine, of Comfy Furniture, was their salesperson. Mr. Blaine said that the fabric was ideal for the styles selected because it required no matching. He also offered that there was plenty of material, that 30 yards is adequate for a job of this nature. The fabric was a small paisley print, with the right side having a lovely sheen and vibrant coloration. The Blacks placed the order on July 7, 1993. They were planning a family reunion for Thanksgiving and felt that ordering in July would give them plenty of time to completely decorate their living room. The new pieces would provide plenty of seating for the family reunion. The Blacks indicated to Mr. Blaine that they needed the furniture for the reunion. Mr. Blaine asserted that the furniture would be ready by September 15. The Blacks gave Comfy Furniture a deposit of

$1,000. The loveseat and the chair were delivered to the Black home on September 10, but the furniture was upholstered with the fabric's reverse side showing. The Blacks were devastated.

The legal issue is whether the Blacks are entitled to damages for the breach of the contract to upholster the furniture?

The legal principle surrounding this problem is the expectation interest in a contract. The expectation interest is the expectation of gain from the performance of the contract. The damages are assessed to give the nonbreaching party the measure of gain that he or she would have received if the contract was performed as agreed. Sometimes special or consequential damages are awarded in addition to the expectancy interest.

CASE A

The Cahill family ordered a sofa from the Acme Furniture Company in red tapestry, on June 1, 1994, due to be delivered in 6 weeks, on July 15, 1994. The Cahills paid $600 for the sofa at the time of the order. After 10 weeks, Acme delivered a gold sofa to the Cahill home. The Cahills called Acme to complain and Acme picked up the sofa with the promise that it would be reupholstered in red. The sofa was delivered in green 6 weeks later. In the meanwhile, the Cahills decorated their living room to match the red sofa. After the sofa was delivered in green, 16 weeks after the initial order, the Cahills sued Acme for breach of contract and for damages resulting from the breach, which included the cost of redecorating their living room to match the red sofa. The legal rule is that the nonbreaching party can only collect damages to recoup the expected gain from the contract if performed as agreed. The nonbreaching party cannot receive damages for expenses incurred that were not in contemplation at the time the contract was formed. The Cahills are entitled to damages for the upholstering of the sofa in the incorrect color and are entitled to compensation for the loss of the use of their sofa for 16 weeks as well as the cost of a new red sofa.

CASE B

Jane Smith ordered a new car from Lunar Motors on June 1, 1994. The Lunar coupe in black was ordered but the salesperson suggested that the grey floor model, which was just used for demo drives, would represent a $300 savings off of the sticker price of the Lunar coupe. Ms. Smith agreed to purchase the floor model for $12,700 rather than pay $13,000 for the special order car. The salesperson once again asserted that the floor model was new, was only used for demo drives, and only had 5 miles on the odometer. Ms. Smith returned to Lunar Motors on June 3, 1994, paid the

$12,700 for the grey floor model Lunar coupe and drove home. While driving home, Ms. Smith noticed that the car veered dramatically to the left. Ms. Smith took the car to her mechanic who reported that the car was in an accident previously and had been repaired but the frame was bent in such a manner as to distort the alignment. Ms. Smith contracted to and expected to receive a new, undamaged car with mileage and wear and tear due to demo drives. Ms. Smith did not contract to receive a damaged car. The salesperson asserted the car was like new. The holding of the court is that the nonbreaching party is entitled to the gain expected from the performance of the contract as agreed, and if the contract is not performed as agreed, the nonbreaching party is entitled to receive the benefit that she would have received if the contract had been performed as agreed. Ms. Smith is entitled to a complete refund of the $12,700 she paid for the car plus the daily cost of the loss of the use of the automobile to be tabulated by the fair market rental value per day of a Lunar coupe.

To synthesize the holdings from the fictitious cases, you would find a common theme that ties together the rules of law from both decisions. Basically, both cases hold that the nonbreaching party in a contract is entitled to receive the benefit of the deal that would have been received if the contract had been performed as agreed. First, craft a general statement of the law. Then, mention the legal rules from Case A and Case B as they pertain to the general statement of the law.

Example

Whether the Blacks are entitled to damages compensating them for the breach of the contract to reupholster the loveseat and the chair? Damages are assessed in a breach of contract action (to give the nonbreaching party the measure of gain that he would have received if the contract had been performed as agreed) in a very specific manner. The nonbreaching party can only collect damages to recoup the gain expected from the contract if the contract had been performed as agreed. *Case A*; *Case B*. If the contract is not performed as agreed, the nonbreaching party is entitled to the benefit he would have received if the contract had been performed as agreed. *Case B*. The nonbreaching party cannot be compensated for expenses incurred that were not in contemplation at the time the contract was formed. *Case A*. In the alternative, the nonbreaching party can be compensated for expenses incurred that were in contemplation at the time the contract was formed. *Case A*. In our problem, the Blacks contracted to have the chair and loveseat upholstered in paisley fabric with the correct side showing. The furniture was upholstered with the wrong side of the fabric showing. When ordering the furniture, the Blacks stipulated that they needed the pieces for a family reunion and that the pieces would provide the necessary seating. The Blacks were without their furniture because of an error of Comfy Furniture, and the need for the seating was mentioned at the time of the contract formation. The Blacks should receive the gain they expected from the performance of the contract as agreed as well as compensation for the expense of providing alternative seating for the family reunion based on the rental cost of chairs.

An ineffective case synthesis based on our hypothetical problem would be as follows.

> Whether the Blacks are entitled to damages from Comfy Furniture for breach of contract? In *Case B,* the court held that "the nonbreaching party is entitled to the gain expected from the performance of the contract as agreed and if the contract is not performed as agreed, the nonbreaching party is entitled to receive the benefit that she would have received if the contract had been performed as agreed." *Case B.* The Blacks were the nonbreaching party and anticipated a loveseat and a chair to be upholstered in paisley with the correct side showing. Therefore, the Blacks are entitled to be compensated by a damage award to put them in a position as if the contract had been performed as agreed.
>
> Whether the Blacks are entitled to be compensated for not having adequate seating for the family reunion? *Case A* holds that the nonbreaching party cannot receive damages for expenses incurred that were not in contemplation at the time the contract was formed. *Case A.* The Blacks alerted Mr. Blaine, the salesperson, that the couches were needed for a family reunion at Thanksgiving. The Blacks indicated that the additional seating provided by the chair and the loveseat would be necessary at the reunion when ordering the furniture. Since the need for the seating, to be provided by the furniture, was in contemplation at the time the order was placed, the Blacks should be compensated for not having adequate seating at the time of the reunion; the damages should be measured by the cost of providing alternative seating.

This example, although clear and coherent, does not synthesize the decisions and unify the concepts articulated in the cases. Each holding is addressed separately, although one holding relates to the other and the authority is presented more as a list than as a cohesive unit.

When you have found a relevant statute for a problem, give it the highest regard because statutes on point govern before case law. (See Chapters 1 and 2.) Generally, synthesize statutes separately from case law holdings. However, if you find cases that interpret and apply the relevant statutes, synthesize the statute text with the application found in case law. Always apply the plain meaning rule to statutes. The plain meaning of the statute text is derived from a reading of each word at its face value.

The problem below illustrates the synthesis of a statute and a case.

Problem

FACT PATTERN

On August 7, 1992, our client, Jane Howard, obtained an $800 loan from Rough & Tough Pawn Shop, using her grandmother's engagement ring as collateral. Howard agreed to make monthly payments on the loan for a minimum of 13½ months. After 12 months, Rough & Tough had the right to sell the ring and to refund Howard the difference between her outstanding debt and the price received for the ring.

On September 11, 1992, Howard received a postcard from Rough & Tough stating that its shop and its assets will be sold to Able Pawn. The postcard also stated that Able would assume the business of Rough & Tough, including the items pawned and the loans outstanding. The postcard alerted Howard to pick up the ring and to pay off her note by September 29, 1992, if Howard wanted to reclaim her property. Howard decided to continue to make her monthly payments to Able Pawn, where her loan would be transferred.

On October 1, 1992, Able Pawn was robbed and all of the jewelry was stolen, including Howard's ring. The premises were protected by a security alarm system and a guard dog. The jewelry was sold to Village Jewelers in Lincoln Park.

ISSUE

The issue to be examined is whether Rough & Tough had authority to sell its interest in Howard's ring?

STATUTORY AUTHORITY

The applicable statute is from the Pawnbrokers Regulation Act, 205 ILCS 510/10 (1992).

> *Sale of Property.* No personal property received on deposit or pledge, or purchased by any such pawnbroker, shall be sold or permitted to be redeemed or removed from the place of business of such pawnbroker for the space of twenty-four hours after the delivery of the copy and statement required by Section 7 of this act required to be delivered to the officer or officers named therein; and no personal property pawned or pledged shall be sold or disposed of by any such pawnbroker within one year from the time when the

pawner or pledger shall make default in the payment of interest on the money so advanced by such pawnbroker, unless by the written consent of such pawner or pledger.

RELEVANT CASE LAW

This decision interprets and applies the relevant statute so the statute and the decision should be synthesized together.

Jacobs v. Grossman

310 Ill. 247, 141 N.E.2d 714 (1923)

DUNCAN, J.

This case is brought to this court on a certificate of importance and appeal from a judgment of the Appellate Court for the First District, affirming a judgment of the municipal court of Chicago in favor of the appellee and against appellant in the sum of $330. Appellee, Minnie Jacobs, on April 8, 1921, began an action of replevin in the municipal court of Chicago against appellant, Harry Grossman, a licensed pawnbroker, to recover possession of a diamond ring delivered by herself to appellant to secure the payment of $70 borrowed from him. A replevin bond was given for $800, and a writ of replevin issued. It was returned April 12, 1921, served but no property found. Appellee then filed a count in trover, alleging possession of the ring of the value of $400 and the conversion of it by appellant. The case was heard before the court without a jury.

On June 3, 1919, appellee placed in pawn with appellant, a licensed pawnbroker doing business at 426 South Halsted Street, Chicago, the ring, and received thereon the sum of $70. Interest on the loan was paid to June 7, 1920. The pawn ticket issued to appellee contained this statement, "This office protected by the Chicago Electric Protective Company," and described the location and name of the pawnbroker as "Metropolitan Loan Bank, 426 South Halsted St." The ticket further described the goods pawned, the amount loaned, and the time of redemption. Between October 7 and 10, 1920, appellant sold all his interest in whatever pledges he had to Jacob Klein, another duly licensed pawnbroker at 502 South Halsted Street, for the sum of $16,000 or $17,000, which represented the principal sums loaned on said pledges with interest thereon. The pledges were sold by appellant to Klein upon the express understanding that the pledgors might redeem from Klein in the same manner as they could from appellant, had he not sold his interest in the pawns. It was admitted that Klein is a reputable business man, and it was also conceded by appellant that no notice was given by him, either expressly or impliedly, to the appellee of the transfer of her property. On January 8, 1921, the pawnshop of Klein was entered by four armed robbers. The robbers ordered the clerks employed there to hold up their hands, and they forcibly took from a safe a large number of articles, including the diamond ring in question of appellee, which has never been recovered.

There is an unimportant dispute in the record evidence as to whether appellee or her sister, after the sale of appellant's business to Klein, had called on Klein and secured an additional loan upon a diamond ring other than the one in question. The Appellate Court found that the evidence on this point showed that appellee's sister and not appellee, was involved in that transaction. Appellant admits in his reply brief that he does not rely in any way on this testimony to show actual notice to appellee of the change in the possession of the pledge in question. As to the other material facts above set out, there is no dispute between the parties.

Counsel for appellant relies for a reversal of the judgment on two propositions: First, that a pawnbroker is bound only to use ordinary care for the safety of the pawner's property, and, if the property is lost or destroyed without the negligence of the pawnee, then he is not liable; second, that a pawnbroker has the right to assign or sell to another his interest in an article pledged to him.

A pawn is a species of bailment which arises when goods or chattels are delivered to another as a pawn for security to him on money borrowed of him by the bailor. It is the pignari acceptum of the civil law, according to which the possession of the pledge passes to the creditor, therein differing from a hypotheca. It is a class of bailment which is made for the mutual benefit of the bailor and bailee. All that is required by the common law on the part of a pawnee in the protection of the property thus entrusted to him is ordinary care and diligence. Consequently, unless a failure to exercise such care and diligence is shown, a pawnee is not answerable for the loss of the article pledged. 30 Cyc. 1169; *Standard Brewery v. Malting Co.*, 171 Ill. 602, 49 N.E. 507. This is an elementary principle, and there can be no question as to the accuracy and correctness of appellant's first proposition.

But the question arises as to whether or not appellant was guilty of negligence in transferring the interest of the pawner without giving her any notice of such transfer. Appellant's duty to her was to safely keep and protect the property pledged. It was a legal obligation on his part to appellee, from which he could not relieve himself by transferring the pledge to another without her consent. Appellee relied upon him to keep and protect her property where it would be reasonably safe, and he had in substance assured her by the language on the ticket that her property was insured or safeguarded. He violated this duty or obligation to her by transferring the possession of her property to another, to be kept at another place, which the evidence does not show to be protected by a protective company, and without giving her notice of such custody and transfer.

Whatever may be the right of the parties in a bailment for the mutual benefit of the bailor and the bailee, it is unquestionably the law that the parties may increase or diminish these rights by stipulations contained in the contract of bailment. 30 Cyc. 1167; *St. Losky v. Davidson*, 6 Cal. 643. The sum and substance of appellant's contract was that he would keep appellee's property at his office or shop described as aforesaid, and which was protected as aforesaid. The pawning of the ring by appellee under the circumstances imposed a personal trust upon appellant to personally keep the property at his shop and under the assurance of protection as aforesaid, and he could not at his will, without the consent of appellee, transfer the possession and custody thereof to another without such consent. The rule is stated in 3 R.C.L. 112, that any attempt on the part of the bailee in an ordinary simple bailment of a pawn to sell, lease, pledge, or otherwise part with the title or possession of the bailment, constitutes a conversion in every case where the bailment can be properly regarded as a personal trust in the bailee.

There is another controlling reason for holding that appellant is liable for the loss of the ring, and for holding that he could not transfer the possession of the article pawned to him to another and escape liability for a conversion. Section 10 of the Pawnbroker's Act (Smith-Hurd Rev. St. 1923, c. 107½) provides, in part, as follows:

> No personal property pawned or pledged shall be sold or disposed by any such pawnbroker within one year from the time when the pawner or pledger shall make default in the payment of interest on the money so advanced by such pawnbroker, unless by the written consent of such pawner or pledger.

Appellant claims that the proper interpretation of this statute is that it prohibits the sale of an article, including the interest of the pledger or pawner as well as his own, and does not refer to a sale of only the interest of the pawnbroker or pledgee. The statute is not subject to such construction. It should be construed to mean what it says: That the property must not be sold or disposed of by the pawnbroker without the written consent of the pledgor. The statute does not confine itself to a sale, but also forbids any disposition of the same without consent as aforesaid. It cannot be seriously disputed that appellant did dispose of the property without the consent of appellee, within the meaning of the foregoing section of the statute.

The judgment of the Appellate Court is affirmed.

Judgment affirmed.

SAMPLE SYNTHESIS

Whether Rough & Tough has the authority to sell its interest in Howard's ring? Unless the pawner gives written consent, no pawned property shall be sold or disposed of by any pawnbroker within one year from the time when the pawner defaults in the payment of interest on the money advanced by the pawnbroker. 205 ILCS 510/10 (1992). Where a pawnbroker neglected to give notice of the intent to sell his interest in a pawner's diamond ring and neglected to receive written consent for such sale, the pawnbroker lacked authority to transfer his interest in the ring to another. *Jacobs v. Grossman,* 141 N.E. 714, 715 (Ill. Ct. App. 1923). Although Rough & Tough gave Howard notice of its intent to sell the shop and its assets, R & T failed to obtain Howard's written consent to sell her ring. Therefore, a court will probably find that Rough & Tough lacked the authority to sell its interest in Howard's ring to another pawnbroker.

The sample synthesis above synthesizes the statute and the *Jacobs* case around the issue of a pawnbroker's authority to sell its interest in a pawned item without the consent of the pawner. Notice how the statute is mentioned first because its authority ranks higher than the case. The *Jacobs* case follows the statute because the holding is more detailed on the issue of a pawnbroker's duty to give notice before selling his interest in the pawner's ring and the facts are similar to Jane Howard's situation. Two sources of primary authority, a statute and a case, are used together in this sample synthesis because both sources relate to a single legal issue.

Seven Steps for Effective Synthesis

1. Brief your authority.
2. Outline the problem.
3. Organize the primary authority.
4. Under each issue, organize your primary sources by hierarchy of authority.
5. Compare and contrast the case holding and statutory text.
6. Formulate a statement of the law that incorporates all of the primary sources that will be used under the sub-issue heading.
7. Attribute the authority for any legal statement by using proper Bluebook citation.

CHAPTER SUMMARY

This chapter demonstrates the methods of synthesis used in a memo. Synthesizing authority requires finding a common theme from two or more sources that ties together the legal rule. Cases are synthesized because it is hard to find a single decision that articulates the precise rule of law required for a memo. Often one case holding will expand another so the two holdings can be combined, or synthesized, to reflect an accurate statement of the law.

Statutes should be given the highest regard in the hierarchy of authority. If you find case law that applies or interprets a statute, synthesize the statute and the case holding.

Key Terms

Analytical outline   Primary authority
Cause of action   Reasoning
Facts   Synthesis

EXERCISES

1. Read the following fact pattern and cases carefully. Draft an IRAC paragraph in which you synthesize the holdings of the cases. The issue that you will address is provided as well. Remember that proper synthesis requires you to relate the authority to a common legal theme. The problem's issue will guide you in synthesizing the authority.

FACTS

On November 29, 1993, Michael Jones purchases a used truck from Grimy's Auto and Truck Service. At the time of the purchase, Grimy's stated that the engine was completely overhauled and consisted of rebuilt and reconditioned parts, that all parts were guaranteed, and that invoices for all new parts would be provided. On November 13, 1994, after using the truck for almost one year, Jones discovered that several engine parts were not rebuilt or reconditioned and that other engine parts were defective. These defects caused the truck to break down, resulting in lost wages and lost profits for Jones. Jones made repairs to the truck on November 13, 1994, December 13, 1994, and December 16, 1994. Jones did not attempt to return the truck and did not notify Grimy's that the truck was defective. The truck is currently disabled in Columbus, Ohio. Jones wants to sue Grimy's for damages for breach of contract.

ISSUE

Whether Jones continued to use the truck for more than a reasonable time after noticing the defects and failed to properly reject the truck and to notify Grimy's as to the defects?

CASE A

A buyer of goods must alert the seller as soon as he discovers that the goods are not as agreed on. A buyer must rescind a sales contract as soon as he discovers the breach or after he has had a reasonable time for examination. The buyer waives the right to rescind a contract for the sale of goods by continuing to use allegedly defective goods for more than a reasonable time.

CASE B

To meet the requirements of an effective rejection the buyer must reject the goods within a reasonable time and seasonably notify the seller.

2. Read the following fact pattern and cases carefully. Draft an IRAC paragraph in which you synthesize the holdings of the cases. The issue that you will address is provided as well.

FACTS

Robert and Jane Moore live in Evingston and have to repair the gutters on their house. There is eight feet between their house and their neighbor's. The properties are adjoining; the neighboring Kandler house is north of the Moore house. The Moore's contractors and carpenters must enter the Kandler property to work on the gutters on the north side of the house. Mrs. Kandler is not very pleased that workers are entering her property. The Moores came to our office to find out what they should do. The Moores specifically asked if they should obtain an easement to grant them a right of way on Mrs. Kandler's property to make the repairs.

ISSUE

What legal access would allow the contractors and carpenters, repairing the gutters on the Moore house, to enter the adjoining property belonging to Mrs. Kandler?

STATUTORY AUTHORITY

Ch. 12 § 99: If the repair and maintenance of an existing single family residence cannot reasonably be accomplished without entering onto the adjoining land, and if the owner of the adjoining land refuses to permit entry onto that adjoining land for the purpose of repair and maintenance of the single family residence, then the owner of the single family residence may bring an action in court to compel the owner of the adjoining land to permit entry for the purpose of repair and maintenance where entry will be granted solely for the purposes of repair and maintenance.

CASE Y

The need to enter the land of an adjoining property for the purpose of making repairs to one's own property should not mandate that an easement be acquired. An easement grants a right of way, but only the landowner can create an easement. The adjoining landowner may view the repairs as a nuisance and would not grant the easement. Sometimes repairs must be performed on a single family residence that require entering the adjoining land. Statute Ch. 12 § 99 was created to avoid the need to obtain an easement to enter adjoining land when the sole reason for the right of way is to make repairs on a single family residence.

11. Outlining and Organizing a Memorandum

CHAPTER OVERVIEW

In Chapters 6 through 10, you learned about the components of a legal memorandum. This chapter teaches you how to organize the discussion section of your memorandum. You are shown some outlining techniques. (These are suggested techniques only. You may have a technique of your own that works well. Feel free to use it.) In this chapter, you also learn how to draft thesis paragraphs for your discussion.

A. Purpose of Outlining

The key to a well-organized memo is a well-drafted outline. **Outlining** allows you to organize your discussion easily so that it is smooth and cogent. An outline ensures that you cover all of the legal rules and apply all of the legally significant facts to those rules.

B. Steps to Outlining

What Are the Stages of Outlining?

The outline should be done in two stages, each of which consists of a number of steps. In the first stage, you compile a **list of legal authorities,** which includes the names of and the citations to authorities, a note about the legally significant facts presented in any case, and a statement that summarizes each authority's significance to the issues presented in your research problem. See Illustration 11-1.

In the second stage, you **arrange the discussion sections** concerning each issue and, in some cases, arrange each paragraph. See Illustration 11-2.

What Are the Steps in the First Stage, the Compilation of the Authorities?

1. Draft the statement of the facts, the questions presented, and the conclusions.
2. Research your issues.
3. Read the cases.
4. Brief the authorities as discussed in Chapter 5. Once you have briefed the authorities, you will have written a holding for each case. These holdings should be used in your list of authorities. These holdings will summarize the significance of the authorities. If the holdings are well written, they will incorporate important facts derived from the authorities.
5. Write a summary statement for each statute or other noncase authority you plan to cite.
6. Prepare a list of each of the relevant authorities. Note that not all authorities will be relevant. Some will not be helpful. Include only those that help you to determine the law involved in your case. For your list, include the name of the authority. If the authority is a case, list the holding or summary statement of the significance of the authority. Note the complete citation. It is also helpful to list whether the authority is a primary binding, primary persuasive, or secondary authority.

Now review Illustrations 11-1 and 11-4. Illustration 11-1 is a list of the significant authorities for the memo in Illustration 11-3. Illustration 11-4 is a list of authorities for the memo in Illustration 11-5, which follows the pattern of the outline in Illustration 11-2. To see the actual outline for the memo in Illustration 11-5, see Illustration 11-7. Each of the statements listed in each outline of authorities was derived from a holding found in a case brief prepared for the memos. A summary statement for the statute also was included in the list.

ILLUSTRATION 11-1. *List of Authorities*

---

1. Crane Rev. Stat. § 808 (Williams 1994):   A civil battery occurs when one individual touches another individual without his or her consent and a physical injury occurs.

2. Eve v. Scott, State of Crane Supreme Court: A contact between a nonconsenting individual with an object such as a bat thrown by an offender is sufficient to be a touching within the context of the civil battery statute because the object would be an extension of the offender's body. (primary binding)

3. Wayne v. Robert, State of Crane Supreme Court: A person intends his or her conduct when he or she undertakes an action with a knowing mind.

4. Hawes v. Jackson, State of Crane Supreme Court: If a person consents to the touching, a battery has not occurred.

ILLUSTRATION 11-2. *Outline of Discussion*

Element or Sub-issue 1
Issue: Did a touching occur?
Rule: Objects are extensions of body parts
Contact with an object can be touching (*Eve*)
Application of law to facts: Bucket contacted McMillan
Conclusion: A touching occurred
Element or Sub-issue 2
Issue: Did Mann intend to hit McMillan?
Rule: A person intends an act when it is done purposefully (*Wayne*)
Application of law to facts: Mann purposefully threw the bucket at
   McMillan and said she intended to strike her
Conclusion: Mann had intent
Element or Sub-issue 3
Issue: Did McMillan consent to touching?
Rule: If a party consented to the touching, no battery occurred. (*Hawes*)
Application of law to facts: McMillan did not consent
Conclusion: A touching without consent as in this case can be a battery
Element or Sub-issue 4
Issue: Did McMillan suffer the requisite physical injuries as a result of
   the contact?
Rule: Physical injuries must result from contact for battery (Statute)
Application of law to facts: McMillan sustained cuts and eye irritation
   from bucket and sand contact
Conclusion: McMillan had requisite physical injuries

ILLUSTRATION 11-3.   *Memorandum: McMillan Battery Action*

MEMORANDUM

To: William Mark

From: Ivy Courier

Date: November 7, 1995

Re: McMillan Battery Action

QUESTION PRESENTED

Did an actionable battery occur when Mann intentionally struck McMillan with a bucket, without McMillan's consent, causing McMillan to suffer physical and monetary injuries?

CONCLUSION

Mann's intentional striking of McMillan with a bucket and sand was an actionable battery.

FACTS

Our client, Mary McMillan, a 36-year-old bank teller, wants to bring an action for battery against Carol Mann, a 36-year-old mother, who threw a metal bucket filled with sand at McMillan at a local park. While McMillan sat on a park bench, she teased Mann's 7-year-old son. Mann did not like this teasing and threw a bucket filled with sand at Mary. Sand landed in McMillan's eyes while she was wearing soft contact lenses. As a result, McMillan's contacts had to be replaced. The bucket also cut McMillan's eye and cheek. She had stitches in both places. McMillan asked Mann to pay for her doctor bills and for the new contacts. Mann refused and added, "I'm not sorry. I meant to hurt you."

DISCUSSION

The issue presented is whether Mann's intentional touching of McMillan with a bucket rather than her person is an actionable battery. A battery is the intentional touching of another without consent, which causes injury. Crane Rev. Stat. § 808 (Williams 1994). A touching can occur when an object rather than an individual's body contacts the other party. *Eve v. Scott; Wayne v. Robert.* In this case, Mann intentionally struck McMillan with a bucket without McMillan's consent and that touching resulted in injuries. Therefore, a battery occurred.

The threshold issue is whether a touching occurred when the bucket struck McMillan. A contact between a nonconsenting party and object rather than the actor's body can be a battery. *Eve v. Scott; Wayne v.*

ILLUSTRATION 11-3. *Continued*

Robert. In *Eve,* one person hurled a baseball bat at another person, resulting in injuries. The court found that the baseball bat was an extension of the person and that a contact between the bat and the nonconsenting person met the requirement of a touching under the Crane battery statute. In this case, Mann threw the bucket at McMillan, and the bucket contacted her face. Following the reasoning in the *Eve* case, the bucket would be an extension of Mann's body, and the contact between McMillan and the bucket would be considered a touching under the civil battery statute.

Next, the question to consider is whether under the statute Mann intended to touch McMillan when she struck her with the bucket. A person intends his or her conduct when he or she undertakes an action with a knowing mind. *Wayne v. Robert.* In the *Wayne* case, one co-worker, Robert, aimed a golf ball at the face of another co-worker, Wayne, and deliberately struck Wayne in the face. Following a bench trial, the judge found that Robert aimed a shot at Wayne with the purpose of striking him. *Wayne.* In McMillan's case, Mann aimed the bucket at McMillan purposefully trying to strike her. Mann later told McMillan that she deliberately threw the bucket at her. McMillan probably will be able to establish that Mann had the statutory intent.

The next factor to consider is whether McMillan consented to the contact. If a person consents to the touching, a battery has not occurred. *Hawes v. Jackson.* In our case, McMillan did not consent to Mann's throwing of the bucket at her face. Therefore, McMillan did not consent to any contact.

Finally, the question is whether McMillan suffered physical injuries. A battery occurs only if a plaintiff sustains physical injuries as a result of the touching. Crane Rev. Stat. § 808 (Williams 1994). McMillan sustained cuts on her face and eye irritation as a direct result of the bucket striking her face and the sand flying out of the bucket into her eyes. McMillan will be able to show that she sustained physical injuries as a result of the contact with the bucket.

After you have prepared a detailed list of authorities, you are ready to organize your issues and to determine each of the legal elements that your memo should address. Each legal theory is defined by several factors called **elements.** You can think of the elements as pieces of a puzzle. You must consider each element before you complete your discussion. You can think of your discussion of these elements as a discussion of the sub-issues of the questions presented. Your discussion of some of these sub-issues will be cursory; some elements can be discussed in a single sentence. Most sub-issues, however, will be discussed in one or more paragraphs, generally organized in the IRAC (Issues, Rules Application, and Conclusion) format discussed in Chapter 9.

ILLUSTRATION 11-4. *Outline of Authorities*

---

1. 42 U.S.C. § 2000e (1968): The term "employer" means a person engaged in an industry affecting commerce who has fifteen or more employees for each working day in each of twenty or more calendar weeks in the current or preceding calendar year.

2. Zimmerman v. North American Signal Co., 704 F.2d 347 (7th Cir. 1983): Salaried workers or full-time workers counted as employees for every day of the week on the payroll whether they were present at work or not. Hourly paid workers are counted as employees only on the days when they are actually at work or days on paid leave. (primary binding)

3. Musser v. Mountain View Broadcasting, 578 F. Supp. 229 (E.D. Tenn. 1984): "Current calendar year" is the year of discrimination. (primary persuasive)

4. Wright v. Kosciusko Medical Clinic, 791 F. Supp. 1327, 1333 (N.D. Ind. 1992): "Each working day" is literal and must be a day on which an employer conducts normal, full operations. (primary persuasive)

5. Norman v. Levy, 767 F. Supp. 144 (N.D. Ill. 1991): Part-time workers counted only on the days that they actually work. (primary persuasive)

6. Knight v. United Farm Bureau Mut. Ins. Co., 950 F.2d 377 (7th Cir. 1991): The "economic realities" of the relationship between an employer and his or her worker must be weighed by applying five factors: 1) the amount of employer control and supervision over employee; 2) the responsibility for the operational costs; 3) the worker's occupation and the skills required; 4) the form of compensation and benefits; and 5) the length of the job commitment. *Knight,* 950 F.2d at 378. Control is the most important factor. *Id.* Knight is an insurance agent, is not permitted to sell insurance for any other companies, is required to attend weekly staff meetings in the office, and works a specified number of hours in the office (primary binding). *Knight,* 950 F.2d at 378. Company provided supplies and paid for business expenses. *Id.* Essential to company operation. *Id.* Paid commissions with no deductions. *Id.* Knight not an employee.

7. Mitchell v. Tenney, 650 F. Supp. 703 (N.D. Ill. 1986): The "economic realities" of the relationship between an employer and his or her worker must be weighed.

8. Vakharia v. Swedish Covenant Hosp., 765 F. Supp. 461 (N.D. Ill. 1991): When an employee is economically dependent on employer, court is likely to find employment relationship. Plaintiff in *Vakharia* was a physician dependent on the hospital for business. *Id.* at 463. (primary persuasive)

ILLUSTRATION 11-5.   *Memorandum: Sex Discrimination Case*

MEMORANDUM

To: Wallace Maine

From: Thomas Wall

Date: November 15, 1993

Re: Sex Discrimination Case against Whole In One No. C93 CIV 190, G12399990

QUESTIONS PRESENTED

1. Under Title VII, was Whole In One an employer when 14 people, including 3 full-time and 11 part-time workers, worked on any one day for 24 weeks and when 10 full-time employees were on the Whole In One payroll?

2. Under Title VII, was Walker an independent contractor rather than an employee when she worked exclusively for Whole In One, paid taxes quarterly rather than through deductions, and worked with limited company supervision?

3. Under Title VII, was Radiant an independent contractor rather than an employee when she worked with limited company supervision using company supplies and equipment and had taxes and medical deductions taken from her salary?

CONCLUSIONS

1. Whole In One was an employer. Under Title VII, an employer has at least 15 employees working for 20 or more weeks during the relevant year. Salaried employees are included in this number for each week they are on the payroll, while hourly workers are only counted on the days they actually work. In 1993, the year of the alleged discrimination, 14 workers, 3 full-time and 11 part-time people, worked for Whole In One on any day during the 24-week restaurant and golf season. However, 10 full-time workers were on the payroll. As these part-time workers are only counted on the days that they work, the number of part-time individuals included in the count of employees is 11 for each day of the 24-week season. Because full-time workers, however, are counted for each day of a week that they are on the payroll, all 10 of Whole In One's full-time workers would be included in the count of employees. In total, Whole In One had 11 part-time workers and 10 full-time workers "working" for 20 or more weeks during the relevant year, bringing the total count of employees to 21. Therefore, Whole In One was an employer under Title VII.

2. Walker was an employee. The Seventh Circuit will weigh five factors to determine whether she was an independent contractor or an employee for this Title VII lawsuit. The primary focus will be on the

ILLUSTRATION 11-5. *Continued*

company's control of Walker. Although Walker worked from home, set her own hours and had an impact on her commission pay, the company controlled her work by reviewing and revising it, restricting Walker's employment opportunities, and providing supplies for her. Therefore, the company exerted control over Walker and she would be considered an employee.

3. Radiant was probably an employee. To determine whether she was an employee or independent contractor for this Title VII lawsuit, the court will focus on five factors, primarily the amount of control the company exerted over Radiant's work. Whole In One provided Radiant with an office, supplies, a two-year contract and additional training. Whole In One paid her regularly and deducted taxes from her salary. Although Whole In One did not actively supervise Radiant's work on a daily basis, she still worked in the company offices and was under the control of Whole In One. Therefore, the court probably will find that Radiant was an employee.

FACTS

Victoria Radiant and Karen Walker, two former Whole In One Enterprises workers, brought a federal sex discrimination lawsuit based upon Title VII against our client, Whole In One Enterprises, owned by Nancy and Craig Black. The lawsuit, filed in the U.S. District Court for the Northern District of Illinois, stems from the dismissal of the two women by the Blacks during 1993.

The Blacks own Whole In One Enterprises, which operates a miniature golf course and restaurant in Glenview, Illinois. During the 24-week 1993 restaurant season, 10 people worked full-time and 14 people worked part-time for Whole In One. However, no more than 14 people worked on any one day. Of those 14 people, only 3 were full-time employees. The other full-time employees regularly took days off during the summer restaurant and golf season.

Among the full-time workers was Karen Walker who worked as a public relations director for Whole In One. Walker responded to an ad which said that "an employer" sought an individual to perform public relations work. Whole In One hired Walker without a contract and prohibited her from working for other firms. However, Walker worked from home and set her own hours. Whole In One required Walker to attend weekly staff meetings at the company offices where Whole In One would review and revise Walker's work. The company supplied Walker with paper, pencils, stamps, telephone service and paid for her life and health insurance. Whole In One did not withhold taxes from Walker's commissions.

Victoria Radiant, who had a two-year employment contract with the company, provided marketing services to Whole In One from October of 1991 until she was fired in 1993. Although Radiant worked in the company office, Whole In One management rarely supervised her work.

ILLUSTRATION 11-5.   *Continued*

The company paid for her continued education, provided her with bonuses and deducted taxes from her weekly salary.

APPLICABLE STATUTE

The term "employer" means a person engaged in an industry affecting commerce who has fifteen or more employees for each working day in each of 20 or more calendar weeks in the current or preceding calendar year. 42 U.S.C. § 2000e(b) (1988).

DISCUSSION

This memo first will address whether Walker and Radiant can successfully establish that Whole In One was an employer within the meaning of 42 U.S.C. § 2000e(b) (1988), commonly called Title VII. Next, the discussion will focus on whether Walker can establish that she was an employee protected by Title VII. Finally, the memo will explore whether Radiant was an employee protected by Title VII. If Whole In One was not an employer, then the Title VII claim will be dismissed. If the court finds that neither individual is an employee, the individual's claim will be barred.

I. Was Whole In One an Employer Under Title VII?

Before a federal court can consider Walker's and Radiant's claims, the plaintiffs must establish that Whole In One was an employer under the definition established in Title VII. An employer is "a person engaged in a business affecting commerce who has fifteen or more employees for each working day in each of 20 or more calendar weeks in the current or preceding calendar year." 42 U.S.C. § 2000e(b). The focus of this discussion will be how to calculate whether 15 employees worked for Whole In One on each working day in each of 20 or more calendar weeks and how to determine which year's employment records are relevant. The Seventh Circuit has held that full-time employees are "working" each day of a week during a week for which they are on the payroll, but part-time workers are counted only on the days that they actually work. *Zimmerman v. North American Signal Co.,* 704 F.2d 347 (7th Cir. 1983). In 1993, the year of the alleged discrimination, 14 workers, 3 full-time and 11 part-time people, worked for Whole In One on any day during the 24-week restaurant and golf season. In addition, 10 full-time workers were on the payroll. Based on the counting method established in *Zimmerman,* these figures indicate that Whole In One had at least 15 employees working for each working day in each of 20 or more calendar weeks. Therefore, Whole In One was an employer under Title VII.

The central focus of this discussion will be how to calculate the number of employees. First, the relevant year must be determined. The statute states that the time to be considered is "20 or more calendar

ILLUSTRATION 11-5. *Continued*

weeks in the current or preceding year." 42 U.S.C. § 2000e(b). The current year of the discrimination was 1993. Because the statute specifies "or" the preceding year, 1992 also is relevant. However, in a persuasive decision a Tennessee district court held that the "current calendar year" is the year in which the alleged discrimination occurred. *Musser v. Mountain View Broadcasting*, 578 F. Supp. 229 (E.D. Tenn. 1984). If the court follows *Musser*, the employment records from 1993 would be relevant because Whole In One fired Walker and Radiant in 1993.

The phrase "each working day" must be clarified. "Each working day" should be taken literally and must be a day on which an employer conducts normal, full operations. *Zimmerman*, 704 F.2d at 353; *Wright v. Kosciusko Medical Clinic*, 791 F. Supp. 1327, 1333 (N.D. Ind. 1992). Whole In One operated the golf course and restaurant seven days a week. Therefore, Whole In One must have 15 employees working on all seven days of a week to be considered an employer under Title VII.

The final issue is who should be counted on each of the working days. The Seventh Circuit has determined that a salaried or full-time employee is counted as working for every day of the week that they are on the payroll, whether or not they were actually at work on a particular day. *Zimmerman v. North American Signal Co.*, 704 F.2d 347 (7th Cir. 1983). However, part-time workers are counted only on the days that they actually work. *Id.*; *Wright*, 791 F. Supp. at 1327; *Norman v. Levy*, 767 F. Supp. 144 (N.D. Ill. 1991). In 1993, the year of the alleged discrimination, 14 workers, 3 full-time and 11 part-time people, worked for Whole In One on any day during the 24-week restaurant and golf season. As these part-time workers are only counted on the days that they work, the number of part-time individuals included in the count of employees was 11 for each day of the 24-week season. Because full-time workers, however, are counted for each day of a week that they are on the payroll, all 10 of Whole In One's full-time workers should be included in the count of employees. In total, Whole In One had 11 part-time workers and 10 full-time workers "working" for 20 or more weeks during the relevant year, bringing the total count of employees to 21. Therefore, Whole In One was an employer under Title VII.

II. Are Walker and Radiant Employees or Independent Contractors?

If the plaintiffs can show that Whole In One was an employer, the court still must determine whether Walker and Radiant were employees entitled to Title VII protection or independent contractors. To determine whether an individual is an independent contractor or an employee, the "economic realities" of the relationship between an employer and his or her worker must be weighed. *Knight v. United Farm Bureau Mut. Ins. Co.*, 950 F.2d 377 (7th Cir. 1991); *Norman v. Levy*, 767 F. Supp. 144 (N.D. Ill. 1991); *Mitchell v. Tenney*, 650 F. Supp. 703 (N.D. Ill.

ILLUSTRATION 11-5. *Continued*

1986). The Seventh Circuit will weigh five factors to determine the economic reality of the relationship: 1) the amount of control and supervision the employer exerts over the worker; 2) the responsibility for the costs of the operation; 3) the worker's occupation and the skills required; 4) the method and form of compensation and benefits; and 5) the length of the job commitment. *Knight,* 950 F.2d at 378. Control is the most important factor. *Id.* When an employer controls a worker in such a manner as to make that worker economically dependent on the employer, the court is likely to find that an employment relationship exists. *Vakharia v. Swedish Covenant Hosp.,* 765 F. Supp. 461 (N.D. Ill. 1991).

The *Knight* case involved an insurance agent who was not allowed to sell insurance for any other company and who was required to attend weekly staff meetings in the office and work a specified number of hours in the office. *Knight,* 950 F.2d at 378. The insurance company provided Knight with supplies and paid for business expenses. *Id.* These agents were trained by the insurance company and were crucial to the company's continued operation. *Id.* Knight was paid on commission and did not have taxes deducted. *Id.* Knight also was free to leave the company and work elsewhere. *Id.* Based on these facts, the *Knight* court failed to find that the agent was an employee.

Although Walker's work situation was factually similar in many ways to that of the plaintiff in *Knight,* the *Knight* case can be distinguished based on the nature of the occupations. Knight worked in the insurance sales field. Most often, individuals who work in such positions are independent contractors rather than employees of a company. In addition, the Seventh Circuit indicated in the dicta of the *Knight* case that it might have found that Knight was an employee. *Id.* at 381.

In contrast to *Knight,* the U.S. District Court for the Northern District of Illinois found that control of an individual's livelihood could establish an employment relationship. *Vakharia v. Swedish Covenant Hosp.,* 765 F. Supp. 461 (N.D. Ill. 1991). The plaintiff in *Vakharia* was a physician who was dependent on the hospital for business. *Id.* at 463. The district court found that this individual depended on the hospital for patients and that when the hospital reduced the number of patients it assigned to the plaintiff, the plaintiff's livelihood was affected. *Id.* The court held that when an employer has this type of control over an individual's livelihood an employment relationship may be established.

The facts in our case are similar to the facts in the *Vakharia* case. In our case, Whole In One barred Walker from working for other companies and required that she attend weekly staff meetings at the company offices where Whole In One would review and revise Walker's work. Because Walker was barred from working for other individuals and was required to attend these meetings where Whole In One would revise her work, it seems that Walker could establish the central element of control necessary to prove an employment relationship. In addition,

ILLUSTRATION 11-5.   *Continued*

these facts show that Walker, like the plaintiff in *Vakharia,* was economically dependent on her employer, Whole In One. Therefore, an employment relationship should be established.

However, the plaintiffs will be able to show more than control. They will be able to establish that Whole In One bore the cost of the operation of the business. Whole In One supplied Walker with paper, pencils, stamps, telephone service and paid for her life and health insurance. These facts indicate that Whole In One was responsible for the cost of Walker's services to the company. Therefore, it would help to establish that Walker was an employee.

The factors that would mitigate the establishment of an employment relationship, however, are that Walker worked from home and set her own hours and Whole In One did not withhold taxes from Walker's commissions. Despite these factors, the court is likely to focus on the control Whole In One had over Walker and is likely to find that she was an employee rather than an independent contractor.

III. Was Radiant an Employee or an Independent Contractor?

Whether Radiant was an employee again turns on the amount of control Whole In One exerted over Radiant's work. The court will focus on the same factors established in *Knight* to determine whether an employment relationship exists. *Knight,* 950 F.2d at 378. Control will be the key factor the court will consider. *Id.* Radiant had a two-year employment contract with the company to provide marketing services. Whole In One also provided her with an office, supplies, and additional training. The company paid her regularly and deducted taxes from her salary. Based upon these facts, the company exerted control over Radiant. Therefore, the court is likely to find that Radiant was an employee of Whole In One.

What Steps Should You Follow in Preparing Your Outline of Each of the Issues?

The first step in organizing your outline is to write a thesis paragraph. This is the first paragraph of your discussion. It is a summary of the legal issue you plan to discuss. In the thesis paragraph you introduce the issue, define the applicable rule of law, introduce each legal element, apply the legally significant facts to the rule of law, and provide a short conclusion, usually one sentence long.

1. Thesis Paragraph

The best format for the thesis paragraph is the IRAC format. (For a full discussion of this format, see Chapter 9.) The first sentence of a thesis paragraph introduces the overall issue presented in the memo. The second sentence explains the rule of law. The next sentence applies the rule of law to the facts of your case, and the final sentence states a conclusion. A general outline for a thesis paragraph, then, is:

1. Introduce the legal issue or question presented
2. Summarize the legal rule for question presented and each legal element to be discussed
3. Apply the legally significant facts to the legal rule
4. Conclude

Review the thesis paragraph in Illustration 11-6, which is the first paragraph of the discussion section of the memo in Illustration 11-3. The first sentence introduces the issue: whether a battery occurred when Mann struck McMillan with the bucket. This sentence mirrors the question presented. See Illustration 11-3. The second sentence is the rule of law. In this sentence you introduce each of the legal elements or factors that will be discussed. In the *McMillan* case, the elements are touching, intent, lack of consent, and resulting physical injury. Each of these elements is discussed separately in the succeeding memo paragraphs. A thesis paragraph should introduce the reader to as many legal elements as possible in the thesis paragraph. The third sentence of this thesis paragraph is the application of the law to the facts. In this sentence, you explain to the reader the relationship between the relevant law and the facts of your case. In Illustration 11-6, the fact that Mann struck McMillan with the bucket without McMillan's consent was applied to the rule of law stated in the second sentence. The final sentence is a conclusion. This sentence explains to your readers your view of how the law and facts relate to each other. In the *McMillan* case, the writer concluded that a battery occurred.

ILLUSTRATION 11-6. *Thesis Paragraph*

The issue presented is whether Mann's intentional touching of McMillan with a bucket rather than her person is an actionable battery. A battery is the intentional touching of another without consent which causes injury. Crane Rev. Stat. § 808 (Williams 1994). A touching can occur when an object rather than an individual's body contacts the other party. *Eve v. Scott*; *Wayne v. Robert*. In this case, Mann intentionally struck McMillan with a bucket without McMillan's consent and that touching resulted in injuries. Therefore, a battery occurred.

OUTLINE OF THESIS PARAGRAPH
FOR *McMILLAN* CASE

— Introduce the battery issue or question presented
— Summarize the legal rule: battery is the intentional touching of another without consent which results in physical injury; touching can be with an object

— Apply the legally significant facts to the legal rule: touching occurred when bucket struck McMillan
— Conclusion: battery occurred

Next, read the sample thesis paragraph below.

Before a federal court can consider Walker's and Radiant's claims, the plaintiffs must establish that Whole In One was an employer under the definition established in Title VII. An employer is "a person engaged in a business affecting commerce who has fifteen or more employees for each working day in each of 20 or more calendar weeks in the current or preceding calendar year." 42 U.S.C. § 2000e(b). The focus of this discussion will be how to calculate whether 15 employees worked for Whole In One on each working day in each of 20 or more calendar weeks and how to determine which year's employment records are relevant. The Seventh Circuit has held that full-time employees are "working" each day of a week during a week for which they are on the payroll, but part-time workers are counted only on the days that they actually work. *Zimmerman v. North American Signal Co.*, 704 F.2d 347 (7th Cir. 1983). In 1993, the year of the alleged discrimination, 14 workers, 3 full-time and 11 part-time people, worked for Whole In One on any day during the 24-week restaurant and golf season. In addition, 10 full-time workers were on the payroll. Based on the counting method established in *Zimmerman*, these figures indicate that Whole In One had at least 15 employees working for each working day in each of 20 or more calendar weeks. Therefore, Whole In One was an employer under Title VII.

An outline for the thesis paragraph above might look like the following example.

THESIS PARAGRAPH

Issue: Is Whole In One an employer?

RULE

Under Title VII, an employer has at least 15 employees working for 20 or more weeks during the relevant year. 42 U.S.C. § 2000e(b) (1968). (**first element**) Salaried employees are included in this number for each week they are on the payroll (**second element**), while hourly workers are only counted on the days they actually work. (**third element**) *Zimmerman* (primary binding).

APPLICATION OF LAW TO FACTS

In 1993, Whole in One had 14 workers, 3 full-time and 11 part-time people on any day during the 24-week season. Ten full-time workers were on the payroll. Part-time workers are only counted on the days that they work; they number 11 for each day of the 24-week season. All 10 full-time workers are counted each day of a week. In total, Whole In One had 11 part-time workers and 10 full-time workers "working" for 20 or more weeks during the relevant year, bringing the total count of employees to 21.

CONCLUSION

Therefore, Whole In One was an employer under Title VII.

The outline and thesis paragraph in the above example introduce multiple sub-issues or legal elements. Each of these elements is discussed fully in the sample memo contained in Illustration 11-5. The thesis paragraph, however, introduces the reader to the elements and provides a preview of the elements that will be discussed.

2. Determine Which Element to Discuss First

The next step is to determine which element to discuss first. If a legal claim has a "**threshold**" **issue** or **element,** it should be discussed first. A threshold issue is an issue that, if decided one way, would eliminate any further consideration of the legal claim. For example, in a breach of contract case, you must decide first whether a contract was formed before determining whether a breach occurred. Because courts sometimes change current law or approach legal claims differently than expected or than the law provides, you should fully discuss all sub-issues or elements, even if your threshold issue would dispose of the legal claim.

For the memo in Illustration 11-3, the touching is the threshold issue. If Mann did not touch McMillan, then McMillan could not bring an action for battery. Therefore, this issue must be considered first.

3. List of Elements or Sub-Issues

Next make a list of the elements or sub-issues to discuss. In the *McMillan* case, the elements list might be as follows:

Touching
Intent
Lack of consent
Physical injury

4. Add Authority

Now add the authority or authorities that relate to each element:

Touching (*Eve, Wayne*)
Intent (*Wayne*)
Lack of consent (Statute)
Physical injury (Statute)

5. Refine Issues

You might refine the issues so that they include facts from your case or incorporate further questions that are raised by the issues. For example, the issue of touching involves a secondary question of whether contact with an object rather than a person is a touching sufficient to constitute a battery. Your new list might be as follows:

Touching (*Eve, Wayne*)
   Object rather than person (*Eve, Wayne*)
Intent (*Wayne*)
Lack of consent (Statute)
Physical injury (Statute)

6. Arrange the Order of Elements

Now arrange the order of the elements. Touching is the threshold element or sub-issue, so you should discuss it first. The order of the other issues is a value judgment. If one or more elements can be easily discussed in a single sentence, often it is best to consider them after the threshold issue. If none of the elements is a threshold issue, then consider those elements that can be discussed easily first.

7. Organize into IRAC Paragraph

After you have determined the order of the elements, organize each element or sub-issue into an IRAC paragraph. Introduce the issue, present the rule, apply the law to the facts of your case, and conclude. For the *McMillan* memo, the discussion outline for each element might be as follows:

Element or Sub-issue 1
   Issue: Did a touching occur?
   Rule: Objects are extensions of body parts
      Contact with an object can be touching (*Eve, Wayne*)

Application of law to facts: Bucket contacted McMillan

Conclusion: A touching occurred

Element or Sub-issue 2

Issue: Did Mann intend to hit McMillan?

Rule: A person intends an act when it is done purposefully (*Wayne*)

Application of law to facts: Mann purposefully threw the bucket at McMillan and said she intended to strike her

Conclusion: Mann had intent

Element or Sub-issue 3

Issue: Did McMillan consent to touching?

Rule: If a party consented to the touching, no battery occurred. (*Hawes*)

Application of law to facts: McMillan did not consent

Conclusion: A touching without consent as in this case can be a battery

Element or Sub-issue 4

Issue: Did McMillan suffer the requisite physical injuries as a result of the contact?

Rule: Physical injuries must result from contact for battery (Statute)

Application of law to facts: McMillan sustained cuts and eye irritation from bucket and sand contact

Conclusion: McMillan had requisite physical injuries

Review this outline and compare it to the text of the memo in Illustration 11-3. The discussion is derived entirely from the outline and follows it closely.

C. Example of Outlining

You should follow this same process for more complicated issues. The memo shown in Illustration 11-5 discusses several complicated issues and sub-issues. Review the discussion of the question of whether Whole In One is an employer.

I. Was Whole In One an Employer Under Title VII?

Before a federal court can consider Walker's and Radiant's claims, the plaintiffs must establish that Whole In One was an employer under the definition established in Title VII. An employer is "a person engaged in a business affecting commerce who has fifteen or more employees for each working day in each of 20 or more calendar weeks in the current or preceding calendar year." 42 U.S.C. § 2000e(b). The focus of this discussion will be how to calculate whether 15 employees worked for Whole In One on each working day in each of 20 or more calendar weeks and how to determine which year's employment records are relevant. The Seventh Circuit has held that full-time employees are "working" each day of a week during a week for which they are on the payroll, but part-time workers are counted only on the days that they actually work. *Zimmerman v. North American Signal Co.,* 704 F.2d 347 (7th Cir. 1983). In 1993, the year of the alleged discrimination, 14 workers, 3 full-time and 11 part-time people, worked for Whole In One on any day during the 24-week restaurant and golf season. In addition, 10 full-time workers were on the payroll. Based on the counting method established in *Zimmerman,* these figures indicate that Whole In One had at least 15 employees working for each working day in each of 20 or more calendar weeks. Therefore, Whole In One was an employer under Title VII.

The central focus of this discussion will be how to calculate the number of employees. First, the relevant year must be determined. The statute states that the time to be considered is "20 or more calendar weeks in the current or preceding year." 42 U.S.C. § 2000e(b). The current year of the discrimination was 1993. Because the statute specifies "or" the preceding year, 1992 also is relevant. However, in a persuasive decision a Tennessee district court held that the "current calendar year" is the year in which the alleged discrimination occurred. *Musser v. Mountain View Broadcasting,* 578 F. Supp. 229 (E.D. Tenn. 1984). If the court follows *Musser,* the employment records from 1993 would be relevant because Whole In One fired Walker and Radiant in 1993.

The phrase "each working day" must be clarified. "Each working day" should be taken literally and must be a day on which an employer conducts normal, full operations. *Zimmerman,* 704 F.2d at 353; *Wright v. Kosciusko Medical Clinic,* 791 F. Supp. 1327, 1333 (N.D. Ind. 1992). Whole In One operated the golf course and restaurant seven days a week. Therefore, Whole In One must have 15 employees working on all seven days of a week to be considered an employer under Title VII.

The final issue is who should be counted on each of the working days. The Seventh Circuit has determined that a salaried or full-time employee is counted as working for every day of the week that they are on the payroll, whether or not they were actually at work on a particular day. *Zimmerman v. North American Signal Co.,* 704 F.2d 347 (7th Cir. 1983). However, part-time workers are counted only on the days that they actually work. *Id.; Wright,* 791 F. Supp. at 1327; *Norman v. Levy,* 767 F. Supp. 144 (N.D. Ill. 1991). In 1993, the year of the alleged discrimination, 14 workers, 3 full-time and 11 part-time people, worked for Whole In One on any day during the 24-week restaurant and golf season. As these part-time workers are only counted on the days that they work, the number of part-time individuals included in the count of employees was 11 for each day of the 24-week season. Because full-time workers, however, are counted for each day of a week that they are on the payroll, all 10 of Whole In One's full-time workers should be included in the count of employees. In total, Whole In One had 11 part-time workers and 10 full-time workers "working" for 20 or more weeks during the relevant year, bringing the total count of employees to 21. Therefore, Whole In One was an employer under Title VII.

1. After you review the thesis paragraph, make a list of the elements. Your list of elements might be as follows:

Person
Engaged in business affecting commerce
15 or more employees for each working day in each of 20 or more
   calendar weeks current or preceding calendar year.

2. Refine this list. Next to the element to which the authority relates, note the relevant authority from your list of authorities. Some authorities will relate to multiple elements. In such a case, note that authority next to each of the elements to which it relates. Now your list might read as follows:

Person (42 U.S.C. § 2000e(b))
Engaged in business affecting commerce (42 U.S.C. § 2000e(b))
15 or more employees for each working day in each of 20 or more
   calendar weeks current or preceding calendar year (42 U.S.C.
   § 2000e(b)); *Zimmerman v. North American Signal Co.*, 704 F.2d
   347 (7th Cir. 1983); *Musser v. Mountain View Broadcasting*, 578
   F. Supp. 229 (E.D. Tenn. 1984); *Wright v. Kosciusko Medical
   Clinic*, 791 F. Supp. 1327, 1333 (N.D. Ind. 1992); *Norman v.
   Levy*, 767 F. Supp. 144 (N.D. Ill. 1991)

It is better to list the full name of the authority next to the element rather than the number of the authority because the numbers might be confusing later.

3. Your list of elements, however, should be revised again. Often, as in this case, the authorities will guide you as to how to further delineate the elements. Several authorities noted in the above memo focus on the word "employees" and indicate that different types of employees are counted differently for the purpose of the statute. For example, full-time or salaried workers are counted for each day that they are on the payroll, while part-time workers only are counted on the days that they are actually at work. Add this distinction to your list of elements. Now rewrite your list as follows:

Person (42 U.S.C. § 2000e(b))
Engaged in business affecting commerce (42 U.S.C. § 2000e(b))
15 or more employees
   — part-time: *Zimmerman v. North American Signal Co.*, 704
      F.2d 347 (7th Cir. 1983); *Wright v. Kosciusko Medical Clinic*,

791 F. Supp. 1327, 1333 (N.D. Ind. 1992); *Norman v. Levy,* 767 F. Supp. 144 (N.D. Ill. 1991)
— full-time: *Zimmerman v. North American Signal Co.,* 704 F.2d 347 (7th Cir. 1983); *Wright v. Kosciusko Medical Clinic,* 791 F. Supp. 1327, 1333 (N.D. Ind. 1992); *Norman v. Levy,* 767 F. Supp. 144 (N.D. Ill. 1991)

Each working day in each of 20 or more calendar weeks current or preceding calendar year (42 U.S.C. § 2000e(b)); *Zimmerman v. North American Signal Co.,* 704 F.2d 347 (7th Cir. 1983); *Musser v. Mountain View Broadcasting,* 578 F. Supp. 229 (E.D. Tenn. 1984); *Wright v. Kosciusko Medical Clinic, Inc.,* 791 F. Supp. 1327, 1333 (N.D. Ind. 1992); *Norman v. Levy,* 767 F. Supp. 144 (N.D. Ill. 1991)

4. Note that one case defines the relevant year while another explains the phrase "each working day." Review the outline of elements below.

Person (42 U.S.C. § 2000e(b))
Engaged in business affecting commerce (42 U.S.C. § 2000e(b))
15 or more employees (determining the number of employees)
— part-time: *Zimmerman v. North American Signal Co.,* 704 F.2d 347 (7th Cir. 1983); *Wright v. Kosciusko Medical Clinic,* 791 F. Supp. 1327, 1333 (N.D. Ind. 1992); *Norman v. Levy,* 767 F. Supp. 144 (N.D. Ill. 1991)
— full-time: *Zimmerman v. North American Signal Co.,* 704 F.2d 347 (7th Cir. 1983); *Wright v. Kosciusko Medical Clinic,* 791 F. Supp. 1327, 1333 (N.D. Ind. 1992); *Norman v. Levy,* 767 F. Supp. 144 (N.D. Ill. 1991)
Each working day in each of 20 or more calendar weeks (*Wright v. Kosciusko Medical Clinic,* 791 F. Supp. 1327, 1333 (N.D. Ind. 1992)
Current or preceding calendar year (42 U.S.C. § 2000e(b)); *Musser v. Mountain View Broadcasting,* 578 F. Supp. 229 (E.D. Tenn. 1984))

5. Now you are ready to arrange the order of each of the elements. Determine if any of the elements should be discussed first. For the above memo, the threshold issue is how to determine whether Whole In One had 15 or more employees.

6. After you have determined the order of the elements, organize each element or sub-issue in an IRAC paragraph. For the above discussion, the outline of each element might be arranged as follows:

Element or Sub-issue 1
Issue: For which year is the number of employees relevant?
Rules: The current calendar year or preceding year (42 U.S.C. § 2000e (1968)); the "current calendar year" is the year of the discrimination (*Musser*)

Application of law to facts: Discrimination occurred in 1993
Conclusion: 1993 is the relevant year
Element or Sub-issue 2
Issue: What does the phrase "each working day" mean?
Rule: "Each working day" is literal: a day of normal operations (*Zimmerman*; *Wright*)
Application of law to facts: Whole In One operated the golf course and restaurant seven days a week
Conclusion: Therefore, Whole In One must have 15 employees working on all seven days of a week to be considered an employer under Title VII
Element or Sub-issue 3
Issue: Who should be counted as employees each day?
Rule: Salaried or full-time employees counted for every day of the week that they are on the payroll (*Zimmerman*); part-time workers counted only on the days that they actually work (*Zimmerman*; *Wright*; *Norman*)
Application of law to facts: In 1993, 14 workers, 3 full-time and 11 part-time people, worked for Whole In One on any day during the 24-week season. 11 part-time workers counted on the days that they work. 10 full-time workers counted for each day of a week. In total, Whole In One had 11 part-time workers and 10 full-time workers "working" for 20 or more weeks during the relevant year, bringing the total count of employees to 21.
Conclusion: Therefore, Whole In One was an employer under Title VII.

Review this outline and compare it to the text of the memo in Illustration 11-5. The outline closely parallels the discussion concerning Whole In One. If your outline is well-drafted, your writing of the discussion will flow from it easily.

D. Multi-Issue Memorandum

If you have a multi-issue memorandum, you will use many of the same techniques discussed above.

How Do You Organize a Multi-Issue Memorandum?

1. Determine how many issues you will discuss. Often an attorney will help you make this determination. Decide which issue should be discussed first. Again, consider whether there is a threshold issue. In

the memo above, the first issue is whether Whole In One is an employer. If Whole In One is not an employer, then Title VII will not apply and the later issues do not need to be addressed. Therefore, this issue is the threshold issue and it should be placed first. However, you should still discuss the later issues even if you determine that the first issue would be decided in a manner that would dispose of a case. Courts are unpredictable and might decide the issue differently than you did.

2. Determine the legal elements you will discuss and a logical order for this discussion.

3. Prepare a detailed outline of the discussion. For each issue, note each legal element you will address, the authority related to that element, and the legally significant facts applicable to that element.

4. Write a thesis paragraph. For a multi-issue memo, such as on Whole In One, introduce the issues and explain the rules of law in the thesis paragraphs that introduce each issue. Your organization for a multi-issue memo might be as follows:

Thesis Paragraph
    Introduce all legal issues or questions presented
    Conclusions
Thesis Paragraph for Issue or Question Presented #1
    Introduce the legal issue or question presented
    Summarize the legal rule for question presented #1 and each legal element to be discussed
    Apply the legally significant facts to the legal rule
    Conclusion
  First Legal Element or Sub-Issue
    Introduce the legal element
    Summarize the legal rule
    Apply the legally significant facts to the legal rule
    Conclusion
  Second Legal Element or Sub-Issue
    Introduce the legal element
    Summarize the legal rule
    Apply the legally significant facts to the legal rule
    Conclusion
Thesis Paragraph for Issue or Question Presented #2
    Introduce the legal issue or question presented
    Summarize the legal rule for question presented #2 and each legal element to be discussed
    Apply the legally significant facts to the legal rule
    Conclusion
  First Legal Element or Sub-Issue
    Introduce the legal element
    Summarize the legal rule
    Apply the legally significant facts to the legal rule
    Conclusion

Second Legal Element or Sub-Issue
  Introduce the legal element
  Summarize the legal rule
  Apply the legally significant facts to the legal rule
  Conclusion

5. Use headings to introduce new issues. Use transitions to guide the reader from one issue to another and one paragraph to another.

Illustration 11-7 is an outline of the Whole In One memo shown in Illustration 11-5.

ILLUSTRATION 11-7. *Multi-Issue Outline*

Thesis Paragraph
  Introduce issues
    Whether Whole In One is an employer under Title VII?
    Whether Walker is an employee under Title VII?
    Whether Radiant is an employee under Title VII?
  Heading: Issue 1 or Question Presented 1
    Introduce issue: Was Whole In One an employer under Title VII?
    Rules: (**A**) Under Title VII, an employer has at least 15 employees working for 20 or more weeks during the relevant year. (42 U.S.C. § 2000e(b) (1968)) (**first element or sub-issue**) (**B**) Salaried employees are included in this number for each week they are on the payroll. (**second element or sub-issue**) (**C**) Hourly workers are only counted on the days they actually work. (**third element or sub-issue**) (*Zimmerman*) (primary binding)
    Application of law to facts: In 1993, Whole In One had 14 workers, 3 full-time and 11 part-time people on any day during the 24-week season. Ten full-time workers were on the payroll. Part-time workers are only counted on the days that they work; their number is 11 for each day of the 24-week season. All 10 full-time workers are counted each day of a week. In total, Whole In One had 11 part-time workers and 10 full-time workers "working" for 20 or more weeks during the relevant year, bringing the total count of employees to 21.
    Conclusion: Therefore, Whole In One was an employer under Title VII.
  First Legal Element or Sub-Issue:
    Introduce sub-issue: Which is the appropriate year for counting workers?
    Rules: (**A**) Under Title VII, an employer has at least 15 employees working for 20 or more weeks during the current calendar year or preceding year. (42 U.S.C. § 2000e(b) (1968))

ILLUSTRATION 11-7. *Continued*

(B) The "current calendar year" is the year of the discrimination (*Musser*)

Application of law to facts: Discrimination occurred in 1993

Conclusion: 1993 is the relevant year.

Second Legal Element or Sub-Issue

Introduce sub-issue: Is "each working day" literally interpreted?

Rule: "Each working day" is literal: a day of normal operations (*Zimmerman*; *Wright*)

Application of law to facts: Whole In One operated the golf course and restaurant seven days a week.

Conclusion: Therefore, Whole In One must have 15 employees working on all seven days of the week to be considered an employer under Title VII.

Third Legal Element or Sub-Issue

Introduce sub-issue: Who should be counted?

Rules: (A) Salaried or full-time employee counted for every day of the week that they are on the payroll (*Zimmerman*)

(B) Part-time workers counted only on the days that they actually work (*Zimmerman*; *Wright*; *Norman*)

Application of law to facts: In 1993, 14 workers, 3 full-time and 11 part-time people, worked for Whole In One on any day during the 24-week season. 11 part-time workers counted on the days that they work. 10 full-time workers counted for each day of a week. In total, Whole In One had 11 part-time workers and 10 full-time workers "working" for 20 or more weeks during the relevant year, bringing the total count of employees to 21.

Conclusion: Therefore, Whole In One was an employer under Title VII.

Thesis Paragraph to Introduce Issues 2 and 3

Issues 2 and 3

Introduce issues and elements: Are Walker and Radiant employees or independent contractors?

Rules: (A) "Economic realities" of the relationship between an employer and his or her worker must be weighed. (*Knight*; *Norman*; *Mitchell*) Five factors to determine the economic reality of the relationship: 1) the amount of control and supervision the employer exerts over the worker; 2) the responsibility for the costs of the operation; 3) the worker's occupation and the skills required; 4) the method and form of compensation and benefits; and 5) the length of the job commitment. (*Knight*) (**first element**)

(B) When an employee is economically dependent on the employer, an employment relationship exists. (*Vakharia*) (**second element**)

ILLUSTRATION 11-7. *Continued*

Application of law to facts: Walker worked from home, set her own hours, received pay on commission. Company controlled her work by reviewing and revising it, restricting Walker's employment opportunities, and providing supplies for her.

Conclusion: Therefore, the company exerted control over Walker, and she would be considered an employee.

Application of law to facts: Whole In One provided Radiant with an office, supplies, a two-year contract, additional training, paid her regularly, and deducted taxes from her salary. She worked in company offices under the control of Whole In One.

Conclusion: Therefore, the court probably will find that Radiant was an employee.

Reintroduction of Issue 2: Was Walker an employee or an independent contractor?

First Legal Element or Sub-Issue

Introduce sub-issue: What factors will the court weigh to determine economic realities?

Rule: "Economic realities" of the relationship between an employer and his or her worker must be weighed. (*Knight*; *Norman*; *Mitchell*) Five factors to determine the economic reality of the relationship: 1) the amount of control and supervision the employer exerts over the worker; 2) the responsibility for the costs of the operation; 3) the worker's occupation and the skills required; 4) the method and form of compensation and benefits; and 5) the length of the job commitment. (*Knight*. Facts: Knight worked in the insurance sales field, traditionally an independent contractor setting.)

Application of law to facts: Walker worked from home, set her own hours. Received her pay on commission. Company controlled her work by reviewing and revising it.

Conclusion: Walker was an employee.

Second Legal Element or Sub-Issue

Introduce sub-issue: Was Walker economically dependent on Whole In One?

Rule: When an employee is economically dependent on the employer, an employment relationship exists. (*Vakharia*. Facts: A physician dependent on the hospital for business establishing employment relationship.)

Application of law to facts: Similar facts for Walker. Whole In One barred Walker from working for other companies.

Conclusion: Because Walker was barred from working for other companies, employment relationship existed.

ILLUSTRATION 11-7. *Continued*

Reintroduction of Issue 3: Was Radiant an employee or an independent contractor?

Rule: Five factors weighed, primarily control of her by the company. (*Knight*) See also the Rules discussed below the thesis paragraph introducing Issues 2 and 3. There is no need to discuss the Rule in as much detail in Issue 3 as in Issue 2.

Application of law to facts: Whole In One provided Radiant with an office, supplies, a two-year contract, additional training, paid her regularly, and deducted taxes from her salary. She worked in company offices under the control of Whole In One.

Conclusion: Therefore, the court probably will find that Radiant was an employee.

Once you complete your outline, you are ready to begin writing your discussion. Follow your outline and use the applicable law and the facts from cases when they are useful. Illustration 11-8 reprints the last paragraph in Illustration 11-5 and the original outline for that paragraph. Once you have completed your draft, compare the draft to the outline to ensure that you have incorporated all of the components in your outline and that your text matches your outline organization.

ILLUSTRATION 11-8. *Writing from an Outline*

Outline

Issue 3: Was Radiant an employee or an independent contractor?

Rule: Five factors weighed, primarily control of her by the company. (*Knight*) See also the Rules below the thesis paragraph introducing Issues 2 and 3. There is no need to discuss the Rule in as much detail in Issue 3 as in Issue 2.

Application of law to facts: Whole In One provided Radiant with an office, supplies, a two-year contract, additional training, paid her regularly, and deducted taxes from her salary. She worked in company offices under the control of Whole In One.

Conclusion: Therefore, the court probably will find that Radiant was an employee.

Paragraph Drafted from Outline

III. Was Radiant an Employee or an Independent Contractor?

Whether Radiant was an employee again turns on the amount of control Whole In One exerted over Radiant's work. The court will focus

ILLUSTRATION 11-8.   *Continued*

on the same factors established in *Knight* to determine whether an employment relationship exists. *Knight,* 950 F.2d at 378. Control will be the key factor the court will consider. *Id.* Radiant had a two-year employment contract with the company to provide marketing services. Whole In One also provided her with an office, supplies, and additional training. The company paid her regularly and deducted taxes from her salary. Based upon these facts, the company exerted control over Radiant. Therefore, the court is likely to find that Radiant was an employee of Whole In One.

CHAPTER SUMMARY

Outlining is an important component of legal writing. It helps you organize the discussion section of your legal memorandum. To outline a legal memorandum, first draft a list of legal authorities. Second, arrange the discussion sections concerning each issue and, if necessary, arrange each paragraph of the memorandum.

The list of legal authorities should include the names and citations to the authorities, a note about the legally significant facts contained in the authority, if any, and a statement that summarizes the significance of the authority.

The legal issues of the discussion should be organized in the IRAC format discussed in Chapter 9. Each element of a legal issue should be addressed in this format.

Before you can begin writing your memorandum, you must organize your thesis paragraph. The thesis paragraph is the first paragraph of your discussion. It summarizes the legal issues you will discuss in the memorandum. This paragraph also should be organized in IRAC format, if possible.

You have been shown how to draft questions presented, issues, conclusions, brief answers, facts statements, and discussion sections. In addition, you have been taught how to synthesize authorities and how to use a legal writing convention called IRAC.

Key Terms

Elements	Threshold issue
List of legal authorities	Thesis paragraph
Outlining	

EXERCISES

1. Review the following memo. Prepare an outline based on this memo. (This is the reverse of the process you would normally use.)

MEMORANDUM

To: Margaret Sterner

From: Marie Main

Date: January 28, 1995

Re: *Harris v. Sack and Shop*

QUESTION PRESENTED

Is Sack and Shop, a grocery store, liable for injuries sustained by Harris, a store patron who slipped on a banana peel that had been on the grocery store floor for two days?

BRIEF ANSWER

Probably yes. Sack and Shop, a grocery store, probably will be liable based on negligence for injuries sustained by Harris, a store patron who slipped on a banana peel that had been on the grocery store floor for two days.

FACTS

Our client, Sack and Shop Grocery Store, is being sued for negligence by Rebecca Harris.

Harris went to the store to purchase groceries on July 8, 1994. While she was in the produce section, she slipped on a banana that had been left on the floor by a grocery store employee. The employee had dropped it on the floor two days earlier and had failed to clean it up after a patron asked him to do so.

Harris sustained a broken arm and head injuries as a result of the slip and fall.

DISCUSSION

The issue presented in this case is whether Sack and Shop Grocery Store was negligent when Rebecca Harris slipped in the store's produce section. A grocer will be found negligent if a store employee breached the store's duty of reasonable care to its patrons and, as a result of that breach, the patron was injured. *Ward v. K Mart Corp.*, 554 N.E.2d 223 (Ill. 1990). In *Ward,* the grocery store employee failed to clean up a banana peel for two days and that peel caused a patron to be injured. Similarly in our case Sack and Shop failed to remove the banana peel. Therefore, Sack and Shop is likely to be found liable for the injuries Harris sustained.

The first element to consider is whether Sack and Shop owed a duty of reasonable care to Harris. A grocery store owes a duty of care to any patron. *Ward,* 554 N.E.2d at 226. Harris was a customer in the store. Therefore, Sack and Shop owed her a duty of care.

The next question to consider is whether Sack and Shop breached its duty of reasonable care to Harris. A store will be found to have breached its duty of reasonable care to a patron if a store employee fails to properly and regularly clean the floor of the store. *Olinger v. Great Atlantic & Pacific Tea Co.,* 173 N.E.2d 443 (Ill. 1961). In *Olinger,* the store was found liable because a store employee failed to clean the floor for one day and a patron slipped on a substance on the floor. 173 N.E.2d at 447. No one had told any store employee about the slippery substance. *Id.* at 447. Nonetheless, the Illinois Supreme Court found the store liable, saying that the store employees had sufficient time to notice the substance if they had used ordinary care. *Id.* In our case, Sack and Shop's employee had two days to clean the floor before Harris fell. In addition, a customer had placed the store employee on notice of the banana. Therefore, Sack and Shop breached its duty of care to Harris.

The plaintiff, however, still must establish proximate cause, that is that the injury resulted as a natural consequence of Sack and Shop's breach of its duty. A store owner's failure to clear debris from a store floor, resulting in injury to a patron who slipped on the floor, was found to be the proximate cause of the patron's injuries. *Id.* at 449. In this case, Sack and Shop's failure to clean the peel from the floor was a breach of its duty of care to Harris. This breach resulted in injury to Harris. Sack and Shop's breach will be found to be the proximate cause of Harris' injuries.

The final element that must be established is that the plaintiff, Harris, suffered injuries. Harris sustained a broken arm and head injuries as a result of the slip and fall. Therefore, she will be able to show that she was injured.

CONCLUSION

Sack and Shop owed Harris a duty of reasonable care. The store is likely to be found to have breached that duty of reasonable care because an employee failed to remove a banana peel from the grocery store floor during the preceding two days. The injuries Harris sustained were directly caused by a slip on a banana peel. Therefore, Sack and Shop is likely to be found liable to Harris.

Research

2. The answers to the following exercises will vary depending upon the jurisdiction and the person researching the issues.

After you have reviewed the facts presented and the information available to you, map out your research strategy. What specific sources will you use? Indicate what you hope to learn from each source and what type of authority you will find in each source.

Using the facts specified below, research the question of intentional infliction of emotional distress in your jurisdiction. Find answers only to the questions presented in the memo below.

Next, outline the discussion section. Provide a detailed outline and list of authorities. Incorporate your authorities into your outline.

Write the discussion section only for the memo below.

MEMORANDUM

To: Karen Abbey

From: Gail Mark

Date: January 28, 1995

Re: *Kahn v. Randall,* Civ. 95 No. 988, File No. 8988977

QUESTION PRESENTED

Does Janice Kahn have a valid claim for intentional infliction of emotional distress against Ronnie Randall after Kahn saw Randall turn his car to strike Kahn's 11-year-old child in front of her, causing her to suffer from anxiety, headaches, and vomiting?

CONCLUSION

Janice Kahn probably has a valid claim for intentional infliction of emotional distress against Ronnie Randall. Kahn saw Randall turn his car to strike her 11-year-old child. Seeing this accident caused Kahn to suffer, daily, from anxiety, headaches, and vomiting. Randall's act could be considered extreme and outrageous conduct if it was done with intent. Several witnesses can testify that Randall said that he intended to harm Kahn, and Kahn states that Randall turned the car to strike her son. Two factors, however, might show that Randall lacked intent: the statement that he made to the police that he did not intend to hit the child, and the fact that his blood alcohol level was .11, possibly preventing him from formulating the needed intent.

FACTS

While driving a car, Ronnie Randall struck Janice Kahn's son at 5:00 P.M. on August 29, 1993. It was bright and clear. No skid marks appeared on the dry street following the accident.

Janice Kahn was working in her garden about five feet from the accident scene at the time of the accident. Her son was playing a game in the street before Randall's car struck him. Kahn did not see the car strike her 11-year-old son. When she first looked up from her garden, she thought her son was dead. He was covered with blood and had several broken bones. However, Kahn's son was conscious after the accident.

Immediately after the accident, Randall, who had a blood/alcohol level of .11, was cited for drunk driving and driving with a suspended driver's license. Police charged him with drunk driving and had suspended his license two weeks earlier, after the car he was driving had struck another child at the same spot. Randall has a history of alcohol abuse.

Following the accident, several witnesses said Randall was upset and wobbled as he walked. One witness said that Randall intentionally turned the steering wheel to hit Kahn's son. Kahn stated that Randall often swerved down her street to get her attention.

Rhonda Albert, Kahn's neighbor, said she heard Randall say he would get even with Kahn after Kahn broke off a 10-year relationship with him.

During Kahn and Randall's 10-year relationship, Randall was close to Kahn's son. He took him to ball games, including one in April, and attended the son's baseball games. Randall knew that Kahn's son was the most important person in her life.

Since the accident, Kahn vomits daily and has nightmares about the accident. Dr. Susan Faigen, Kahn's internist, states that the vomiting and nightmares are the result of the accident.

Research Memo

3. Read the statement below. Research the issues and then prepare a six page, typed memo. Be sure that it is double spaced. The jurisdiction for this problem is your state.

> You are a paralegal with the Law Office of Warren T. Sales. You have been asked to research the following questions and provide answers. These are the facts that Mr. Sales presented to you.
>
> Your client is Sue A. Buyer. She lives at 3225 Wilmette Avenue, Glenview, your state. The defendants are Lee R. Merchant, owner of Mowers R Us, in Glenview, Your state, and Manny U. Facture, the owner of a manufacturing concern, which is not incorporated, called Mowers, of Rosemont, Your state. Ms. Buyer went to the defendant's store, Mowers R Us, to purchase a lawnmower for her new home. She was a first-time homeowner and was unfamiliar with lawnmowers. She had never operated a lawnmower because her brothers had always mowed the lawn when she was a child.
>
> When she went to Mowers R Us, she asked to speak with the owner. She told Mr. Merchant: "I don't know anything about these mowers and I need to talk with an expert." Mr. Merchant said, "I'm the owner and you couldn't find a better expert anywhere in

the Chicagoland area. I have been in the business of selling mowers for more than 40 years. I only sell mowers and the equipment to clean and repair them. Are you familiar with the type of lawnmower you would like?"

"No, I don't know anything about lawnmowers. I just know that I have to have a lawnmower that will mulch my grass clippings because I cannot bag the clippings. The village of Glenview does not permit me to bag the clippings, so the clippings must remain on my lawn."

"You're absolutely correct. You must have a mulching mower," Mr. Merchant said. "That type of mower will grind the grass clippings and you will not notice them on your grass. I have the perfect mower for you. It is a used model that will fit into your price range, only $200. It's a good brand, a Roro, and will mulch the grass as well as any of the new mowers. This one is true blue. You can purchase a separate mulching blade, which will easily attach to it, for an additional $50," he added.

"Do you think that I need the mulching blade," Ms. Buyer asked. "I've never used a lawnmower so I don't know what to expect and you appear to be the expert."

"I think that you could do without the mulching blade unless you want the grass ground up very fine."

"I think that I would like it ground up fine. I'll defer to your judgment. If you think a mulching blade is necessary, then I'll buy that with the mower. Do you think that this is the best mower for mulching?"

"Absolutely, I told you it is a true value. It will mulch with the best of them."

"If you think it can do the job, I'll trust your judgment," said Ms. Buyer. "I'll take the mower and the mulching blade. Can you install the mulching blade? I don't know anything about the installation."

"Sure, we can install any blade for another $30."

"OK. Do you clean up the machine, too?"

"We can do it for an additional $40 or you can do it yourself with the special, industrial strength, non-toxic, non-irritant, mower cleaner."

"Well, I have sensitive skin. Do you really think that the mower cleaner is safe for me to use? I have never used any type of industrial strength cleaner," Ms. Buyer said.

"Absolutely, I've used the cleaner many times and it is very safe and won't hurt your sensitive skin at all."

Ms. Buyer purchased the mower, the blade, and the cleaner, and used the mower after Mr. Merchant installed the new mulching blade. It barely cut the grass and certainly didn't mulch the clippings into fine pieces as Mr. Merchant had claimed.

She brought the mower back to Mr. Merchant. He said that he had made no warranties about the mower. He showed her the language on the receipt which said that he did not expressly warranty anything.

Ms. Buyer brought the mower to a Roro dealer. The owners of the Roro dealership, Abe Saul and Lou T. Wright, said that the mower Ms. Buyer had purchased from Mowers R Us was not a mulching mower. It was a mower built before mulching was popular. Therefore, it would not perform the mulching task. It was designed merely to cut the grass. "Any merchant who has been in business even for one year should have known that mowers built before 1970 were not designed for mulching," Mr. Wright said. He showed Ms. Buyer where the manufacturing date appeared on the mower. "Manufactured in August 1969," it said on the plate with the serial number. "Also, mulching blades cannot be placed on these old mowers. Any mower dealer should know that too," Mr. Wright added. "However, this mower isn't defective. It can cut the grass without mulching it."

The mower wasn't Ms. Buyer's only problem. She also had used the cleaner with gloves. She broke out in a rash all over her hands. The dermatologist stated that the cleaner was caustic and permeated the gloves, causing the rash on Ms. Buyer's hands.

Ms. Buyer is bringing an action against Mr. Merchant and Mr. Facture in the Circuit Court of Cook County, Law Division, in your state. Your research is limited to actions Ms. Buyer has against Mr. Merchant for breach of an implied warranty of fitness for a particular purpose.

Research Memo

Answer the following question fully and provide authority (i.e., cases, secondary sources, if necessary, or laws) to support your position. Indicate whether the authority is primary or secondary authority and whether it is mandatory or persuasive authority. Remember that your goal is to find the best primary binding authorities.

4. You are a paralegal with the firm of Probing and Will. You must research whether Sarah Wakefield can renounce Adam Antwernt's will and collect a portion of the estate.

Your firm's client is Sarah Wakefield. She was married to Adam Antwernt. Antwernt died on June 6, 1994, in your state, following a long illness. Wakefield was Antwernt's second wife. She had been married to him for more than 20 years and lived in their home in the Highlands of your state. Antwernt purchased the home with his first wife, Carry MacOver. MacOver died in 1965. When Antwernt married Wakefield he never changed the deed for the home to include Wakefield. Wakefield kept her maiden name. Antwernt adopted a son with MacOver in 1964. The son, who is now 30 years old is Grayson Antwernt.

Antwernt drafted his will in May of 1992. He and his wife were getting along fine. However, he excluded her from his will. He did not leave her any property. Instead, he left all of his property to Grayson. Antwernt's will was admitted to probate on July 8, 1994.

Wakefield wants to know whether Antwernt's will is valid and whether he can divest her of their marital property, or whether she can renounce the will and collect a portion of the estate.

Grayson is out of town and his attorney told Wakefield that she will get her share of the estate once Grayson returns. He is scheduled to return on July 5, 1995.

What rights does Mrs. Wakefield have to the estate? How must she exercise those rights in your state? Draft an outline of the memo.

Part III.

12. Persuasive Writing

CHAPTER OVERVIEW

Persuasive writing is used to convince a court, an opposing party, or an individual to adopt your client's assessment of the facts and the applicable law. Persuasive writing eloquently articulates a position. This form of writing is used in many legal documents, the most common of which are litigation documents. Transaction documents such as contracts and leases are also persuasive forms of writing because they advocate a client's position or protect a client's rights.

Persuasive writing is used for litigation memos that are filed with the court. **Litigation memos** are persuasive documents detailing the legal and factual arguments to grant or deny a client's motion to dismiss and other procedural motions. As the word persuasive indicates, this style of writing is used to persuade. Persuasive writing is argumentative but the argument is based on the law, not just on whim or fury.

A. The Nature of Persuasive Writing

What Kinds of Documents Are Persuasive?

Persuasive writing is used in drafting advocacy memos in support of motions designed to convince a court to rule a certain way. Persuasive writing is also used in writing trial and appellate briefs. **Trial briefs** explain the leading legal issues anticipated to emerge in a trial while they emphasize the client's position. Trial briefs outline a case, offer the elements that will be proven, and include witnesses' names and pertinent facts and evidence. Trial briefs are submitted to the court in some but not all jurisdictions. Trial briefs are usually submitted in federal court. Regardless of whether an attorney files a trial brief with the court, he or she would use it to prepare for trial. **Appellate briefs** are formal documents submitted to the court in accordance with federal, state, or local court rules. Appellate briefs are filed in cases in which the parties are dissatisfied with a trial court judge's decision concerning a legal issue, evidentiary point, or finding of fact in a bench trial or a jury's verdict. By their nature, appellate briefs are designed to persuade the court that an error occurred in the trial. For example, an appellant may claim that the trial court erred when the jury was allowed to consider some evidence. Litigation paralegals are often called upon to write persuasively. Also, at times transaction paralegals write persuasively, for example, in demand letters and default notices. Anytime you write a document that vehemently articulates your client's position, you are writing persuasively.

This chapter will focus on persuasive writing used in litigation documents. Initially, the **complaint** filed by the plaintiff is the first document that triggers the need to write persuasively. A complaint sets out the legal claim and issues combined with the specific facts. Additionally, advocacy memos are written persuasively.

Which Aspects of Persuasive Writing Do Paralegals Perform?

Generally, in small firm practice, paralegals draft complaints, answers, and interrogatories. Infrequently, paralegals draft memoranda in support of motions filed with the court and trial briefs. Appellate briefs are rarely drafted by paralegals because this is a specialized practice area of the law reserved for attorneys who have developed this expertise. However, paralegals should be knowledgeable about all facets of persuasive writing. Often paralegals are requested to work on portions of a persuasive document or to extract the citations from a document to compile an authorities table. Paralegals are not authorized to sign court documents and pleadings. Only attorneys are licensed to practice law and to sign pleadings.

What Is the Difference Between Objective and Persuasive Writing?

Objective writing is neutral and seeks to inform the reader as to all of the relevant law. In persuasive writing, the writer takes a position and attempts to convince the court and the reader that this position is correct. Persuasive writing seeks to solve a problem in favor of the client and conforms to the attorney's theory of the case. Law and facts that are harmful to the client's position are minimized and, if the jurisdiction permits, omitted.

B. Techniques

Is There a Formula for Persuasive Writing as There Is for Objective Writing?

Yes there is. As you learned, the formula for objective writing uses the IRAC structure in the discussion. See Chapter 9, The IRAC Method. The fundamental difference is that IRAC is the structure for crafting an objective discussion that poses a question and explores the answers neutrally; whereas in persuasive writing, the first "A" of the **ARAC** sequence is the writer's assertion (his or her position), followed by the Rule, the Application, and the Conclusion (the rest of the ARAC sequence proves the writer's assertion). To write persuasively, use the ARAC or CRAC structure (ARAC and CRAC being virtually synonymous: ARAC is the acronym for Assertion, Rule, Application, Conclusion, and CRAC is the acronym for Conclusion, Rule, Application, Conclusion).

The ARAC formula sounds quite similar to IRAC, yet there is an important difference. Instead of posing a question or viewing an issue objectively, you make an assertion based on the theory of your case and then support it with the relevant legal rule, the factual foundation, and legal analysis—that is, you explain why that rule of law relates to your assertion and then you draw a conclusion. Notice that there are important similarities between ARAC and IRAC—the Rule, the Application, and the Conclusion are essential components of both formats. The Rule provides the legal basis of the argument, the Application relates the legal rule to the instant problem or case, and the Conclusion demonstrates the nexus between the rule and the facts and provides a resolution. Just as in objective writing, the application segment is most important and should never be skipped, for it tells the reader why the rule of law applies to this factual and legal scenario.

The following is an example of a paragraph from an objective memo written in IRAC format:

> (ISSUE) Did Jones indicate acceptance of the truck and waive his right to seek damages by repairing and continuing to use the truck for more than a reasonable time? (RULE) A buyer must rescind a sales contract as soon as he discovers the breach, or after he has had reasonable time for examination. He waives this right to rescind by continuing to use the goods for more than a reasonable time. *Olson Rug Co. v. Smarto,* 204 N.E.2d 838, 841 (Ill. App. 1965). In *Olson,* the court found that the Smartos indicated acceptance and waived their right to rescind the contract by continuing to use the carpeting for more than one year after the defects were discovered. *Id.* (APPLICATION) Our problem differs from *Olson* because Jones did not discover that the truck was defective until

he made the first repair on December 13, 1994, over one year after he purchased the truck. However, one year is more than reasonable time for examination. (CONCLUSION) Therefore, Jones indicates acceptance of the truck, waiving his right to recover damages, by repairing and continuing to use the truck after more than a reasonable time for inspection passed.

For purposes of comparison, an ARAC paragraph follows. Notice how it is written in a persuasive tone, beginning with the writer's assertion.

(ASSERTION) The plaintiff failed to give notice of defects within a reasonable time. The plaintiff did not put the defendant on notice, as to the truck's defects, until over one year after the defects were discovered. (RULE) "A buyer must notify a seller of defects within a reasonable time thereof notwithstanding acceptance." *Stamm v. Wilder Travel Travelers,* 358 N.E.2d 382, 385 (Ill. Ct. App. 1976). Furthermore, if a buyer fails to reject a good within a reasonable time, acceptance takes place. *Vitromar Piece Dye Works v. Lawrence of London, Ltd.,* 256 N.E.2d 135, 137 (Ill. Ct. App. 1969). (APPLICATION) Here, the plaintiff made various repairs and replaced components over a one year period. The truck was purchased in November 1993, and repairs were made between December 1993 and March 1995. The plaintiff failed to notify Grimy's of any defects until over one year after the purchase date. (CONCLUSION) Since the plaintiff did not notify Grimy's as to the defects within a reasonable time, he has accepted the truck.

The IRAC paragraph begins with a question and the answer is reached by using a neutral exploration of the law and by applying the facts. The ARAC sequence begins with a premise, an Assertion of what the party considers to be true, and the Rule, Application, and Conclusion that follow support the assertion. A close examination of various sentences in the IRAC and the ARAC paragraphs further underscores the differences between persuasive and objective writing. Aside from beginning the sequence with an assertion, persuasive writing uses strong adjectives and conjures emotional reactions. The Application portion of the objectively written paragraph is as follows:

Our problem differs from *Olson* because Jones did not discover that the truck was defective until he made the first repair on December 13, 1994, over one year after he purchased the truck. However, one year is more than reasonable time for examination.

What Are Some Techniques Used in Persuasive Writing?

Comparing objective and persuasive writing emphasizes the techniques used to craft an argument. Look at how the objective application segment differs from the persuasive application: Here, the plaintiff made various repairs and replaced components over a one year period. The truck was purchased in November 1993, and repairs were made between December 1993 and March 1995. The plaintiff failed to notify Grimy's of any defects until almost two years after the purchase date.

First, persuasive writing tries to depersonalize the opposing party. Notice how Grimy's is referred to by name whereas Jones is referred to as "the plaintiff." Another hallmark of persuasive writing is using language to arouse emotion or form an opinion. An example of this technique is used in the persuasive sentence "The plaintiff failed to notify Grimy's of any defects until almost two years after the purchase date." Labeling behavior is a persuasive writing technique.

Are There Any Other Tools That Are Helpful for Persuasive Writing?

In persuasive writing, an attorney cannot ignore relevant law or facts but can make an effort to enhance or emphasize facts and law favorable to his or her client's position and minimize facts and law that are unfavorable. The facts are slanted so that favorable information is highlighted and harmful information is minimized. A frequently used method is to write the facts that are favorable to your client in the active voice and to write the facts that are harmful in the passive voice. Passive voice deemphasizes the actor. Therefore, if you want to deemphasize your client's actions, use passive voice, as in the *Grimy* example above. The body of the brief is generally written in the CRAC or ARAC format.

A portion of a facts statement from an objective memo follows:

> On November 28, 1993, Mr. Jones paid $15,225 to Grimy's Auto and Truck Repair Service, Inc., of Stream Grove, Illinois, as payment in full for the purchase of a 1985 Kenworth truck. As part of the purchase agreement, Grimy's represented to Jones that it had completely overhauled the engine, using newly rebuilt parts for which Grimy's would provide invoices. Grimy's represented that the parts were guaranteed. Also, Grimy's stated that the trac-tor/trailer was in as-good-as-new condition and was ready for standard interstate trucking. Because of an equipment failure, on November 13, 1995, Mr. Jones received an invoice totaling $3,604.18 from a repair shop for replacement of the nos. 5 and 6 cylinders.

Notice how both parties are referred to by name. The facts are reiterated in chronological order. Emotional adjectives are not included.

A facts statement from a persuasive document follows for comparison:

> Grimy's Auto and Truck Repair Service, Inc., of Stream Grove, Illinois, sold the plaintiff a 1985 Kenworth truck on November 28, 1993, which was represented as being completely overhauled. At the time of purchase, the truck was in as-good-as-new condition and was ready for standard interstate trucking. Two years after the purchase, on November 13, 1995, the plaintiff received an invoice for $3,604.18, from a repair shop, for the replacement of the nos. 5 and 6 cylinders.

The passage of time between the purchase and the repair is emphasized, whereas the representations made by Grimy's are deemphasized. The party being represented is referred to by name and the opposition is depersonalized.

Are There Any General Rules for Writing Persuasively?

First, persuasive writing begins at the level of word choice, sentence structure, and paragraph formation. When you receive an assignment requiring persuasive writing, follow the pre-writing techniques outlined in Chapter 3, Getting Ready to Write. When you receive your assignment, ask yourself: What is the purpose? The purpose of the document determines its form. Is the document for a trial court or an appellate court? If so, it is either a trial or an appellate brief. Is the document a letter demanding an individual to perform in a specific manner? Then the document is a demand letter. The purpose determines the rhetorical stance. If the document is a letter, you know that it does not have to be drafted in ARAC format but must be persuasive. If the document is a memo to be used to prepare for trial or to convince a judge to rule on behalf of your firm's client, then it must be written following the ARAC format. Next, you must assess the intended audience. Reader awareness is important. Who will read the document? What type of education does he or she have? How should the document sound? It is at this level that the persuasive tone of the document is determined. Select powerful, emotional words and you will sway the reader toward your side if you can substantiate your position with law and facts. Generally, short sentences are used for beneficial information, and long, clause-ridden sentences are used to obscure detrimental facts.

When Does the Need to Write Persuasively Arise?

Once again, remember that paralegals are not authorized to sign court documents and pleadings. Only attorneys are licensed to practice law and to sign court documents and pleadings.

C. Types of Persuasive Writing

1. Complaints

What Is a Complaint?

A complaint is the document filed with the trial court that initiates the proceedings. A complaint is a short statement of the facts of the case, and a statement of why the plaintiff is entitled to win. The jurisdiction determines the contents of the complaint. Some jurisdictions, such as federal court, require a statement of the basis for jurisdiction. Some jurisdictions require fact pleading that identifies all facts alleging a valid cause of action. Notice, required in some jurisdictions, is a short statement of the case's basis, or grounds, and why the plaintiff is entitled to win.

The parties must be clearly identified. Note whether a party is a corporation or a partnership, and its state of residence and address. In some federal complaints, a diversity statement is included to indicate the basis for the case being heard in federal court. An example of a diversity statement is: "The plaintiff is a citizen of Illinois. The defendant is a corporation doing business in the state of Ohio. The matter in controversy, exclusive of interests and costs, exceeds $50,000."

Paragraphs are numbered in a complaint. State all claims the plaintiff has and use separate counts for different claims. At the end of the complaint, ask the court for specific remedies. This request is called the prayer for relief.

How Do You Know What to Include in a Complaint?

Interview your client. Determine the facts of the case. Do some preliminary research to determine what facts are necessary to support each element of a legal claim the plaintiff might have. You must plead each element of a claim. If you fail to do so, a defendant will file a motion to dismiss the complaint for failure to state a claim. Often, statutes and court cases establish the elements of the cause of action, the "magic language," that should be included in a claim. Review relevant statutes and court cases before drafting the complaint. However, you do not cite to a statute or court case in a claim, except when required in the jurisdictional statement. Outline all of the information, legal and factual, to support allegations in the complaint.

When you have gathered the information, use a form book or ask to see examples of complaints created by members of your firm or legal department. Form books are excellent resources for they include all of the necessary elements to include when drafting a complaint. Remember that the forms are always tailored to your client's situation because the facts are unique to each case. Another excellent source is *American Jurisprudence Proof of Facts 2d* published by Lawyer's Cooperative. *Proof of Facts* has a checklist of necessary facts and legal rules that you should include to build a case.

Each paragraph should contain one simple, thorough thought. Do not incorporate multiple ideas into one numbered paragraph. By keeping the statement simple, you will know what a defendant is admitting or denying.

Your complaint should allow the reader to understand the plaintiff's story and to see it in his or her mind.

The damages and the relief sought should always be included in the complaint.

An example of a complaint follows:

ILLUSTRATION 12-1. *Sample Complaint*
_____

IN THE CIRCUIT COURT OF MILL COUNTY, ILLINOIS, COUNTY DEPARTMENT, LAW DIVISION

MICHAEL JONES,	)	
	)	
Plaintiff	)	No. 95L 27901
	)	
v.	)	
	)	
GRIMY'S AUTO AND TRUCK SERVICE,	)	
INC., an Illinois Corporation	)	
	)	
Defendant.	)	

COMPLAINT AT LAW

This is an action brought in the Circuit Court of Mill County, Illinois, to recover for the breach of warranty of merchantability arising out of the sale of a defective truck that was said to have been completely overhauled and consisting of newly rebuilt, reconditioned parts. The defendant was aware that Michael Jones purchased the truck for the purpose of using the vehicle for interstate trucking. Plaintiff seeks money damages for lost wages and profits and for the expense of servicing the truck. Plaintiff demands a trial by jury.

PARTIES

The Plaintiff is a citizen of Illinois and engages in the business of interstate trucking. Defendant, Grimy's Auto and Truck Service, Inc.,

ILLUSTRATION 12-1. *Continued*

is a corporation organized under the laws of Illinois with its principal place of business in that state.

BREACH OF WARRANTY OF MERCHANTABILITY

1. On or about November 28, 1993, and for some time before that, Defendant Grimy's Auto and Truck Service, Inc., was in the business of buying, reconditioning, and then selling used trucks. The business is located at 2300 Stream Road, village of Stream Grove, county of Cook, and state of Illinois.

2. On November 28, 1993, Plaintiff, Michael Jones, purchased from Defendant, Grimy's Auto and Truck Repair Service, a 1984 Kenworth C/D Serial Number 239999L with Title Number AB1234 and paid the agreed purchase price of Fifteen Thousand Two Hundred Twenty Five ($15,225.00) Dollars, in full (a copy of said sales documents attached as Exhibit "A"), the price normally charged for reconditioned, rebuilt trucks intended for interstate trucking.

3. The price agreed upon between the Plaintiff and the Defendant for the purchase of the truck was a price for a truck with a recently overhauled engine with all new or rebuilt parts, and one ready for road use in interstate trucking.

4. Jones agreed to purchase the truck, after Defendant was informed that the truck would be used in interstate trucking, and after Defendant made the following representations:

   a. the engine of the truck was completely overhauled and consisted of newly rebuilt, reconditioned parts;
   b. all parts in the rebuilt engine would be guaranteed and Plaintiff would be supplied with invoices for parts purchased to overhaul the engine; and
   c. the tractor/trailer was "like brand new" and ready for use of the type and extent generally involved in the interstate trucking industry.

5. The truck was not as represented by agents and/or employees of Defendant GRIMY'S AUTO AND TRUCK SERVICE because the heads were old and had not been reconditioned, and other parts, including at least two pistons, two rods, two sleeves, and injectors, were not new, were defective, and had not been reconditioned.

6. As a consequence of the failure of the truck to be as agreed, the truck broke down and the Plaintiff was thus without work for an extended period of time resulting in lost wages and profits.

7. As a consequence of the failure of the truck to be as represented, Plaintiff was required to expend the following additional sums in repair of the vehicle:

ILLUSTRATION 12-1. *Continued*

   a. $3,604.18 for replacement of nos. 5 and 6 cylinders, which took
      place between December 23, 1993, and January 5, 1994;
   b. $40.88 for repair of the shut-down solenoid on December 8,
      1994;
   c. $99.88 for repair of rear lights on December 15, 1994;
   d. $312.49 for replacement of broken path tube in no. 6 cylinder
      on December 15, 1994;
   e. $120.00 for tow of vehicle on February 2, 1995;
   f. $247.00 for tow of vehicle to GRIMY'S AUTO AND TRUCK
      SERVICE on March 16, 1995; and
   g. Estimated repair costs of $9000.00 to repair vehicle, which is
      currently disabled in Columbus, Ohio.

Therefore, the Plaintiff, Michael Jones, demands judgment against
Defendant, Grimy's Auto and Truck Service, Inc., in the following
amounts:

   a. $6000.00 in lost profits;
   b. $8000.00 in lost wages;
   c. $4424.43 in expenditures in repair of the vehicle;
   d. $15,225.00 for loss of use of said vehicle; and
   e. Such other damages occurring as a consequence of the breach
      of said contract, plus the costs of this action.

                                   _____
                                          Attorney for Plaintiff

Ted Kane, Esq.
Wall & Smith, P.C.
123 West Monroe Street
Mill, Illinois 60666
(999) 888-8888

Read the complaint carefully. Notice how the complaint tells the story
of the plaintiff's grievance while listing the factual elements necessary
to support a cause of action. The form books will help you draft the
complaint by listing the elements that you must prove to substantiate
the facts.

2. Answer

After the complaint is filed, the defendant responds to, or answers,
the complaint. One option is that the defense may file a **motion** to
dismiss either the entire action or at least one of the counts, to narrow
the issues for trial. If the plaintiff files a five count complaint and the

defendant is successful in dismissing two counts then the defense only has to contend with three counts at trial. The rules of civil procedure for the appropriate jurisdiction provide the basis for dismissal of a complaint. For actions in state court, you look to the relevant state's code of civil procedure. In federal court you would look to the Federal Rules of Civil Procedure. The defendant must file an **answer** to any counts for which the defendant does not seek a motion to dismiss.

What Is an Answer and What Is Its Purpose?

The answer is designed to address each of the points the plaintiff states in the complaint. It is called a pleading because it is a statement of the defendant's position concerning the case. Some of the plaintiff's allegations will be admitted by the defendant; many more, however, will be denied; in some cases, a defendant will state that he or she has insufficient information to admit or deny an allegation. The answer also is the time to plead any affirmative defenses. Affirmative defenses are claims a defendant may present that would bar the plaintiff's recovery. In some jurisdictions, verified answers must be filed to verified complaints. These complaints and answers are signed by the parties, and can be used in court as evidence.

When Is an Answer Filed?

An answer is usually filed within a time period stated in the court rules. Many jurisdictions provide for a 20-day period between the service date and the filing of an answer. In some cases, the defendant will file a motion to dismiss an action rather than answer the complaint within the same time frame. Such a motion is filed when the complaint fails to state a claim or the court lacks jurisdiction or authority to hear a claim. Sometimes complaints will contain multiple claims for legal relief. Defendants can answer those claims while simultaneously filing a motion to dismiss other claims. See Illustration 12-2 for an example of an answer to one count of a complaint, and Illustration 12-3 for an example of a motion to dismiss other counts of the same complaint.

What Are the Components of an Answer?

The top of the answer is the caption. It indicates the name of the court in which the case is filed, the case docket number, the name of the case, and the word "answer." Each document filed with the court should have a title, such as the word "answer," that identifies the type of pleading or motion being filed. Next comes the body of the answer. And finally, a signature line appears for the attorney. Each document filed with the court must be signed, usually by the attorney. Paralegals should never sign the answer. Verified complaints or answers must be signed by the party involved in the lawsuit who is filing the document. Most states require that you include a statement called a certificate of service, which certifies that copies of the document have been sent to the other parties who are of record in the action, and is generally signed by an attorney and contains the date and the name of the document being sent.

How Do You Draft the Body of an Answer to a Complaint?

First, ask the assigning attorney whether a sample answer is available for you to review. Check form books for the appropriate jurisdiction and review your firm's bank of pleadings, if available. Next, read the complaint. Discuss the allegations, both factual and legal, with the assigning attorney. Outlining is important here. Make a list of allegations your client knows are true, a list of the allegations that are to be denied, as well as a list of the allegations for which your client does not know enough information either to admit or to deny the statement. Next, consider any affirmative defenses (you might need to consult the assigning attorney). Finally, begin drafting your answer according to examples from your firm's files or from a form book. For each statement in the answer, you should note the corresponding paragraph in the complaint. For example, to admit an allegation, you would state "the defendant admits the allegation contained in paragraph 3 of the complaint." This allegation would correspond to the statement in the complaint.

ILLUSTRATION 12-2. *Sample Answer*

IN THE CIRCUIT COURT OF MILL COUNTY, ILLINOIS
COUNTY DEPARTMENT, LAW DIVISION

MICHAEL JONES,	)	
	)	
Plaintiff	)	No. 95L 27901
	)	
v.	)	
	)	
GRIMY'S AUTO AND TRUCK SERVICE,	)	
INC., an Illinois Corporation,	)	
	)	
Defendant	)	

ANSWER OF DEFENDANT
GRIMY'S AUTO AND
TRUCK SERVICE

Defendant, Grimy's Auto and Truck Service, for its answer to the Plaintiff's Complaint, states that it is a corporation organized under the laws of Illinois with its principal place of business in that state and the defendant further states as follows:

ILLUSTRATION 12-2. *Continued*

1. The defendant admits the allegations contained in paragraph 1.

2. The defendant admits that on November 28, 1993, Michael Jones purchased from Grimy's Auto and Truck Repair Service a 1984 Kenworth C/D Serial Number 239999L with Title Number AB1234 and paid Fifteen Thousand Two Hundred Twenty Five ($15,225.00) Dollars. The defendant further states that it lacks sufficient knowledge to admit or deny the remaining allegation of Paragraph 2.

3. The defendant denies the allegations contained in paragraph 3 of the complaint.

4. The defendant denies the allegations contained in paragraph 4 of the complaint.

5. The defendant denies the allegations contained in paragraph 5 of the complaint.

6. The defendant states that it lacks sufficient knowledge to admit or deny that Plaintiff was without work for an extended period of time resulting in lost wages and profits. The defendant denies the remaining allegations contained in paragraph 6 of the complaint.

7. The defendant denies the allegations contained in paragraph 7 of the complaint.

Defendant, Grimy's Auto and Truck Repair Service, denies that plaintiff is entitled to judgment in any sum whatsoever and further prays for judgment in its favor and against the plaintiff together with the costs incurred in the defense of this suit.

Respectfully submitted,

By _____

One of the Attorneys for Defendant
Grimy's Auto and Truck Service

Maggie Bourn
Coolar, Bourn, Lopez & Post
20 N. Wacker Drive, Suite 1910
Chicago, Illinois 60606-1229
(312-111-1111)
I.D. #11122

The denial can simply be the word "denied," though some attorneys prefer a full statement. Lawyers sometimes use the words "averment" or "avers" in the complaint or answer. To aver is to declare or allege; an averment is an allegation or declaration. These are old fashioned terms, though some attorneys still use them.

3. Motions

What Is a Motion?

A motion is a vehicle by which an attorney asks a court to act. A motion to dismiss the claim is a defense motion. The defense may assert that the complaint fails to state a cause of action and is therefore substantially insufficient in law. Another motion that the defense may make is that the complaint should be dismissed if it appears beyond a doubt that the plaintiff can prove no set of facts in support of his claim that would entitle him to relief. The language of the motion is based on the statute, either on the state or federal level, and is usually derived from a form book. The motion itself should contain only a brief statement of the relief sought and a synopsis of the reasons supporting the motion. The format of the motion can be obtained from a form book. The actual motion should be written in direct, simple language. Motions are usually quickly decided by the judge prior to the trial, and are used to narrow the number of counts in the complaint that must be decided at trial. If you move to dismiss counts four and five of a five-count complaint, and the judge rules in your favor, then you only have to deal with counts one through three at trial. Consult a text on litigation for a more detailed explanation of pre-trial procedure.

What Would a Motion to Dismiss the *Grimy* Matter Look Like?

ILLUSTRATION 12-3. *Sample Motion to Dismiss*

IN THE CIRCUIT COURT OF MILL COUNTY, ILLINOIS
COUNTY DEPARTMENT, LAW DIVISION

MICHAEL JONES,	)	
	)	
Plaintiff	)	No. 95L 27901
	)	
v.	)	
	)	
GRIMY'S AUTO AND TRUCK SERVICE,	)	
INC., an Illinois Corporation	)	
	)	
Defendant.	)	

MOTION TO DISMISS

The Defendant, Grimy's Auto and Truck Service, Inc., who moves to strike and dismiss the Complaint of Plaintiff, pursuant to § 2-615

ILLUSTRATION 12-3.   *Continued*

of the Illinois Code of Civil Procedure, 735 ILCS 5/2-615 (1994), and in support states as follows:

> 1. The complaint is substantially insufficient in law as to state a cause of action because plaintiff exercised ownership over the truck and indicated acceptance of the vehicle by making repairs and replacing parts over a two-year period, and plaintiff failed to reject the truck in a timely manner because Grimy's was not alerted to the defects until two years after plaintiff was first aware of them.

5 September 1995

By Harry H. Harrison, Esq.

1515 Byrd Street
Mill, Illinois
(999) 888-1234
Attorney for Grimy's

What Is a Memo in Support of Motion or an Advocacy Memo?

Another document that is written persuasively is the Memorandum in Support of Motions. A common synonym is a litigation memo in support of, or against, a motion. The motion to dismiss is based on the applicable state or federal statute and the language is generally gleaned from a form book or an in-house form where the applicable information is inserted in the blanks. When a motion to dismiss is filed in response to a complaint, a memo is attached articulating the legal and factual argument as to why the judge should rule in favor of the motion. This memo is called an advocacy memo. A common use for this type of memo is to support or oppose a motion to dismiss for failure to state a claim, for insufficient facts, or for a judgment on the pleadings. This technique is used to hasten the resolution of the litigation process and to narrow the issues that are involved. Sometimes a judge will rule on one issue, leaving only two issues outstanding to be resolved at trial. Sometimes a judge will rule on the entire matter and dismiss it entirely.

Memoranda are submitted to the court to support the requested relief, articulated in the motion, especially when there is a disputed issue of importance. The memorandum in support of a motion (also called an advocacy memo) should contain the complete argument. Ask the attorney assigning the project for examples of memos in support of motions that have been drafted at your office. Follow the format in the examples. The components of an advocacy memo are:

1. *Introduction:* identifies the party filing the motion, states the purpose, and describes the issues it addresses.
2. *Statement of facts (or other basis for the argument):* what the case is about. Here you provide the necessary factual information to indicate why the motion should be granted. Careful outlining of the beneficial and detrimental facts is important here. You want to emphasize any facts that support your client's position and detract from information that can hinder your client's case. Use the active voice and short, succinct sentences to state beneficial facts, and use the passive voice in long, clause-ridden sentences to obscure detrimental information. Keep the facts short. Your audience is a busy, overburdened judge. Select words that are simple and express the facts succinctly. It is not necessary to go into elaborate detail.
3. *Argument:* combines facts and law to show that the motion should be granted. This section of the memo requires time devoted to the pre-writing process. You should carefully assess the purpose of the memo in support of the motion to dismiss. Basically, either you want the entire matter dismissed or you are using the memo to narrow the issues that will arise at trial. Because you can often successfully dismiss one or two counts in a five-count complaint (leaving only three or four counts to contend with at trial) examine your goals carefully. Next, assess the audience. Who is the judge? Has anyone at your firm or legal department ever appeared before him or her? Is it a municipal court, appellate court, or supreme court? Is it a state court or a federal court? How busy is the court? Is the docket overloaded? Select your language, voice, and the length of the document accordingly.

   After performing research and gathering the facts, it is time to outline. This is the most important stage of the pre-writing process. Outline the assertions that you want to make, and prove with the relevant law and facts. Assertions are statements regarding the client's position that you are alleging to be true. The argument is written in ARAC format. ARAC is the acronym for Assertion, Rule, Application, and Conclusion.

   Sometimes a judge focuses most carefully on the beginning of the argument and gets distracted before finishing the memo. Therefore, list your assertions in the following order: The strongest and broadest assertion always comes first, especially if it is supported by case law from the highest court and is on point; the narrowest and weakest assertion is addressed in the last ARAC sequence.

4. *Conclusion:* summarizes the basic arguments contained in your memo, and states the relief you seek.

ILLUSTRATION 12-4. *Memorandum in Support of a Motion to Dismiss*

IN THE CIRCUIT COURT OF MILL COUNTY, ILLINOIS
COUNTY DEPARTMENT, LAW DIVISION

MICHAEL JONES,	)	
	)	
Plaintiff	)	No. 95L 27901
	)	
v.	)	
	)	
GRIMY'S AUTO AND TRUCK SERVICE,	)	
INC., an Illinois Corporation	)	
	)	
Defendant.	)	

DEFENDANT'S MEMORANDUM IN SUPPORT OF
DEFENDANT'S MOTION TO DISMISS

Statement of Facts

On November 28, 1993, the defendant, Grimy's Auto and Truck service, sold a 1984 used truck to Michael Jones for the agreed purchase price of $15,225. Grimy's is in the business of buying, reconditioning, and then selling used trucks. **The purchase agreement was based on defendant's representation that the engine of the truck was completely overhauled and consisted of newly reconditioned parts; that all the parts in the rebuilt engine would be guaranteed and plaintiff would be supplied with invoices for parts purchased to overhaul the engine; that the tractor/trailer was "like brand new" and ready for road use in interstate trucking.** While in possession of the truck, the plaintiff repaired the vehicle on his own and replaced various components, altering the original motor. Furthermore, the plaintiff did not notify the defendant of the defects until two years after they had been discovered. The plaintiff, Michael Jones, alleges that the truck was not in the agreed condition as represented by Grimy's. Jones further alleges that the heads in the truck were old and had not been reconditioned and other parts, including at least two pistons, two rods, two sleeves, and injectors were not new, were defective, and had not been reconditioned. The defendant has moved for an order dismissing the complaint pursuant to § 2-615 of the Illinois Code of Civil Procedure because the plaintiff has failed to state a cause of action.

ILLUSTRATION 12-4. *Continued*

[Read the sentence, above, that is in bold type. This sentence is a good example of how long, complex sentences are used is obscure facts that are not beneficial to your client. The sentence is written in passive voice to obscure facts.]

THE DEFENDANT'S MOTION TO DISMISS SHOULD BE GRANTED BECAUSE PLAINTIFF WAIVED HIS CLAIM FOR BREACH OF WARRANTY OF MERCHANTABILITY BY ACCEPTING THE TRUCK THROUGH HIS CONDUCT AND BY FAILING TO NOTIFY DEFENDANT OF THE DEFECTS IN A TIMELY MANNER

[The caption, above, states the defendant's overall assertion. This is a terse statement of what the defendant is trying to prove.]

Section 2-615 of the Illinois Code of Civil Procedure provides for dismissal of a complaint if it is insufficient in law. 735 ILCS 5/2-615 (1994). Defendant's motion to dismiss, pursuant to § 2-615, alleges that the complaint was insufficient in law because the plaintiff waived his claim for breach of contract.

PLAINTIFF'S CONDUCT CONSTITUTES ACCEPTANCE

[This caption is one component of the caption at the beginning of the argument, and guides the judge through the argument.]

The Uniform Commercial Code states that acceptance of goods occurs when the buyer:

1. after a reasonable opportunity to inspect the goods signifies to the seller that the goods are conforming or that he will take or retain them in spite of their non-conformity; or
2. fails to make an effective rejection, but such acceptance does not occur until the buyer has had reasonable opportunity to inspect them; or
3. does any act inconsistent with the seller's ownership; but if such act is wrongful as against the seller it is an acceptance only if ratified by him.

Ill. Rev. Stat. Ch. 26, ¶ 2-606.

The plaintiff repaired and altered the original engine, indicating that he accepted the truck. If a buyer repairs, alters, or modifies a good he has indicated that he intends to accept the good as his own. *Brule C. E. & E., Inc. v. Pronto Foods Corp.*, 3 Ill. App. 3d 135, 139, 278 N.E.2d 477, 480 (1971). When a buyer rejects a good, yet continues to use it, his actions are inconsistent. The buyer's continued use amounts

ILLUSTRATION 12-4. *Continued*

to a waiver of the right to reject the good and instead signifies acceptance. This type of conduct satisfies the three elements for acceptance as set forth in the Uniform Commercial Code. *Id*. In the instant case, Jones replaced two cylinders and a broken path tube and repaired the shut-down solenoid and the rear lights. The plaintiff has significantly altered the original engine that Grimy's installed in the truck. The plaintiff's act of rejecting the truck after making repeated repairs and changing the original motor is inconsistent. Since Jones altered the truck engine and continued to use the vehicle, he waived his right to reject the truck and instead indicated, by his behavior, his acceptance.

Jones exercised ownership over the truck by making repairs. When a buyer acts in a way in which he would have no right to act unless he was the owner, he has accepted the goods. *Pirie v. Carroll*, 28 Ill. App. 2d 181, 185, 171 N.E.2d 99, 102 (1960). By repairing the engine himself and replacing some of the parts without alerting Grimy's as to the defects, Jones exercised ownership over the truck.

PLAINTIFF FAILED TO GIVE NOTICE OF DEFECT WITHIN A REASONABLE TIME

The plaintiff did not put Grimy's on notice as to the truck's defects until two years after the first mechanical problem was discovered. "A buyer must notify a seller of defects within a reasonable time thereof notwithstanding acceptance." *Stamm v. Wilder Travel Travelers*, 44 Ill. App. 3d 530, 535, 358 N.E.2d 382, 385 (1976). Furthermore, if a buyer fails to reject a good within a reasonable time, acceptance takes place. *Vitromar Piece Dye Works v. Lawrence of London*, 119 Ill. App. 2d 301, 306, 256 N.E.2d 135, 137 (1969). Here, the plaintiff made various repairs and replaced components over a two-year period. The truck was purchased in November 1993 and repairs were made between December 1993 and December 1994. The plaintiff failed to notify Grimy's of any defects until two years after the purchase date. Since plaintiff did not notify Grimy's of defects within a reasonable time he accepted the truck.

PLAINTIFF WAIVED HIS CLAIM FOR BREACH OF WARRANTY OF MERCHANTABILITY

Plaintiff waived his claim for breach of contract because his conduct was inconsistent with his intent to enforce that claim. An individual may waive a known existing right "either expressly or by conduct inconsistent with an intent to enforce that right." *Whalen v. K-Mart Corp.*, 166 Ill. App. 3d 339, 342, 519 N.E.2d 991, 994 (1988). An individual may not seek judicial enforcement after a known right has been relinquished. *Id*. Jones accepted the truck through his actions. Replacing parts on his own and altering the original motor are acts inconsistent with his intent to reject the truck. Since Jones's conduct is inconsistent with his intentions he has waived his right to claim a breach of contract.

ILLUSTRATION 12-4. *Continued*

Conclusion

For these reasons, the defendant respectfully requests that this court issue an order dismissing this complaint for failure to state a cause of action.

Respectfully submitted,

_____

Harry H. Harrison, Esq.
Attorney for the Defendant

How Do You Organize an Argument?

1. Rely on the pre-writing skills addressed in Chapter 3, Getting Ready to Write. Discern the purpose and audience.
2. Determine the client's allegations or assertions. What is the client's assessment of the facts? The attorney assigning the project will provide guidance for the client's legal argument. You should ask the attorney about the arguments that he or she will make on the client's behalf. Once you establish the client's stance (an example of this is the large heading at the beginning of the argument in the memo in support of the motion to dismiss), break this down into components, or elements. The elements are illustrated in the captions in the preceding memo illustration.
3. Research to find relevant and timely legal support for all of your assertions. Remember that the most recent cases from the highest court in the appropriate jurisdiction are at the top of the hierarchy of authority.
4. Outline. Use the ARAC format to apply the law to the facts and draw a conclusion that supports the assertion made.

An outline of the persuasive argument used in the memo in support of the motion to dismiss follows:

Heading: Plaintiff waived his claim for breach of contract by accepting the truck through his conduct and by failing to notify defendants of defects in a timely manner.
 Assertion 1—Jones's actions of repairing the truck's engine demonstrated his acceptance of the vehicle.
 Rule or Rules of law.
 Application: This demonstrates why the rule or rules of law support your assertion in the instant case. Discuss all repairs made with specificity.
 Conclusion: A succinct restatement of your assertion. Always conclude what you assert.

Assertion 2—Jones indicated his acceptance by acting in a manner that was inconsistent with Grimy's ownership of the truck.
Rule or Rules of law.
    Application: Discuss all engine and vehicle parts replaced by Jones.
    Conclusion: Restate the assertion with some additional information to show why you are concluding in this manner.
Assertion 3—Jones failed to give proper notice as to the truck's defects within a reasonable time.
    Rule or Rules of law as to what is a reasonable period of time.
    Application: Discuss the actions Jones took, and the dates on which that they occurred, and when he actually alerted Grimy's as to the truck's defects. Do not draw conclusions but let the facts illustrate the untimely notice. This is the factual foundation where you state the legally significant facts.
    Conclusion: Conclude what you asserted but with more precision. Your conclusion that the notice was not timely will flow logically because your application laid the factual foundation.
Assertion 4—Failure to give timely notice caused Jones to waive his claim for breach of contract.
    Rule or Rules of law: Cases and/or statutes supporting your assertion.
    Application: Lay the factual foundation indicating the length of time between knowledge of the first flaw or defect and when notice to Grimy's was actually given.
    Conclusion: Conclude what you assert but with more precision.

Outlining carefully in the pre-writing stage is an efficient allocation of your time. Writing is much easier once you have carefully outlined the argument. Preparing an after-the-fact outline, that is, outlining an argument that you already wrote, is a good way to revise and to check organization.

4. Trial Briefs

What Is a Trial Brief?

This term is used in two ways. Attorneys file trial briefs to support motions that ask the court to take a particular action. These are essentially memoranda in support of motions. Often, however, attorneys want to explain the reasons why a court should take the requested action. In such cases, attorneys file trial briefs that provide an argument as to why the judge should grant the request. A trial brief is also a document that is provided to a court just before trial. Some briefs are filed with the court. Others are used merely for an attorney's trial preparation, helping attorneys to hone their cases. These briefs may include witness lists, motions to limit evidence (called motion in limine), and stipulations (that is, evidence attorneys are willing to accept as true without proof).

How Do You Draft a Trial Brief or Memorandum in Support of a Motion?

First, research the legal issues. After you have your authorities and the facts of your case, you are ready to outline your brief. Make a list of the legal arguments you plan to address. Prepare a list of the relevant facts. Decide upon an order for your legal arguments. Next, draft the brief or memorandum.

When you begin drafting your briefs, concisely state the purpose of the brief or memorandum and the motion it supports. Next, explain the relevant facts. Summarize the legal arguments that support your request for action. Explain each argument in detail. Be sure to apply the supporting legal authorities to the facts of your case. Next, summarize your arguments. And finally, repeat your request for action.

The procedure for drafting a trial brief that is filed just before trial will vary by court rule.

5. Summary Judgment Motions

What Is a Summary Judgment Motion?

A summary judgment motion asks a trial court to rule in favor of party without a trial. Such a motion is made when the facts are not disputed and the only issue to be decided is a question of law. State and federal courts provide for summary judgment motions. However, some states may combine the motion to dismiss with the summary judgment motion calling in a summary disposition motion.

What Should Be Included in a Motion for Summary Judgment and How Do You Draft One?

A motion for summary judgment should include a brief statement of the purpose of the motion. Next, state the relevant facts. Provide any supporting evidence that is not controverted. For example, if your firm represents the dependant and the plaintiff makes a statement in a deposition that is favorable to your case and there is no evidence to counter that statement, it is uncontroverted. Deposition pages, and often the entire deposition, should be included with the motion, and the deposition pages should be cited in the motion. Check your local rules to determine whenever you are permitted to use pages rather than the entire document. Other evidence such as affidavits often are filed with motions for summary judgment. Once you have stated the facts and told the court that the facts are not disputed, you should begin to explain why the motion should be granted. Explain the legal issues and provide legal authorities that support your argument. Finally, repeat your request that the court grant your motion for summary judgment.

6. Appellate Briefs

Briefs, for trial court and appellate court, are another vehicle for persuasive writing. Appellate court briefs follow detailed rules as to format, structure, and copies required by the particular court. Please check the rules of the particular appellate court where you are filing the brief to find out the requirements. The rules are in the particular jurisdiction's code as well as in many lawyer's desk books.

The parts of the sample brief, which follows, are labeled for your reference. Appellate briefs are very specialized documents written to appeal an error of law made by the trial court. Judges and counsel read these briefs. Many of the same persuasive writing techniques used in drafting memos in support of motions to dismiss are used in drafting appellate briefs. Both documents are persuasive in nature and are formal documents designed to sway a court to rule in your party's favor.

ILLUSTRATION 12-5.   *Sample Appellate Brief*

No. 88 L 2377

IN THE APPELLATE COURT OF ILLINOIS
FIRST JUDICIAL DISTRICT

This is the cover sheet which has the docket number, the parties, the court hearing the appeal, request for oral argument, and counsel's name.

Michael Martin	)	
	)	On Appeal from the Circuit Court of Cook County, Illinois County Department, Law Division
v.	)	
Drake Industries	)	Honorable Sam Smith, Judge Presiding

ILLUSTRATION 12-5. *Continued*

Brief of Appellant

John Johnson, Esq.
12 South Erie
Chicago, Illinois 60000
Attorney for Appellant

Oral Argument Requested

<table>
<tr><td>POINTS AND AUTHORITIES*</td><td></td><td>*This is a table of contents listing the captions and headings as well as the cases, statutes, and other authorities falling under the headings. Paralegals often work on this section.</td></tr>
<tr><td>DRAKE INDUSTRIES IS BOUND BY THE LEASE BECAUSE DRAKE INDUSTRIES ACCEPTED THE LEASE, THUS DRAKE IS A WILLFUL HOLDOVER TENANT AND A TENANT AT SUFFERANCE</td><td>6</td><td></td></tr>
<tr><td>A. Drake Industries Demonstrated Acceptance of the Lease Making It Valid and Binding, Even Though the Lease Was Never Signed</td><td>6</td><td></td></tr>
<tr><td>McFarlane v. Williams, 107 Ill. 33 (1833)</td><td>6</td><td></td></tr>
<tr><td>Housing Authority of the County of Franklin v. Moore, 5 Ill. App. 3d 833, 284 N.E.2d 456 (1972)</td><td>6</td><td></td></tr>
<tr><td>Cuthbert v. Stempin, 78 Ill. App. 3d 562, 396 N.E.2d 1197 (1979)</td><td>7</td><td></td></tr>
<tr><td>Baragiano v. Villani, 117 Ill. App. 372 (1904)</td><td>7</td><td></td></tr>
<tr><td>Henderson v. Virden Coal Co., 78 Ill. App. 437 (1897)</td><td>7</td><td></td></tr>
<tr><td>B. No Notice Was Necessary to Demand Possession of the Property from the Defendant.</td><td>8</td><td></td></tr>
<tr><td>Illinois Compiled Statutes, ch. 735, § 5/9-213 (1994)</td><td>8</td><td></td></tr>
<tr><td>Poppers v. Meager, 148 Ill. 192, 35 N.E. 805 (1894)</td><td>8</td><td></td></tr>
<tr><td>C. Defendant, by Willfully Remaining in Possession of the Property After Expiration of the Lease, Became a Tenant at Sufferance.</td><td>8</td><td></td></tr>
<tr><td>General Parking Corp. v. Kimmel, 79 Ill. App. 3d 883, 398 N.E.2d 1104 (1979)</td><td>8</td><td></td></tr>
<tr><td>D. By Holding Over Possession of the Property, Defendant Could Be Treated as a Holdover Tenant or as a Trespasser.</td><td>9</td><td></td></tr>
<tr><td>Sheraton v. Lewis, 8 Ill. App. 3d 309, 290 N.E.2d 685 (1972)</td><td>10</td><td></td></tr>
</table>

ILLUSTRATION 12-5. *Continued*

No. 88 L 2377

IN THE APPELLATE COURT OF ILLINOIS
FIRST JUDICIAL DISTRICT

This repeats the
information on the
cover sheet.

Michael Martin	)	
	)	On Appeal from the Circuit
	)	Court of Cook County,
	)	Illinois County Department,
	)	Law Division
v.	)	
	)	
	)	Honorable Sam Smith,
Drake Industries	)	Judge Presiding

Brief of Appellant

INTRODUCTION

This is an appeal
from an order
deciding that
Drake Industries
had a month-to-
month tenancy.

ISSUE PRESENTED FOR REVIEW

This is the
question before
the court.

By following all of the terms of the unsigned lease, did the tenant create a valid lease that upon expiration makes a tenant a holdover tenant or a tenant at sufferance?

STATEMENT OF FACTS

These are the facts,
written from the
appellant's
perspective.

Michael Martin appeals from the Circuit Court of Cook County's holding that Drake Industries had a tenancy from month to month. The holding requires that Michael Martin give thirty days' notice to Drake Industries to vacate the premises. Michael Martin appeals from that order.

Michael Martin is the owner of record of the real property and struc-

ILLUSTRATION 12-5. *Continued*

ture located at 2700 North Bosworth, Chicago, Cook County, Illinois. Drake Industries, an Illinois corporation, entered into a lease for Martin's property on January 1, 1975. Terms of the lease called for seven hundred dollars ($700) per month rent until expiration of the lease on December 31, 1986.

In November of 1986, Martin gave a new lease to Drake Industries to be signed and returned by December 31, 1986. The lease specified new terms calling for an increase in the rent to eight hundred and fifty dollars ($850) per month, to be paid on the first day of every month. The lease term was from January 1, 1987 through June 30, 1994. The lease was unsigned and was never returned to Martin. Drake Industries, however, continued its tenancy without interruption, and followed the terms of the new lease, by paying the increased rent on the first day of each month, including July 1, 1994.

Martin made a written demand of the tenant to deliver up and surrender possession of the premises on July 15, 1994. Martin filed an action for forcible entry and detainer against Drake Industries on August 16, 1994, based on their refusal to leave the premises. Martin contended that Drake Industries entered into a valid oral lease that expired on June 30, 1994, and that Drake Industries is now a holdover tenant and a tenant at sufferance.

The trial was held on September 1, 1994, with Drake Industries still in possession of the premises. The trial court determined that a month-to-month tenancy existed between the parties. Martin now appeals from that order.

ARGUMENT

DRAKE INDUSTRIES IS BOUND BY THE LEASE BECAUSE DRAKE ACCEPTED THE LEASE. DRAKE INDUSTRIES IS A WILLFUL HOLDOVER TENANT AND A TENANT AT SUFFERANCE.

> This is the persuasive discussion, or argument. It is written in ARAC format. The headings and captions guide the reader to the points, or assertions, made in the argument.

This court should reverse the trial court's decision finding that Drake Industries has a month-to-month tenancy. Drake Industries demonstrated acceptance of the unsigned lease and willfully held over after the lease term expired.

A. *Drake Industries Demonstrated Acceptance of the Lease Making It Valid and Binding, Even Though Lease Was Never Signed*

Drake Industries accepted the lease and all of its terms. A tenant is bound by the terms of a lease, whether or not the lease is signed, if the tenant accepted the lease. *McFarlane v. Williams,* 107 Ill. 33, 43 (1883);

ILLUSTRATION 12-5. *Continued*

Housing Authority of the County of Franklin v. Moore, 5 Ill. App. 3d 883, 890, 284 N.E.2d 456 (1972). A tenant's occupancy and use of the premises demonstrated an acceptance of the terms of the lease, whether or not the lease was signed. *Cuthbert v. Stemin,* 78 Ill. App. 3d 562, 570, 396 N.E.2d 1197, 1203 (1979); *Housing Authority,* 5 Ill. App. 3d at 890, 284 N.E.2d at 461; *Baragiano v. Villani,* 117 Ill. App. 372, 375 (1904). "By accepting the lease and thus acting upon it, it became valid and binding, and the lessor and lessee were bound by its covenants, although it was not signed by lessee." *Henderson v. Virden Coal Co.,* 78 Ill. App. 437, 442 (1897).

Herein, defendant demonstrated acceptance of the lease by the actions taken, even though the lease was never signed. The lease was tendered to defendant on November 25, 1986, specifying that the term would begin on January 1, 1987, and terminate on June 30, 1994. The lease also specified a rent of $850 per month to be paid on the first day of every month. The lease was never returned to Martin with a signature upon it, but defendant continued occupancy of the premises and complied with the terms of the lease by paying $850 rent on the first day of every month. By following the terms of the lease along with the continued occupancy and use of the premises defendant accepted the lease and all of its terms, making a signature unnecessary.

Defendant also acted upon the lease by paying the rent on the first day of each month. Since defendant accepted and acted upon the lease, the lease became valid and binding and defendant was bound by all the covenants within the lease, even though defendant never signed the lease.

B. No Notice Was Necessary to Demand Possession of the Property from Defendant

No notice to quit or a demand of possession is necessary when the lease term has expired. Martin was not required to give notice and defendants had a duty to surrender possession of the property. When a tenancy is for a certain term, and the term expired, the tenant is then bound to surrender possession and no notice to quit is necessary. 735 ILCS § 5/9-213 (1994). It is the tenant's duty to surrender possession upon expiration of the lease. *Poppers v. Meager,* 148 Ill. 192, 202, 35 N.E. 805, 808 (1894).

Since the defendant accepted the lease and the lease was valid, no notice to quit or demand of possession was necessary upon expiration of the lease. Defendant had a duty to surrender possession of the premises to Martin on June 30, 1994, so no notice was necessary.

C. Defendant, by Willfully Remaining in Possession of the Property After Expiration of the Lease, Became a Tenant at Sufferance

Defendant became a tenant at sufferance after remaining in possession of the premises after the lease term expired. Defendant's possession

ILLUSTRATION 12-5.   *Continued*

can be terminated whenever Martin wished. "A tenant who remains in possession after his lease expires becomes a tenant at sufferance whose possession can be put to an end whenever the landlord wishes." *General Parking Corp. v. Kimmel,* 79 Ill. App. 3d 883, 886, 398 N.E.2d 1104, 1107 (1979). The lease expired on June 30, 1994, and defendant refused to give up possession of the property when Martin demanded possession on July 15, 1994. The tenant, defendant, became a tenant at sufferance at the expiration of the lease; the defendant's possession can be ended at any time the landlord, Martin, desires.

D. By Holding Over Possession of the Property, Defendant Could Be Treated as a Holdover Tenant or as a Trespasser

Defendant, by not surrendering possession of the premises and by willfully holding over, after the expiration of the lease, could be treated as either a holdover tenant or as a trespasser. Martin, as the landlord, can elect to treat defendant as either a holdover tenant or as a trespasser. If a tenant holds over after the expiration of the lease, the landlord can exercise his exclusive right to treat the tenant as a trespasser or permit the original terms of the lease to still be in effect. *Sheraton v. Lewis,* 8 Ill. App. 3d 309, 310, 290 N.E.2d 685, 686 (1972). Herein, defendant held over possession of the premises by remaining in possession after July 31, 1994, even though the lease expired on June 30, 1994. Martin, as landlord, had the option to treat the defendant either as a holdover tenant under the same terms of the previous lease or as a trespasser. Martin elected to treat defendant as a trespasser so defendant is required to relinquish possession of the premises.

CONCLUSION

For these reasons, Michael Martin respectfully requests that this court reverse the trial court's order that the defendant had a tenancy from month to month.

Respectfully submitted,

_____

James Michaels
Attorney for Michael Martin

James Michaels, Esq.
330 Jamestown Avenue
Chicago, Illinois 60001

Are There Any General Tips for Writing an Appellate Brief?

1. Draft the facts using the active voice for beneficial facts, and the passive voice for harmful facts. Rely on short, succinct sentences for emphasis, and long, convoluted sentences to obscure information.

2. Start with the broadest and strongest assertion.

3. Use your strongest case or statute first. Rely on the hierarchy of authority to determine the strength of the source. The newest case from the highest court in the appropriate jurisdiction is stronger than an older case from a lower court.

4. Rely on the ARAC format when crafting the argument. ARAC stands for Assertion, Rule, Application, Conclusion.

5. Always revise your writing. Do an after-the-fact outline to determine if the organization, logic, and flow of the argument is effective.

6. Check the local court rules for the form of the appellate brief for the particular court where you intend to file.

7. Ask to see samples of briefs drafted by members of your firm or legal department.

8. Before filing the brief, always update the validity of your authority by Shepardizing and, in addition, by using Insta-Cite on WESTLAW or AutoCite on LEXIS.

7. Other Forms of Persuasive Writing

Are There Any Instances When Persuasive Writing Is Used in a Transaction?

Contracts and leases that favor one side are persuasive documents. Letters articulating a client's position are persuasive documents. This is particularly the case with demand letters. Default notices and eviction notices are also persuasive documents.

The following is an example of persuasive writing, in letter format, stating a client's position in regard to a partnership agreement. This type of letter, because it reaches legal conclusions and makes representations, must be signed by an attorney but often paralegals participate in the drafting process.

ILLUSTRATION 12-6.   *Sample of Persuasive Writing, Letter Format*

---

1 DuPage National Center
New York, NY 10010

December 19, 1995

Mr. Hal Smith
Cloth & Cloth
33 City Center
New York, New York 10021

Re: Bobbin & Thread Company
        Withdrawal and Distribution Agreement (the "Agreement")

ILLUSTRATION 12-6.   *Continued*

Dear Mr. Smith:

We represent Bobbin & Thread Co. Our client has referred to us the now superseded Liquidation and Distribution Agreement dated as of November 15, 1995, for the Company and your letter of October 27, 1995, describing the above defined Agreement. Mr. Jones, of Bobbin & Thread, believes that consummation of the Agreement will provide substantial financial and tax benefits to the general partners and their affiliated Class B limited partners while providing no real benefit to Mr. Jones and the other Class A limited partners. In light of these concerns, Mr. Jones and the Class A limited partners have asked us to analyze their rights and obligations under the Bobbin & Thread Company Agreement of Limited Partnership dated October 1, 1994, as amended (the Partnership "Agreement").

Having reviewed the Partnership Agreement, we believe that the consent of Mr. Jones and the other Class A limited partners is required before the transactions contemplated by the Agreement can be consummated. We also believe that consummation of the transactions contemplated by the Agreement by the general partners without the consent of the Class A limited partners would constitute a breach of fiduciary duty.

I would be happy to discuss this matter with you at your convenience.

Very truly yours,

_____

Farrell Henry, Esq.

CHAPTER SUMMARY

In this chapter you learned about the nature of persuasive writing and its role in litigation and in transactions. The ARAC formula for drafting a persuasive discussion was explored and examples of persuasive documents were included. Paralegals are becoming more and more involved in writing persuasive documents. Look upon this chapter as a starting point for developing persuasive writing techniques that will become refined with experience.

Key Terms

Answer	Litigation memo
Appellate brief	Motion to dismiss
ARAC	Persuasive writing
Argument	Summary judgment
Brief	Trial brief
Complaint	

EXERCISES

1. Take the discussion portion of an objective memo and reformulate it into persuasive format. Take a position and rewrite the issues and make them assertions.

2. Use the persuasive material that you created in the first exercise, and extract the points and authorities from the document that you drafted. Write the headings and captions to indicate the assertions that you are making, and organize the headings, captions, and authorities into a table of points and authorities like the table included in our appellate brief sample.

3. Draft a letter that articulates a position so that it has a persuasive tone. The following fact pattern will guide you through the process:

> Dr. Jones owns an orthopedic clinic. Ms. Smith received treatment from the clinic following a car accident. Ms. Smith was diagnosed as having whiplash. Ms. Smith has not paid for services she received that were rendered by the clinic. Dr. Jones sent three bills requesting payment. Ms. Smith's response to the final bill is that she should not pay because the accident was not her fault and Mr. Driver should pay because he was at fault. At this point, Dr. Jones retained your firm to help collect the amount owed. Ms. Partner assigned the project of drafting the letter requesting payment from Ms. Smith to you.

4. Find a form for a complaint in your jurisdiction.

5. Where do you find the rules for filing an appellate brief for your jurisdiction?

13. In-House and Objective Client Documents

CHAPTER OVERVIEW

You learned about an objective memorandum in the previous chapters. This chapter discusses other objective documents you may write as paralegals. Paralegals often are asked to write objective summaries of client interviews, meetings, a case's progress, or a deposition. The format for each document will vary. Every attorney and firm has a style it prefers for each document. This chapter will provide some examples of such documents and a few tips for drafting them. Each document should be outlined, drafted, and rewritten before it is submitted to an attorney or placed in a file.

A. Client or Witness Interview Summary

What Is a Client or Witness Interview Summary?

A **client** or **witness summary** is a written record of an interview you conduct with a client or witness. It also might be a summary of an interview an attorney conducts and you attend. It should contain client or witness statements, information about documents an individual brought to the interview, or information about any other tangible evidence that may be relevant to a legal claim, such as photographs, written contracts, receipts, and the like that you learn about during the interview. Your impressions of the client or witness should be prepared on a separate piece of paper to avoid potential disclosure during the discovery process. A witness statement might be discoverable, but your impressions are likely to be protected from disclosure by the **attorney-client privilege.**

The summary of the client or witness statements, documents, or evidence should be **objective;** your impressions could be subjective.

What Questions Should You Ask Yourself Before You Begin to Write?

Before you begin to write your statement, ask yourself: Who, What, Where, When, and Why (the five journalistic "W"s).

1. Client's Statements

For the client statement, consider the following questions:

- Who does the legal question involve?
- What are the circumstances?
- What happened?
- What is the essence of the legal problem?
- What does the client hope to get as a result of speaking with the lawyer or paralegal?
- Where did the problem arise? (Be specific. Note the state, the county, and the municipality, if any. Note any location, such as a home, a store, or the like.)
- When did the problem arise?
- Why is the client seeking legal advice?

If you are summarizing a discussion with an established client, these questions may vary. But this list will provide you with some guidance when you summarize any discussions you might have with a client.

Note the client's statements. If the statements are important, write direct quotations. This will provide an attorney with a feel for the client's statements.

2. Witness Statements

For witness statements, consider the following questions and comments:

- What is the witness's name, address, phone number, date of birth, social security number, and employment record?
- What does the witness know about the incident? What did the witness see? What did the witness hear? If relevant, did the witness smell anything? What other observations did he or she make?

- Describe any documents or evidence in detail. Note where it is located and its condition.
- Finally, provide your impressions of the client or the witness. Does the individual speak clearly? Is the person articulate? Does the person present himself or herself well? Is the individual well dressed and well kept? What is the person's demeanor? Note these comments in a separate paper so that they can be protected by attorney-client privilege and cannot be obtained in the discovery process.

How Do You Draft a Client or Witness Summary?

Next, draft the statement and place it in the file or provide a copy to the assigning attorney. Make a list of the relevant facts. Outline the statement. Often these statements flow best when they are written in chronological order. However, some claims may be presented in topical order. A chronological organization is based upon the order of events. Start with the first event and end with the last. Another method is to write the statement in reverse chronological order, beginning with the last event and ending with the first. For statements related to an accident, a contract dispute, or a criminal case, chronological organization works well. Write the statement clearly and concisely. Only list relevant facts that the witness observed. Use the witness's words and tone.

Illustration 13-1 is a brief statement of a phone conversation.

ILLUSTRATION 13-1. *Summary of a Phone Conversation*

SUMMARY OF A PHONE CONVERSATION WITH KAREN BURNS, ON MARCH 30, 1990

Karen Burns received the affidavit from Mr. Porer, the plaintiff's attorney, and a recorded statement of her conversation with Mr. Porer. She would not sign the affidavit for several reasons. She said that the statement was inaccurate and contained many grammatical errors. She also is upset with Mr. Porer because he misled her as to his relationship with Robert Lewis. Mr. Porer threatened Ms. Burns. He told her that she perjured herself. He also said that she would be subpoenaed for a deposition. He told her that she had been influenced by Matts's lawyers and they had told her what to say. Apparently, Mr. Porer was very irritated that Ms. Burns would not sign the affidavit.

The summary is concise. It communicates the problems the witness had with the opposing attorney and a statement she made to that attorney. This statement simply conveys the witness statements to the attorney. Below, headings are used to guide the reader in the example contained in Illustration 13-2.

ILLUSTRATION 13-2. *Summary of Witness Interview*

MEMORANDUM

To: The File

From: Cara Marcus

Date: March 28, 1995

Re: Summary of Interview with Wanda Weber, on March 28, 1995

BACKGROUND

Wanda Weber, 1001 Arlington Road, Wilmot, IL, is a newspaper reporter for the *Arlington Herald*. She has held that position for five years. On December 20, 1994, she was a patron at the Welcome Matts Hotel in Cancún, Mexico.

DESCRIPTION OF THE ACCIDENT

On December 20, 1994, at about 10 A.M., Ms. Weber saw Drew Cartoon, an old man, reading the newspaper and drinking a cup of coffee as he walked toward the pool area. Cartoon was not watching where he was walking, she said. He then slipped on the marble flooring next to the pool. She saw him hit his head on the floor. Then she saw blood come from his head. He remained conscious and called for help. The hotel staff held fresh-looking napkins from the serving carts against Cartoon's head. The staff called paramedics. The paramedics arrived and took Mr. Cartoon away while he was still conscious.

DESCRIPTION OF THE POOL AREA

Signs were posted at various locations near the pool asking patrons to walk carefully because the floor was wet. The signs also asked patrons to use the mat placed between the coffee shop and the pool. The mat, the signs said, was to ensure the patrons' safe passage from the shop to the pool. The signs were written both in English and in Spanish. Cartoon did not use the mat. Instead, he crossed from the coffee shop to the pool on a diagonal.

OTHER WARNINGS

When Weber checked in, the hotel staff member told her to walk carefully near the pool and to use the matted walkway rather than travel on the wet marble floor. Weber heard the staff tell this warning to other individuals in the check-in area.

CAM:jc

B. Meeting Summaries

As paralegals you will attend many meetings. If you work in the litigation arena, some meetings may include only the defense attorneys, the clients, and you. Other meetings will include co-counsel. In other practice areas, you may attend a client board meeting. An attorney may ask you to take notes during the meeting and then draft an objective summary of the meeting.

What Should Be Included in a Meeting Summary?

A **meeting summary** should explain the primary purpose of the meeting, any issues discussed, and any matters that were mentioned but which will be explored fully at a later date. The summary should note the meeting participants, the venue (if it is significant), and who did not attend. You should include the date of the meeting and the date of any future meetings that were set. If your client or your opponent's client said anything that was extremely important, you might want to write down the quotation of what was said.

How Do You Draft a Meeting Summary?

First, take copious notes during the meeting. Write down each discussion topic. Note who supported and who rejected an issue discussed. Write quotations for any statement you think might be significant to your case or transaction. Second, review your notes. Third, draft an outline of your summary. List the important topics to be included. Next to the topics, include any important statements and note the individuals who supported or rejected those topics. Fourth, draft the summary in sentence format from your detailed outline. Finally, review your summary. Edit it and rewrite it.

Summary Drafting Checklist

1. Take notes.
2. Review your notes.
3. Write a detailed outline.
4. Draft your summary.
5. Review and revise your summary.

Assume that an attorney asked you to attend an Illinois Department of Transportation hearing concerning the widening of a road. The firm's clients are considering litigation to block the street widening. Here is an example of such a meeting summary.

ILLUSTRATION 13-3. *Meeting Summary*

MEMORANDUM

To: Barry Michaels

From: Cara Marcus

Date: November 15, 1995

Re: Meeting Concerning the Widening of Willow Road, September 27, 1995

This meeting was one of two informational sessions the Illinois Department of Transportation (IDOT) recently held to solicit comments concerning the $55 million project to widen Willow Road between Milwaukee Avenue and the Edens Expressway, and to explain the project to the community.

IDOT will review the comments and compile a list by the fall of 1996. Following that, public hearings will be held in the fall or winter of next year. A final decision concerning the project is scheduled for spring of 1997. The department will spend two years developing the final plans and acquiring property. The construction would begin in 1999.

IDOT representatives said that the proposed plan calls for the widening of Willow Road between Milwaukee Avenue and the Eden's Expressway. One through lane is slated to be added to each side of the street. In addition, left and right turn lanes and median strips will be built. At Pfingsten and Willow roads, the proposal suggests that right turn lanes be added at all four corners of Willow Road.

No changes in the turn lanes are expected at Greenwood and Willow roads. Only additional lanes will be added.

Left turn lanes are proposed for Shermer Avenue on both sides of Willow Road. No change will be made to Willow Road at Shermer.

In Northfield, Willow Road may be widened to five lanes. Overpasses or pedestrian-controlled stop lights may be installed to accommodate the children who cross Willow on their way to school.

The project plans include a median strip the entire length of Willow Road. Villages will be asked where openings should be placed. This median will limit the left turn access into the shopping areas and some streets.

The speed limit is expected to remain the same. However, the speed limit along Willow Road near Sanders may be decreased.

To date, $8 million has been approved, but not appropriated by the state legislature. As soon as a final project plan is devised, the $8 million will be appropriated. The legislature then will determine whether to allocate the remaining money needed for the project.

Planners say that the widening of the Willow Road is necessary to

ILLUSTRATION 13-3.   *Continued*

accommodate the tremendous increase in traffic. When IDOT studied the traffic in 1990, it projected a 15 to 20 percent increase in traffic by the year 2010. Recent IDOT studies show that that figure has been exceeded and planners expect traffic to increase by another 15 to 20 percent.

The first paragraph describes the purpose of the meeting and when it was held. The next paragraph explains the status of the project. The remaining paragraphs provide details concerning the plans that were disclosed during the meeting.

C. Status Memos

What Is a Status Memo, and Who Reads It?

A **status memo** is a summary of the progress of a case or transaction. It is a document that is placed in a file, sent to attorneys or other legal team members, or sent to a client. Some clients require status memos. A status memo is especially useful to an attorney or paralegal who may be added to a transaction or case team after a case has started. Such a memo will provide them with information about the background of a case and a history of the action that already has occurred or is about to occur.

How Often Should a Status Memo Be Prepared?

It will vary. Some clients require a status memo each time you appear in court or at a deposition. Some clients require such memos monthly. Attorneys also have varied expectations. Always ask the assigning attorney how often to post such a memo for attorney and client review. You, however, should make a notation in your file each time you work on a case. Such a status memo can be short and simple, such as "Drafted interrogatories to be served on the defendant." If, however, you meet with a client or attend a hearing or deposition, your summary should be more detailed.

What Should the Detailed Summary Include?

The items included will vary depending upon the timing of your draft. For example, your first draft should note what happened and who was involved in the client's matter. Include where and when the case or transaction arose and why your firm is handling it.

ILLUSTRATION 13-4. *Example of a Status Memo for the File*

MEMORANDUM

To: File

From: Randall Arthur

Date: November 7, 1995

Re: Status of the Case

BACKGROUND

This is an action for breach of contract and quantum meruit. At one point, the plaintiff, Nut Services, Inc., sought to collect damages for promissory estoppel. After the defendant's two successful motions to dismiss, plaintiff decided not to refile that claim.

RELATIONSHIP OF THE PARTIES

The action stems from a series of informal transactions between Rock Tube and Conduit Corporation and Nut Services, Inc. in 1993. At one time, Nut Services acted as an "outside cutter" for Rock Tube and Conduit. At some point, Rock personnel gave cutting business to other cutting houses and to its own in-house operation. Nut, which had relied solely on the business from Rock, was devastated and went out of business.

When Ken Kiser, the president and owner of Nut, decided to go out of business, he offered to sell Rock some of his operation's equipment and tools. For several reasons, Rock agreed to some trades.

TED SIMONS'S RECOLLECTION OF THE TRADES

Ted Simons, a former Rock employee, who now works in Rockville, MD, made the deals with Kiser. Simons stated that Rock wanted the used equipment because it could get it without any lead time. Also, most of the equipment was in good shape. Finally, the agreements called for Rock to give Kiser material instead of cash. That material cost Rock much less than the cash value. The material was useless to Rock.

Complaint Count I

Rock offered and paid $20,000 in cash and $15,000 in materials for the saw and all accessories. The requisition for the check asked for

ILLUSTRATION 13-4. *Continued*

$35,000. Kiser signed the purchase order saying $20,000 cash paid, $15,000 in materials owing.

Complaint Count II

Mort Williams, a Rock worker, received many of these items. The plaintiff took his deposition on July 26, 1995. A summary is in the file as is the abstract and a copy of the transcript. Rock received a forklift, four saws, screw drivers, a cart, a drill, and a press.

Rock agreed to trade $10,000 in cash plus steel worth $18,000 to the plaintiff for this equipment. The steel was useless to Rock, but Kiser had a buyer for it. Eventually Rock paid $12,000 because Kiser would not accept the tender of materials. Both Mark Carter and Sidney White say that the materials were tendered. The $12,000 was to settle the equipment purchase.

Complaint Count III

Simons says he never agreed to purchase these items separate from the other equipment. He says that they were part of the earlier materials trade. There is some duplication of items between the lists attached to the complaint.

IMPRESSIONS OF SIMONS

I think that he is telling the truth. He has no reason to lie. He does not want to hurt Kiser because of his long-standing relationship with Kiser.

PLEADINGS

Plaintiff recently filed a third amended complaint. We have filed an answer. To date, we have filed motions to dismiss the previous complaints. The judge dismissed Count II earlier because plaintiff had not sufficiently pled delivery, but he incorporated the deposition into his pleadings this past round and we decided to answer the complaint.

DISCOVERY

Based upon conversations with Mark Carter, Sidney White, and Simons, I prepared the discovery answers. After attorney Cara Marcus reviewed them, they were sent to the client for review and signature. They should be filed soon. I have also prepared our discovery. Cara Marcus has that for review.

The plaintiff has taken one deposition. Discovery will close in January.

ILLUSTRATION 13-4. *Continued*

SETTLEMENT

Ms. Marcus has tried to settle this case several times. First, she offered $10,000 to the plaintiff on behalf of our clients before the lawsuit was filed. Plaintiff formally demanded $30,000. She next offered $7,000. She later increased the offer to $9,000. Plaintiff then wanted $20,000. Ms. Marcus has settlement authority for $20,000, but the client wants the settlement to be closer to $10,000. The attorneys met with the judge though plaintiff's counsel would not settle. However, the judge indicated that trial could be up to two years away. Ms. Marcus recommended that settlement negotiations be stalled because a delay will force the plaintiff to settle.

D. Deposition Summaries

What Is a Deposition Summary?

A **deposition summary** is a variation of a meeting summary. It explains what happened during a specialized meeting called a deposition. For a deposition, an individual is placed under oath and questioned by one or more attorneys. The purpose of the session is to elicit information from the individual that is relevant to the pending court action. The deposition information, called deposition testimony, is transcribed by a court reporter. This transcript may be used during trial instead of a live witness in some cases, or it might be used to contradict statements a witness later may make during trial. The individual being questioned is called the **deponent.** The deposition summary tells the reader what a deponent said, as well as any serious objections that were raised to the testimony. Evidentiary exhibits also might be noted.

When and Why Do You Draft a Deposition Summary, and Who Will Read It?

If you attend a deposition, you may be asked to write a summary of the proceedings. This summary will be read by the assigning attorney. Often it will also be read by other litigation team members and your client. Some insurance companies routinely require defense attorneys to draft a deposition summary after each deposition. The summary is designed to be a quick overview of a deposition.

How Do You Draft a Deposition Summary?

The process for drafting a deposition summary is similar to that of writing a meeting summary. First, take copious notes during the deposition. This is a summary of the deponent's statements. You should not list any independent facts in the notes. In your notes, be certain to write carefully the name of the deponent, his or her age, any addresses the person provides, and any business or organizational affiliation mentioned. Note if the individual is related to any of the parties in the action. Write down each topic. Second, review your notes. Third, draft an outline of your summary. List the important topics to be included. Next to the topics, include any important statements. Fourth, draft the summary in sentence format from your detailed outline. You need not include every statement made. You might find the use of headings will help organize your summary and will assist your reader in locating topics. Finally, review your summary. Edit your summary and rewrite it.

Summary Drafting Checklist

1. Take notes.
2. Review your notes.
3. Write a detailed outline.
4. Draft your summary.
5. Edit your summary and rewrite it.

ILLUSTRATION 13-5. *Example of a Deposition Summary*

MEMORANDUM

To: File

From: Mary Bourn

Date: July 30, 1990

SUMMARY OF DEPOSITION OF MORT WILLIAMS, JULY 26, 1995

Personal Information and Employment

Mort Williams, 65, lives at Rural Route 1, Box 216, Crystal Lake, Illinois. He is currently a supervisor at Rock Wire and Tubing. He has worked for the corporation for 25 years. He currently supervises shipping, receiving, maintenance, and packaging at the Wauconda plant, at 166 South Western. He has been at the Wauconda plant about eight months.

During 1993 and 1994, Mr. Williams was a shop superintendent at the Lake Forest plant.

During that time, Williams could sign requisitions for equipment, but Ted Simons was the individual who could purchase items.

ILLUSTRATION 13-5.   *Continued*

In 1985, Williams traveled to Nut Services' Niles plant three to five times to inspect some saws Rock was considering purchasing. Williams confirmed that Rock bought some saws from Nut. He said he did not know the details of the purchase, such as the price or value of the equipment. Simons was the only Rock person involved in these details.

Rock received from Nut four cold saws, some hand tools, a tool box, blades, a drill, a press, and a forklift.

Next, he reviewed Exhibit 5, which is attached to the Second Amended Complaint. He did not recognize the signature of Ted S. as the signature of Ted Simons. He noted that some items listed in Exhibit 2 duplicated items listed in Exhibit 5.

The court reporter was Mary Kramer of Weston Roads Associates of Lake Forest, IL. Her phone number is 888-2800. Mrs. Crane did not order a transcript at this time as plaintiff did not order a transcript. If the plaintiff's counsel orders a transcript, Mrs. Crane will order a transcript at that time.

E. Deposition Abstracts

What Is the Difference Between a Deposition Summary and a Deposition Abstract?

A deposition summary is a brief explanation of the deposition proceedings. In contrast, the **deposition abstract** details each relevant statement and notes the specific page of the transcript that contains the statement. Some people will refer to deposition abstracts as deposition summaries. However, one is narrative, while the other normally is not.

Who Will Read the Deposition Abstract?

This summary will be read by the assigning attorney. Often it will be read by other litigation team members, new team members, your client, and expert witnesses.

What Is the Purpose of a Deposition Abstract, and When Is It Drafted?

The primary function of the abstract is to assist an attorney in preparing for trial. Some abstracts are prepared immediately after the deposition transcript arrives in an attorney's office. Others, however, are drafted just before trial. Deposition transcripts can be unwieldy. The abstracts provide attorneys with a quick reference to specific topics or statements addressed. This reference facilitates an attorney's trial preparation, especially the development of direct or cross examination of the deponent. In addition, abstracts help in preparing discovery requests, noting additional facts that must be determined before trial, and in finding evidence to submit as part of a summary judgment motion.

What Format Is Used for a Deposition Abstract?

The format will vary by attorney. Ask the assigning attorney if he or she has a preference. Many attorneys ask you to place a short statement following page references. Do not include every item mentioned at a deposition. Routine introductory questions can be omitted. Include the name and address of the deponent, the date of the deposition, the names of the attorneys, and a list of all exhibits. Mention also any questions that have not been answered by the deponent based on advice of counsel and that have been certified.

Some attorneys prefer a chronological format designed to explain the information contained in the deposition based on the timing of the events. Others prefer a topical organization. Some prefer a summary that is done in the same order as the deposition transcript. Such a summary is merely a condensed version of the deposition with the page numbers highlighted. This type of summary works well if any attorney has organized the deposition questions and the deposition has followed the organization. You might follow such a summary with a short index by topic followed by a page number reference. Focus on the responses and not the questions.

How Do You Draft an Abstract?

First, discuss the case with the assigning attorney if you do not know the important case issues. You need to understand the facts and issues of a case before you begin to abstract the deposition. Ask the attorney how detailed the abstract should be. At some large firms, an associate may take a deposition. However, the partner may be the person who will try the case. The partner may need a more detailed deposition because he or she did not question the deponent during the deposition.

When you begin, focus on the issues and facts that are relevant to the case. The deposition abstract should be concise. To be useful, it should not be as lengthy as the original transcript. Paraphrase statements if possible. Be careful to do so accurately and to reflect the comments the deponent made. However, if a statement is made that you deem to be significant, quote it.

Some individuals obtain a copy of the transcript and highlight the sections for abstracting. They then dictate the summaries. Others receive the deposition on disk and edit it for their abstract. This can be a very efficient method.

ILLUSTRATION 13-6. *Example of a Deposition Abstract*

Nut Services v. Rock Tube and Conduit

Abstract of the deposition of Mort Williams,
taken July 26, 1995, pp. 1-62

Page(s)	Exhibit(s)	Summary of Testimony
6-7		Rock cut tubing between 1993 and 1994.
11-13		Williams was shop superintendent at the Lake Forest warehouse until it closed. Then he went to Wauconda as a superintendent.
21		When Williams was the Lake Forest superintendent, he had authority to requisition items for Rock, but could not buy items.
22		Ted Simons was Williams's immediate supervisor. He could approve purchases.
23		Williams first met Ken Kiser at Kiser's business (called Nut) in Palatine in '85 or '86.
27-29		Williams went to Nut three or four times to see equipment.
32		Williams did not know why Nut and Mr. Kiser were selling cutters. He did not know whether Nut was going out of business.
32		Rock bought four saws, which, in 1988, were still used eight hours a day.
35-36		After Nut went out of business, Rock decided to purchase some of Nut's saws and other equipment. It was Ted Simons's decision.
37		Williams did not discuss the purchase price of that equipment with Ted, nor was he involved at any time during this first trip to Nut's plant, or anytime thereafter, in negotiating the purchase price of any of these things.
40		Rock received some hand tools and some big equipment.
41		Williams could not remember everything about the transaction, and he has no list of everything that was agreed to.
42		Mr. Kiser delivered some items and Rock picked up others.

ILLUSTRATION 13-6. *Continued*

Page(s)	Exhibit(s)	Summary of Testimony
45		Williams and Ted picked up hand tools and a tool box. Williams could not remember all of the tools that they picked up.
46		Williams signed some receipts.
48		Williams does not know what the cost of anything was.
	2	Rock received the items on Exhibit No. 2 attached to the Plaintiff's Complaint.
50-52		Williams does not know what the purchase price or value of the items listed on Exhibit 2.
	5	Williams did not recognize the handwriting or signature in the upper right-hand corner of Plaintiff's Exhibit No. 5 for identification that is attached to Plaintiff's Complaint as Addendum A.
53-54		Rock received the forklift.
58-61		Rock also received 40 saw blades, carts, a drill, and a press.
62	2, 5	There may be some duplication between the items on Exhibit No. 2 and those on Exhibit No. 5.

CHAPTER SUMMARY

In this chapter you learned the purpose and some suggested inclusions of information for a variety of objective documents you will draft as paralegals, including summaries of client and witness statements, meetings, depositions, and summaries of a case's progress. In addition, you learned what a deposition abstract is and how to draft one.

Key Terms

Attorney-client privilege   Deposition summary
Client summary   Meeting summary
Deponent   Objective
Deposition   Status memo
Deposition abstract   Witness summary

EXERCISES

1. Draft a summary of the following exchange with the client. *C* is the client and *A* is the attorney.

A: Hello. What can I do for you today?

C: Hi. I am Arthur Lehman. I am here to find out whether I have a case against my neighbor.

A: What happened?

C: My neighbor and I have been fighting for years. His willow tree droops into my backyard and the leaves go into my pool. He doesn't like me because I won't let him swim in my pool. This weekend, I had a pool party. My neighbor decided to cut down the willow tree and let the branches fall into my backyard. One of the big branches hit me on the head. I just got out of the hospital.

A: When did this happen?

C: 7:00 P.M. on Saturday.

A: How did the neighbor cut the tree?

C: With a chain saw.

A: Did the neighbor know you were there?

C: He could hear the party music. He asked me to keep the noise down, and asked how long I was going to have people at the party. I told him I would keep the noise down and that people would be there until midnight. So he knew someone might be under the tree.

A: What time did this conversation take place?

C: 6:30 P.M., when the party was beginning.

A: Did anyone else hear the conversation?

C: Yes. My other neighbor, who was watering her garden. I then asked her to join the party.

A: What is your neighbor's name?

C: Marc Enrico.

A: What about the female neighbor who heard the conversation?

C: Karen Tate.

A: What happened when Mr. Enrico cut the tree?

C: He was in the tree. He was looking at me, then he cut the big branch. It landed on my head. The guests also saw it.

A: What guests?

C: Cindy Wood, Janice Christopher, and Ivan Jones.

A: What happened to you?

C: My guests called an ambulance. I was taken to the hospital. I passed out. They said I had a head injury so they had to keep me overnight. I needed 16 stitches to my face because the branch cut me.

A: How big was the branch?

C: About six feet long and six inches in diameter.

A: What would you like me to do?

C: Sue the creep.

A: We will review your case this week and determine what if any claims we can make. We will also discuss the matter with your witnesses. Then we will call you about it. Our fees . . .

2. Draft a summary of the witness statement. *P* is the paralegal and *W* is the witness, Karen Tate. You spoke with her October 1, 1995.

W: I could hear the party music. I was watering my garden. Then Arthur asked me to join the party.

P: Did you hear Mr. Enrico say anything to Mr. Lehman?

W: Yes. He asked him to keep the noise down, and he asked how long people

W: would be at the party. He was nasty; he told me a minute earlier that he was angry at Arthur because he didn't ask him to join the party.

A: Did he say anything else to you about Mr. Lehman?

W: Yes. He said he would get him to take notice of him and he would get back at him. He said he felt like punching Arthur.

A: What time did this conversation take place?

W: 6:30 P.M., when the party was beginning.

A: Did you see Mr. Enrico cut the tree branch?

W: Yes.

A: What happened when Mr. Enrico cut the tree?

W: He was in the tree. He was looking at Arthur and the other guests and shaking his fists. He yelled, "I'm going to get you Lehman," then he cut the big branch. It landed on Arthur's head.

3. The attorney has determined that there is a claim. You have interviewed the other witnesses. You also have drafted and filed a complaint after you spoke with Mr. Lehman. The attorney signed the complaint. He then asked you to draft interrogatories and to investigate the defendant. Draft a memo to the file concerning these events.

4. Draft a meeting summary for a meeting you attended concerning the rezoning of a residential parcel of land as industrial-class land. The residents oppose the proposal because the land is between two residential developments. The rezoning would allow for an industrial plant to manufacture rubber tires. The subdivisions are old and the neighborhood is not wealthy. The board did not take any action, but plans to on November 10, 1995. The meeting was September 1, 1995. About 200 residents appeared. Another developer has a plan for a strip mall that would benefit the neighborhood.

5. Draft a deposition summary of the following deposition testimony.

STATE OF ILLINOIS   )   SS   Page 1
COUNTY OF COOK   )

IN THE CIRCUIT COURT OF COOK COUNTY
COUNTY DEPARTMENT—LAW DIVISION

JANICE KAHN,   )

)
      Plaintiff   )   No. 96L 219

)

v.   )

)

)

RONNIE RANDALL,   )

)

      Defendant   )

The deposition of Janice Kahn, called by the defendant for examination, pursuant to notice and pursuant to the provisions of the Illinois Code of Civil Procedure and the Rules of the Supreme Court of the State of Illinois, for the purpose of discovery, taken before Christina M. Marks, CSR and Notary Public in and for the County of Cook and the State of Illinois, at Suite 2900, One University Center, Chicago, Illinois, on May 16, 1996, at 10:00 A.M.

Present:

      Robert Marcus and Associates
      By Carol Pinkus
      2 North Wabash St., Suite 7890
      Chicago, Illinois 60602
        appeared on behalf of the plaintiff

      McQuade, Foley and Viner
      By Sarah Lillian
      8 North LaSalle St. Suite 1650
      Chicago, Illinois 60602
        appeared on behalf of the defendant

Witness   Page 2
  Janice Kahn
Examined by Sarah Lillian

No exhibits were marked

| 1. | JANICE KAHN, | Page 3 |

2. having been first duly sworn, was examined and testified as
3. follows:

4.   EXAMINATION
5. by MS. LILLIAN

6.   Q. Let the record reflect that this is the discovery deposition
7.   of Janice Kahn, K-A-H-N, taken pursuant to the Rules of
8.   Civil Procedure of the State of Illinois and the County of
9.   Cook. Mrs. Kahn, my name is Sarah Lillian, and I represent
10.   Mr. Ronnie Randall. I am going to be asking you a series
11.   of questions today about the facts underlying the lawsuit
12.   that you have brought against Mr. Randall. I would like to
13.   give you some instructions before we start. Because the court
14.   reporter has to take down your answers, she has to be able
15.   to hear what you're saying. So a shake or a nod won't do
16.   it. You have to answer out loud, okay?
17.   A. Okay.
18.   Q. If you would like to stop at any time, please let me know

19.		and I will be happy to accommodate you if you need to
20.		take a break. If there is anything that you don't understand,
21.		I would like you to say so and ask me to rephrase the
22.		question or just tell me that you do not understand. If you
23.		do not say so, I am going to have to assume that you under-
24.		stood the question that I'm asking and that you're answer-
25.		ing, okay?
26.	A.	Okay.
27.	Q.	What is your full name?
28.	A.	Janice Lori Kahn.
29.	Q.	Are you married?
30.	A.	No.

1.	Q.	Have you every been married?	Page 4
2.	A.	Yes, to Albert Kahn before he died.	
3.	Q.	When did he die?	
4.	A.	1986.	
5.	Q.	Prior to your marriage to Mr. Kahn, what was your name?	
6.	A.	Janice Lori Winer.	
7.	Q.	What is your address?	
8.	A.	113 Tinkerway, Northbrook, Illinois.	
9.	Q.	How long have you lived there?	
10.	A.	10 years.	
11.	Q.	Do you own your home?	
12.	A.	Yes.	
13.	Q.	Is it a single family residence?	
14.	A.	Yes.	
15.	Q.	Do you have any children?	
16.	A.	Yes. I have a son.	
17.	Q.	What is your son's name?	
18.	A.	Billy Kahn.	
19.	Q.	Is Billy short for something else?	
20.	A.	Yes. William.	
21.	Q.	When was your son born?	
22.	A.	Ten years ago. April 1, 1986.	

1.	Q.	Do you have any other children?	Page 5
2.	A.	No.	
3.	Q.	Are you employed?	
4.	A.	Yes.	
5.	Q.	Where are you employed and what do you do?	
6.	A.	Middleton High School in Crystal Lake, Illinois, as a teacher.	
7.	Q.	How long have you worked there?	
8.	A.	Fifteen years.	
9.	Q.	Were you employed before you began working at Middle-	
10.		ton?	
11.	A.	No.	
12.	Q.	Have you ever been involved in another lawsuit?	

13. *A.* No.
14. *Q.* Not even as a witness?
15. *A.* No.
16. *Q.* Do you recall March 31, 1995?
17. *A.* Yes.
18. *Q.* What happened on that day?
19. *A.* Ronnie Randall struck my son with his car.
20. *Q.* What were you doing when the accident occurred?
21. *A.* Working in my garden. I planted tomatoes, green peppers,
22.   carrots, and broccoli.
23. *Q.* Where is your garden located on your property?
24. *A.* In the front near the street. It is next to a brick wall. I can't
25.   see the garden from my house.

---

1. *Q.* What direction were you facing in your garden?   Page 6
2. *A.* North.
3. *Q.* Does that direction face the street?
4. *A.* No.
5. *Q.* What do you usually do in your garden?
6. *A.* Weed it.
7. *Q.* What were you doing in your garden when the accident
8.   occurred?
9. *A.* Weeding it.
10. *Q.* Where is the street in relation to your garden?
11. *A.* About five feet.
12. *Q.* Where does your son generally play?
13. *A.* In the backyard.
14. *Q.* Where was he playing on the day of the accident?
15. *A.* He was playing t-ball in the front yard.
16. *Q.* Were you watching him at the time of the accident?
17. *A.* Yes. I could see him.
18. *Q.* Did you see the accident occur?
19. *A.* Sort of.
20. *Q.* Did you or did you not see the accident?
21. *A.* I saw my son, who is 10 years old, on the ground covered
22.   with blood and blood all over the front of the Cadillac.
23. *Q.* Did you actually see the driver strike your son?
24. *A.* No. But I know Ronnie hit him. I saw my son next to
25.   Ronnie's car. I heard him swerve.

---

1. *Q.* Did you know the driver?   Page 7
2. *A.* Yes.
3. *Q.* Who was the driver?
4. *A.* Ronnie Randall.
5. *Q.* How did you know him?
6. *A.* We met at a state fair. We dated for 10 years. I broke up
7.   with him two weeks before the accident.
8. *Q.* Did he know your son?

9.   *A.* He knew my son was the most important person to me and
10.   he tried to kill him to pay me back for dumping him.
11.   *Q.* Are you accusing the driver of intentionally striking your
12.   son?
13.   *A.* Yes. He wanted to get back at me so he hit my boy.
14.   *Q.* What happened to your son on the day of the accident?
15.   *A.* He sustained head injuries and several broken bones. He
16.   can't play t-ball for the rest of the season and we had to
17.   cancel our vacation to the Dells because he's been hurting
18.   so much.
19.   *Q.* Was he conscious when you first saw him after the accident?
20   *A.* He was awake but I thought he was dead at first. He had
21.   blood everywhere. I knew the driver, Ronnie, was drunk
22.   when he hit him. He wasn't even looking where he was
             going.
23.   He always swerves down our street to get my attention.
24.   *Q.* Did your son speak to you right after the accident?
25.   *A.* Barely. I told him that Ronnie was speeding and trying to
26.   run him down on purpose. I was horrified to see the blood
27.   and the broken bones. I couldn't move and I was so angry
28.   at Ronnie because I knew he did this on purpose.
29.   *Q.* Did you go to the doctor after this accident?

---

1.   *A.* I went by ambulance with my son to the doctor.   Page 8
         His doctor
2.   looked me over and said I was suffering from shock. Since
3.   then, I can't sleep or eat. I have nightmares about the acci-
4.   dent. I throw up everyday.
5.   *Q.* Have you seen a doctor for your complaints?
6.   *A.* Yes. She said that they are related to the accident. I just
7.   keep thinking back to that day when the neighbor hold me
8.   that Ronnie intentionally turned the wheel to hit my boy.
9.   *Q.* Was your son able to move after the accident?
10.   *A.* Slightly. He looked just like our neighbors' son did after
11.   Ronnie hit him with his car two weeks ago at the same
12.   curve.
13.   *Q.* That is all of the questions I have. Do you have any ques-
14.   tions?
15.   Ms. Pinkus: No.

---

6. Draft a deposition abstract of the above testimony.

14. Letter Writing

A. Basics of Letter Writing
B. Components of a Letter
C. Types of Letters

CHAPTER OVERVIEW

This chapter explains letter writing basics, such as format and types of letters. It provides examples of a variety of letters you might use in practice.

Letter writing is one of the basic tasks you will perform as paralegals. Most letter writing conventions apply to legal correspondence in much the same way as they do to other business communications. Paralegals should be aware of the components of basic letters as well as some special rules for legal communications.

A. Basics of Letter Writing

What Format Should You Use?

Firm style or personal taste generally determines the format of your letters. The formats are **full block, block, modified block,** and **personal style.** In a full block letter, you do not indent the paragraphs. The paragraphs, the complimentary close, and the dateline are flush left. See Illustration 14-1.

For block format, all paragraphs and notations are flush left, except for the date, the reference line, the complimentary close, and the signature lines which are just right of the center of the page. See Illustration 14-3. In a modified block style letter, the first line of each paragraph is indented about five characters. See Illustration 14-6. In a personal style letter, often written to friends, the inside address is placed below the signature at the left margin.

251

B. Components of a Letter

What Basic Components Should a Letter Include?

A letter is divided into several sections: the date, the name and the address of the addressee called the inside address, a reference line, a greeting to the addressee, the body of the letter and the complimentary closing.

You should draft the first page of a letter on firm letterhead. The **letterhead** is the portion of the firm's stationery that identifies the firm, generally the attorneys and sometimes the firm's paralegals. It usually includes the firm's address and its telephone and facsimile numbers. Additional pages should not carry the firm letterhead but should be placed on matching paper with a **header** on each page. The header identifies the letter and is generally placed on the top right side of the page. A header includes the name of the addressee, the date, and the number of the page:

Cheryl Victor
November 15, 1994
Page Two

What Date Is Noted on the Letter, and Where Is It Placed?

The **date** should be placed at the top of the letter just below the firm's letterhead. The date is one of the key components of a letter concerning any legal matters. Date the letter with the same date as the date of mailing. This date can be crucial in determining a time line in a legal proceeding. Timing in sending documents and correspondence is often important in legal transactions and litigation matters. Therefore, be careful to include the date of mailing rather than the date of writing the letter. For example, if you prepare a letter on July 4 after the last mail pickup, you should date the letter July 5 because that is the date it would actually be "mailed." This may seem like a purely technical distinction if you put the letter in the mail on July 4. However, some court cases and negotiations turn on the date of mailing.

Should You Note How the Letter Was Sent?

If the letter is being sent by a method other than U.S. mail, it should be indicated on the top of the address and then underlined as follows:

<u>Via Facsimile and U.S. Mail</u>
Cheryl Victor
Vice President
Arizona Money Makers
1000 Tempe Road
Phoenix, Arizona 85038

This notation should start at least two lines below the date. See Illustration 14-1.

ILLUSTRATION 14-1. *Full Block Letter*

---

[1]Fuzzwell, Cubbon and Landefelt
888 Toledo Road
Ottawa Hills, Ohio 43606
(419) 535-7738

[2]November 7, 1985

[3]<u>Via Federal Express</u>

Mr. Stuart Shulman
Navarre Industries
708 Anthony Wayne Trail
Maumee, Ohio 45860

[4]Re: Settlement of <u>Kramer v. Shulman</u>

[5]Dear Mr. Shulman:

[6]I have enclosed a copy of the settlement agreement that we drafted and that has been signed by Mr. Kramer. Please sign the agreement and forward it to me at the above address by November 30, 1985.

If you have any questions, please feel free to call me at 535-7738.

[7]Sincerely,

Mara Cochran
Legal Assistant

[8]cc: Randall Fuzzwell
[9]Enc.
[10]MAC/wlk

---

    1. Letterhead
    2. Date
    3. Recipient's address and method of service
    4. Reference line
    5. Greeting
    6. Body of the letter
    7. Closing
    8. Carbon copy notation
    9. Enclosure notation
   10. Initials of drafter/typist

How Should the Inside Address Read?

The next part of the letter, the **inside address,** should contain the name of the person to whom the letter is addressed, the individual's title if he or she has one, the name of the business if the letter is for a business, and the address.

What Is a Reference Line?

The **reference line** is a brief statement regarding the topic of the letter. For example, if the letter concerns a contract for the sale of a particular property, your reference line would say:

Re: Sale of 2714 Barrington Road, Toledo, Ohio.

Some firms and corporations ask that the reference line contain a client number, claim number, or case number, so investigate your firm's style.

What Type of Greeting Should Be Used?

In general, your **greeting** depends on how familiar you are with an individual. An individual whom you do not know should be addressed as "Dear Ms. White." If you know an individual well, you may address that person by first name. If you are uncertain whether to address the individual by first name, use a title and the individual's last name. If you are addressing a letter to a particular person, such as the custodian of records, but you do not know the person's name, try to determine the person's name. If necessary, call a company or agency to determine the appropriate recipient for the letter. Your letter is more likely to be answered quickly if it is addressed to the appropriate person rather than "To whom it may concern."

How Do You Write the Body of the Letter?

The **body of the letter** follows the greeting and should begin with an opening sentence and paragraph that summarizes the purpose of the letter. Draft the body of the letter carefully. Outline the letter before writing it to be sure that you address all of the necessary points. List each point you want to cover. For Illustration 14-1, your outline might read as follows:

1. enclose settlement agreement
2. ask for signature and return date
3. ask addressee to call if he has questions

Consider your audience. If you are writing to a layperson who is unfamiliar with the law, explain any legal terms you use. However, do not provide any legal opinions. If you are addressing your letter to an individual who is familiar with the law, such as a judge, a paralegal, an in-house counsel, or an attorney, you do not need to explain such terms. To do so might be considered condescending.

How Should You End a Letter?

End the letter by inviting a response, such as "Please do not hesitate to call if you have any questions," or by thanking the addressee for assistance, such as "Thank you in advance for your cooperation." Finally, end the letter with a complimentary closing such as "Sincerely," "Very truly yours," or "Best regards" placed two lines below the final line of the body of the letter. Your name should be placed four lines below the closing to allow for a signature. You should include your title, that is, paralegal or legal assistant.

Do not provide legal advice in your letter or represent yourself as an attorney. Ethical codes and state laws prohibit paralegals who are not licensed to practice law from providing legal opinions or from representing themselves as attorneys. To avoid any confusion or possible misrepresentation, include your title after your name when you write a letter.

How Do You Indicate That You Are Sending a Copy of a Letter to Another Person?

If you are copying a third party on the letter and want the original addressee to know this, note it with a "cc" at the bottom left margin of the letter following the closing. The cc indicates **carbon copy** sent to the person listed. (Although photocopies have replaced carbon copies, cc is still used.) Indicate to whom a copy of the letter was sent as: cc: Mike Sterner. If you do not want the original addressee to know that you copied a letter to another person, note on the draft or file copy bcc, which means **blind carbon copy**. That notation should only appear on the draft or file copy of the letter and not on the recipient's letter. See Illustration 14-2.

The next notation is for enclosures, such as court orders, contracts, or releases. Place the abbreviation **Enc.** or **Encs.** at the bottom left margin of the letter. See Illustration 14-1.

Finally, the letter should note your initials in all capital letters as the author of the letter and then the initials in lowercase letters of the person who typed the letter. If your initials are RAS and the typist's are HVS, then the notation under the enclosure or cc notation would read: RAS/hvs.

ILLUSTRATION 14-2. *Letter Confirming Deposition*

Law Offices of Sam Harris
2714 Barrington Road
Findlay, Ohio 45840
(419) 267-0000

January 28, 1991

Ms. Karen Dolgin
2903 W. Main Cross Street
Findlay, Ohio 45840

Re: Deposition of Robert Harrold
    Harrold v. Sofer

Dear Ms. Dolgin:

This letter is to confirm our conversation today in which you stated that you will present the plaintiff, Robert Harrold, for a deposition at the law office of Sam Harris, 2714 Barrington Road, in Findlay, on March 18, 1991, at 2 p.m. This deposition is being rescheduled at your request because the plaintiff had a family commitment set for February 15, 1991, the date originally set for the deposition.

If you have any questions or additional problems, please feel free to call me at (419) 267-0000, extension 608.

Best regards,

Craig Black
Paralegal

cc: Sam Harris
    Wally Sofer
CMB/klm

C. Types of Letters

What Types of Letters Do Paralegals Write?

Paralegals write letters to clients to confirm deposition dates, meeting dates, hearing dates, or agreements. These letters are called **confirming letters**. Other letters provide a **status report** of a case or summarize a transaction. Some letters accompany documents, such as those for document productions, contracts, or settlement releases. These are called **transmittal letters**. Still others are **requests for information**. Some letters explain the litigation process to clients. See Illustration 14-3.

ILLUSTRATION 14-3. *Letter Concerning Deposition Schedule*

Law Offices of Sam Harris
2714 Barrington Road
Findlay, Ohio 45840
(419) 267-0000

January 28, 1991

Wally Sofer
Chief Executive Officer
1000 Hollywood Way
Houcktown, Ohio 44060

Re: Deposition of Wally Sofer
<u>Harrold v. Sofer</u>

Dear Mr. Sofer:

This letter is to advise you that you are required to submit to a deposition by the plaintiff's attorney at 10 a.m. on March 1, 1991, at the law office of Karen Dolgin, 2903 W. Main Cross Street in downtown Findlay. During this deposition, the plaintiff's attorney will ask you questions related to the above-referenced court case, and you will provide answers while under oath and in the presence of a court reporter. Mr. Harris also will be present to represent you during the deposition.

Mr. Harris and I would like to meet with you at least once before the deposition to discuss your case and this important part of your case.

I will call you Wednesday to schedule an appointment next week to prepare for your deposition.

Please bring any accident reports, citations, or other documents that relate to the accident if you have not already provided them to our office.

I look forward to speaking with you this week.

Sincerely,

Craig Black
Paralegal

cc: Sam Harris
CMB/klm

What Are Confirming Letters?

Confirming letters reaffirm information already agreed to by you and the recipient. It is a good practice to follow up any conversation with a client or an opposing attorney or paralegal with a confirming letter that summarizes the conversation, any agreements made, or any future acts to be accomplished. See Illustration 14-2. For example, after you discuss a document production with a client and set a meeting date to review the records, send a letter summarizing the conversation. Such confirming letters provide you with a reminder of the conversation and allow anyone who reviews the file later to know what you and the client discussed should you be unavailable.

If opposing counsel has agreed to produce documents or provide a witness for a deposition at a particular time, write a confirming letter to the opposing counsel summarizing these facts and asking to be contacted if there are discrepancies. Whenever a deposition is rescheduled or continued, it is imperative that a confirming letter be sent to avoid future discovery disputes. Whenever your client is deposed, send him or her a copy of the deposition for review. A sample of such a letter is found in Illustration 14-4.

What Are Status Letters and Transaction Summary Letters?

Often you will be asked to provide a status report of a case, especially to insurance companies and other clients. See Illustration 14-5. These letters provide clients with an overview of the current activities in a court case, transaction, or other legal matter.

Transaction summary letters often follow a business transaction such as a real estate closing. In these letters, you summarize a transaction.

In other letters, you will request information, often from the custodian of records. See Illustration 14-6.

Often you will be responsible for coordinating document productions. Illustration 14-7 shows a sample letter to a client concerning a request to produce documents.

Many letters will be written to accompany documents, releases, and checks. See Illustrations 14-8 and 14-9.

What Is a Demand Letter?

A **demand letter** is a letter that states your client's demands to another party. A common letter paralegals write is a demand letter that seeks to collect debts. Such a letter may need to comply with the requirements of your state's fair-debt collection laws. See Illustration 14-10.

ILLUSTRATION 14-4.   *Letter Enclosing Deposition Transcript*

Law Offices of Sam Harris
2714 Barrington Road
Findlay, Ohio 45840
(419) 267-0000

July 11, 1991

Mr. William Gary
709 Franklin Street
Findlay, Ohio 45840

Re: Deposition on July 8, 1991

Dear Mr. Gary:

Enclosed is a copy of the transcript of your July 8, 1991, deposition. Please review the transcript carefully and note any statements that were incorrectly transcribed. You may not rewrite your testimony, but you should note any inaccurate transcriptions. You may correct the spelling of names and places. If you find any serious mistakes, please call me to discuss these problems.

When you review the deposition, please do not mark the original transcript. Instead, note any discrepancies on a separate sheet of paper. Please note the page and line of any discrepancies. I will have my secretary type a list of the discrepancies, and we will discuss these changes before we send them to the court reporter. These changes must be received by the court reporter within 30 days; therefore, I would appreciate your prompt review of the transcript and would like to review your changes by July 30, 1991. If we fail to provide the changes to the court reporter within 30 days, we will forfeit your right to correct the transcript and any inaccuracies will be part of the record.

If you have any questions, please do not hesitate to call me.

Thank you for your cooperation in advance.

Best regards,

Daniel Blanchard
Paralegal

Enc.
DBB/jas

ILLUSTRATION 14-5. *Status Report Letter*

Cosher, Cosher and Snorer
960 Wyus Boulevard
Madison, Wisconsin 53606

June 12, 1985

Mr. Cal L. Medeep
Pockets Insurance Company
10 Wausau Way
Wausau, Wisconsin 54401

Re: Kelsey v. Cocoa
      Your claim number: C100090888

Dear Mr. Medeep:

This letter is to provide you with a status report concerning the progress of the above-referenced matter. To date, we have requested that the plaintiff answer interrogatories and requests for admissions. I sent a copy of these requests to you about a week ago. The plaintiff is required to answer these requests within 30 days. We will send you a copy of the plaintiff's answers as soon as we receive them. We are scheduled to depose the plaintiff on September 1, 1985.

The plaintiff's attorney is scheduled to depose a representative of Oreo Company on October 13, 1985.

At this time, the court has not scheduled a settlement conference, but is likely to do so before the end of the year.

Please feel free to call if you have any questions.

Sincerely,

Karen Thompson
Legal Assistant

KLT/yml

ILLUSTRATION 14-6.   *Request for Information*

Cosher, Cosher and Snorer
960 Wyus Boulevard
Madison, Wisconsin 53606

August 12, 1995

Carol Jennings
Custodian of Records
Federal Deposit Insurance Corp.
9100 Bryn Mawr Road
Rosemont, Illinois 60018

    Re: Freedom of Information Act Request

Dear Ms. Jennings:

    Based on the Freedom of Information Act, 5 U.S.C. § 552 et seq., I am requesting that your agency provide copies of the following:

    Each and every document that relates to or refers to the sale of the property located at 2714 Barrington Road, Glenview, Illinois 60025.

    The documents should be located in your Rosemont, Illinois, office.

    Under the act, these documents should be available to us within ten days. If any portion of this request is denied, please provide a detailed statement of the reasons for the denial and an index or similar statement concerning the nature of the documents withheld. As required by the act, I agree to pay reasonable charges for copying of the documents upon the presentation of a bill and the finished copies.

    Thank you in advance for your cooperation in this matter.

Sincerely,

Carolyn Wentworth
Paralegal

CAW/dag

ILLUSTRATION 14-7. *Request to Produce Documents*

Carthage, Katz and Kramer
1001 B Line Highway
Darlington, Wisconsin 53840

February 28, 1994

Ms. Karen Taylor
Carrots and Critters Corp.
1864 Merrimac Road
Sylvania, Ohio 43560

Re: Carrots and Critters v. Rabbits and Rodents

Dear Ms. Taylor:

Enclosed please find a request from the defendants asking you to produce documents. The date scheduled for the production of these documents is April 1, 1994. Some documents may be protected from disclosure because they may contain confidential trade secret information, and others may be protected because they are communications between you and your attorney or the result of your attorneys' work. We must respond in writing by March 25, 1994, in order to raise any of these claims.

As we must review the documents to determine whether any documents are protected, we should compile the documents no later than March 15, 1994. This will allow us time to review, to index, and to number each document.

I will be available to assist you in gathering documents to respond to this request. I will call you this week to schedule an appointment.

If you have any questions, please feel free to call.

Sincerely,

Eileen Waters

Encs.
EDW/jnn

ILLUSTRATION 14-8.   *Letter Accompanying Document*

David, Randall & Henry
1600 Thirteenth Street
Wilmette, Illinois 60091

March 4, 1994

Frank J. Nustra
Lake County Recorder of Deeds
18 N. County Street
Waukegan, Illinois 60085

Re: 1785 Central Street
    Deerfield, Illinois 60015

Dear Mr. Nustra:

Enclosed please find two original quit claim deeds, one dated December 30, 1993, and one dated January 2, 1994, relating to the above-referenced property. Both deeds have been marked "exempt" from state and county transfer tax. A check for $50.00 to cover the recording fees ($25 each) is enclosed. Please record these deeds at once and return the originals to Karen Smith at the 1785 Central Street address.

Thank you for your assistance.

Sincerely,

Jennifer Lauren
Legal Assistant

Encs.
cc: Karen Smith
JML/jch

ILLUSTRATION 14-9. *Letter Accompanying Check*

Hellman & Fernandez
Central and Carriage Way
Evanston, Illinois 60202

April 22, 1994

Karen Donohue
Chicago Bar Association
124 Plymouth Court
Chicago, Illinois 60611

Re: Commercial Real Estate Contract Prepared by the Real Property
    Law Committee

Dear Ms. Donohue:

Enclosed please find a check for $30.00 to cover the mailing fees and
the cost of a copy of the Real Estate Contract referenced above. Please
send me a copy of the contract at your earliest convenience.

Thank you for your cooperation.

Sincerely,

Mark Taylor
Paralegal

Enc.
cc: Rachel Kramer
MCT/ear

What Should Be Included in a Demand Letter?

In a demand letter, you should include the fact that your firm
represents the creditor or other client, as well as the client's desire
for full payment of the claim. Specify the amount demanded or state
the action sought, and ask the debtor either to make payment or to
contact your office within a certain number of days. Then state the
action that the firm will take if the demand is not met within the
specified time period.

ILLUSTRATION 14-10. *Demand Letter*

Law Office of Sam Harris
145 Water Street
Madison, Wisconsin 53606

April 1, 1995

Carolyn Wehre
889 Barrington Road
Middleton, Wisconsin 53608

Re: Furniture Crafters Account 4155

Dear Ms. Wehre:

Our office represents Furniture Crafters in the collection of the $468.00 debt due on the above-referenced account. Furniture Crafters request that you pay the full amount of the debt, $468.00 immediately.

You must pay this amount in full or contact our firm at the above telephone number or address within seven days. If we do not hear from you within seven days, we will proceed to court in this matter.

Sincerely,

Marcia Bottoms
Paralegal

MAB/hvs

Rules for Letter Writing

1. "Never give legal advice" is the first rule of letter writing for paralegals.
2. Be informative.
3. Consider your audience. If you are addressing a client, do so courteously and at a level that the client will understand. If you were asked to answer a client's questions, be sure that you do. You should always be respectful to the addressee.
4. Choose your words carefully. You want to make certain that your words express what you intend.

CHAPTER SUMMARY

Letter writing is an essential part of your daily routine as a paralegal. Most letter writing conventions apply to legal correspondence in much the same way as they do to other business communications. However, paralegals should be careful about dating letters concerning legal matters. Letters should be dated with the date of mailing, which may or may not be the date of drafting.

A letter should contain a date, the name and address of the addressee, a reference line, a greeting to the addressee, the body of the letter, and the complimentary closing.

Confirming letters reaffirm information already agreed to between you and the recipient. Status letters provide an up-to-date review of the process of a pending matter. Transaction summary letters explain particular transactions. Letters also are written to accompany documents, such as releases and checks.

As with any written document, letters should be outlined, written, and then rewritten if necessary.

Key Terms

Blind carbon copy (bcc)	Header
Block letter	Inside address
Body	Letterhead
Carbon copy (cc)	Modified block letter
Confirming letter	Personal style
Date	Reference line
Demand letter	Requests for information
Enclosure line	Status report
Full block letter	Transmittal letter
Greeting	

EXERCISES

Prepare the following letters as if you are a paralegal with the law firm of Snorer, Hackett and Blank, 1000 Madison Way, Madison, Wisconsin 53606. Addressee names are identified for you, but you may supply each one's address yourself.

1. Write a letter to Madison Insurance Corporation explaining that your law firm will be representing Carol White for a lawsuit against its insured, Harold Watson, stemming from an automobile accident that occurred on September 1, 1994. The Madison claims adjuster is Howie Mark. Harold Watson's insurance policy number is 1280. You once had a difficult time dealing with Mr. Mark and Madison Insurance in the past, so you send your letter by certified mail. Enclose a copy of the police report. Send a blind copy to your client. You write it at 5 P.M. on December 24. You realize that December 25 is a holiday and that mail will not go out until the next day.

2. Your firm represents a client, Karen Taylor, who sustained a neck injury during an automobile accident between Carter McLaughlin and Robert Carroll. Write a letter to Dr. Wendell Martin asking for a detailed

report concerning the present and future medical problems of that client. Dr. Martin is an orthopedic surgeon. Indicate that you have a signed release from the client to enclose.

3. Your firm represents Margaret Weston in a divorce case. Write a short letter to her informing her of the final hearing date in her divorce case. The date is June 16, 1994, in Lucas County Domestic Relations Court, 900 W. Adams Street, Toledo, Ohio 43602.

4. Your client needs to give testimony at a deposition on November 15, 1994, at 10 A.M. at your offices. Please draft a letter asking William Hesse to be at the deposition. Explain to him that you will meet with him in advance to discuss his testimony.

5. Your firm has just settled a case involving Karen Douglas and your client, the Wentworth Industries in Morristown, New Jersey. The case was settled for $88,000. The Wentworth corporation paid Douglas for injuries she sustained when she fell at a Mexican hotel. You do not want to admit any liability in your letter or admit any ownership interest in the Mexican hotel, the CanCan. You merely want to tender the check to Douglas in full satisfaction of any claims she or her husband have against Wentworth. You also have the signed settlement agreement to send her and the court dismissal of the action.

Appendix. Bluebook Citation

The Bluebook is the guide to citation form for all legal documents, whether office memos or Supreme Court briefs. The Bluebook, formally known as the *Uniform System of Citation, Sixteenth Edition*, governs because of convention and tradition rather than by the mandate of the state legislature. Other forms of citation have been developed, like the University of Chicago Maroon Book, but the Bluebook is so entrenched in custom and usage that it is hard to replace. New forms of citation are emerging due to the advent of nonproprietary cases in which the case is not attributed to a publisher. Generally, the Bluebook is the bible for citation format for all legal personnel. If ever in doubt as to citation format, rely on the Bluebook.

What Is a Citation?

A citation is really an address indicating where the cited material can be found so that anyone reading your document can find the material if they want to. The abbreviations must be consistent so that everyone knows what they mean. We rely on a similar convention with street addresses and postal abbreviations. The abbreviation for avenue is Ave.; the postal abbreviation for New York is NY.

What Documents Are Cited?

Any source of authority that you discuss in any legal document is cited. Any concept or idea that is not your own must be cited; this is called attributing authority to your ideas. Citing credits the source from which the idea or legal rule came. It also tells the reader where she can find the original source. Citations are used for all authority, whether it is primary authority like a case or a statute, or secondary authority like a treatise or a law review article. Also cited are looseleaf services, practitioners' materials, and newspaper articles.

The Bluebook has two citation formats, one for briefs and memos and the other for law review articles. Paralegals rely on the brief and memo format for citation.

What Are the Components of a Citation?

Generally the components of a cite are the name of the particular document, the volume or title where the document is located, the name of the publication that contains the document, and the specific page, section, or paragraph where the document is found. Also included is the year that a case was decided or the publication date of a book or volume of statutes. For example:

Jacobs v. Grossman, 310 Ill. 247, 141 N.E. 714 (1923)

The name of the document is the case name, *Jacobs v. Grossman*. Parallel citations are given in the example so that you can find the case in both sources, the official reporter that is always mentioned first and the unofficial reporter, mentioned second. The first number preceding the reporter abbreviation is the volume number of the reporter. Next is the reporter abbreviation and then the page number where the case begins in the reporter. The year that the case was decided is included in parentheses. Bluebook Table T.1 lists reporter abbreviations.

Using the Bluebook takes practice. The Bluebook is organized by rules. Each rule details the citation format for each type of document. The index is very helpful in finding specific references to the citation format for an individual document like a statute, an administrative regulation, or a law review article.

The following portion of the appendix provides examples of the materials mentioned in the book and sample cite formats based on the Bluebook. These examples will help you navigate your way through the Bluebook. If the illustration here does not provide adequate information, you can turn to the Bluebook rule mentioned to obtain more detailed treatment.

How Are Slip Opinions Cited?

Slip opinions are cited according to Bluebook Rule 10.8.1. You should provide the docket number, the court, and the full date of the most recent disposition of the case.

slip opinion cite:	Gillespie v. Willard City Board of Education, No. C87-7043 (N.D. Ohio Sept. 28, 1987)
with page cite:	Gillespie v. Willard City Board of Education, No. C87-7043, slip op. at 3 (N.D. Ohio Sept. 28, 1987)

How Do You Cite a State Case?

Cite a state case according to Bluebook Rule 10. The first example below shows the citation for an Illinois case cited in a brief prepared for an Illinois Supreme Court case. The second example shows the same case cited in a brief to the United States District Court for the Northern District of Illinois.

Ill. Sup. Ct. brief:	Thompson v. Economy Super Marts, Inc., 221 Ill. App. 3d 263, 581 N.E.2d 885 (1991)
U.S. Dist. Ct. brief:	Thompson v. Economy Super Marts, Inc., 581 N.E.2d 885 (Ill. Ct. App. 1991)

When you use a state decision in a memorandum or a brief, always include the regional citation. See Bluebook Table T.1. If you are citing a state case to a state court in which the case was decided, provide both the official citation, if one exists, and the regional citation, as the first example above shows. Always list the official citation first. When you cite a state case in a memorandum addressed to a federal court or to a court of a state different from the state that decided the case, include only the regional citation as the second example above shows. If you are only using the regional citation, remember to place the abbreviation for the deciding court in parentheses. See Bluebook Rule 10.4.

How Would You Cite Decisions Found in the *Federal Reporter* or the *Federal Supplement*?

Bluebook Rules 10.1-10.6 and Table T.1 provide detailed coverage of the citation format for cases from the *Federal Reporter* and the *Federal Supplement*. The case name is placed first and underlined. Next place the volume number. The reporter abbreviation is next. For the *Federal Reporter*, the abbreviation is "F." The number of the series, second or third, should be placed next to the "F." For the *Federal Supplement*, the reporter is abbreviated "F. Supp." The page number follows the abbreviation for the reporter. Next, place an abbreviation denoting the appropriate court and the date of the decision. Be certain to include a geographic designation for the district courts.

Federal Reporter case:	Zimmerman v. North American Signal Co., 704 F.2d 347 (7th Cir. 1983)
Federal Supplement case:	Musser v. Mountain View Broadcasting, 578 F. Supp. 229 (E.D. Tenn. 1984)

How Would You Cite a Decision Found in the *Federal Rules Decisions* Reporter?

The abbreviation for the *Federal Rules Decisions* is F.R.D. A case would be cited according to Bluebook Table T.1 as follows:

Barrett Industrial Trucks, Inc. v. Old Republic Insurance Co., 129 F.R.D. 515 (N.D. Ill. 1989)

How Would You Cite a U.S. Supreme Court Case?

Once a U.S. Supreme Court case is published in an advance sheet of the *U.S. Reports,* the *U.S. Reports* citation, and only the *U.S. Reports* citation, is the proper citation. Do not include parallel citations. See Rule 10 generally and specially see Rule 10.4 and Table T.1.

| correct: | Erie Railroad Co. v. Tompkins, 304 U.S. 64 (1938) |
| incorrect: | Erie Railroad Co. v. Tompkins, 304 U.S. 64, 58 S. Ct. 817, 82 L. Ed. 1188 (1938) |

However, if a Supreme Court opinion has been published in the *West Supreme Court Reporter* but yet not in the *U.S. Reports*, the *Supreme Court Reporter* citation should be used. See Table T.1.

If a Supreme Court opinion has not yet been published in *U.S. Reports, Supreme Court Reporter,* or *U.S. Reports, Lawyer's Edition,* then you should cite to *United States Law Week.* See Table T.1. The court designation, U.S., should be placed in the parentheses with the full date. See Bluebook Rules 10.4 and 10.5. The citation would read as follows:

UAW v. Johnson Controls, Inc., 59 U.S.L.W. 4209 (U.S. Mar. 20, 1991)

How Would You Cite a Case a Second Time, After It Has Already Been Cited in Full?

You do not need to repeat a case citation in full each time it is used. After you have cited a case in full, the Bluebook permits you to use the following short forms, all of which omit the date and court:

full citation:	Thompson v. Economy Super Marts, Inc., 221 Ill. App. 3d 263, 266, 581 N.E.2d 885 (Ill. Ct. App. 1991)
short citation:	Thompson v. Economy Super Marts, Inc., 221 Ill. App. 3d at 266, 581 N.E.2d at 889
short citation:	Thompson, 221 Ill. App. 3d at 266, 581 N.E.2d at 889

Another acceptable short form is similar to the above samples, except that the name is omitted:

221 Ill. App. 3d at 266, 581 N.E.2d at 889.

This form should be limited to references that are near each other. You do not want to force the reader to reread several pages to determine the case you are citing.

If the citation immediately follows the previous full case reference you may use the short form, *id.* However, this short form should not be used when multiple cases are cited in the prior reference.

When a government is the first party in an action, use the second party name in the short form.

How Would You Cite a Decision Reported Only on WESTLAW?

Rule 10.8.1(b) explains how an unpublished decision found only on either WESTLAW or LEXIS should be cited. For WESTLAW, first provide the name of the case and underline it. The next part of the citation is the docket number. In the example that follows, that number is No. 82-C4585. The next part of the citation is the year that the decision was issued. Next, indicate "WL" for WESTLAW and finally the WESTLAW number assigned to the case. In the parenthesis, place the date.

WESTLAW example: Clark Equipment Co. v. Lift Parts Mfg. Co., No. 82-C4585, 1985 WL 2917 (N.D. Ill. Oct. 1, 1985)

How Should a LEXIS Decision Be Cited?

For LEXIS citations, first state the name of the case, the docket number, the year of the decision, the name of the LEXIS file that contains the case, and the name LEXIS to indicate that the case is found on LEXIS. Next place the date in parentheses.

LEXIS example: Barrett Industrial Trucks v. Old Republic Insurance Co., No. 87-C9429, 1990 U.S. Dist. LEXIS 142 (N.D. Ill. Jan. 9, 1990)

If a decision is published in a hardcopy reporter, you should not use the WESTLAW or LEXIS citation.

How Would You Indicate a Page or Screen Number for the Case?

An asterisk should precede any screen or page numbers. See Rule 10.8.1.

WESTLAW screen no.:   Clark Equipment Co. v. Lift Parts Mfg. Co., No. 82-C4585, 1985 WL 2917 at *1 (N.D. Ill. Oct. 1, 1985)

LEXIS screen no.:   Barrett Industrial Trucks v. Old Republic Insurance Co., No. 87-C9429, 1990 U.S. Dist. LEXIS 142 at *1 (N.D. Ill. Jan. 9, 1990)

How Do You Cite Federal Statutes?

Always cite to the official statutory compilation. The first entry in the citation is the title number, then the abbreviation for the statutory compilation, and then the section or paragraph number. Bluebook Rule 12 details all of the various rules pertaining to citing statutes and codes, state or federal. Always cite to the year of the code's compilation, not the year that the particular statute section was enacted. For example:

12 U.S.C. § 211 (1988)

If a code section is well known by a popular name, then include the name in the citation. For example:

Strikebreaker Act 18 U.S.C. § 1231 (1988)

You may rely on an unofficial version for updating purposes. All of the following are citations to the identical statute.

26 U.S.C. § 61 (1988)
26 U.S.C.A. § 61 (West 1988 & Supp. 1994)
26 U.S.C.S. § 61 (Law. Co-op. 1988)

As with the U.S.C., the year included in the citation is the year that the code volume was published, not the year that the statute was enacted. In the U.S.C.A. example above, the first year mentioned, 1988, is the year that the particular volume of the code was published; the second date, 1994, is the year of the pocket part supplement that updates the code volume. The publication date is either printed on the title page of the bound volume or on the back of the title page.

How Do You Cite a Section of a Constitution, Federal or State?

Bluebook Rule 11 outlines the citation format. The United States Constitution citation refers to the particular article, section, and clause being used. For example:

U.S. Const. art. II, § 2, cl. 1

This cite is used when you are referring to the body of the Constitution. A special citation format is required when you are referring to an amendment. For example:

U.S. Const. amend. II

State constitutions are indicated by the name of the state in the Bluebook abbreviated format. Table T.1 indicates the accepted state name abbreviation; this is not necessarily the postal abbreviation. For example, the state of Washington's postal abbreviation is WA, but the Bluebook abbreviation is Wash. A section of the Washington state constitution would be cited as follows:

Wash. Const. art. I, § 2

Years or dates are not included in citations to constitutions, state or federal, that are current. Parenthetical notations after the citation indicate the year a constitutional provision was repealed or amended. An example is the Eighteenth Amendment to the U.S. Constitution prohibiting the sale of liquor. The Twenty-First Amendment later repealed this. Bluebook Rule 11 provides the following example using the Prohibition amendment:

U.S. Const. amend. XVIII (repealed 1933)

How Do You Cite to a Legislative History of a Statute?

Bluebook Rule 13 details the citation format for all of the components of the legislative process: the bill, the committee report, the debates, and transcripts of the hearings.

How Are the *Code of Federal Regulations* and the *Federal Register* Cited?

Rule 14 of the Bluebook details the citation format for administrative and executive materials, which include the *Code of Federal Regulations* and the *Federal Register*. Title 21 of the C.F.R. part 101 from 1992 is cited as:

21 C.F.R. pt. 101 (1992)

If you were citing to Title 21 of the C.F.R. § 101.62 from 1993 it would be written as:

21 C.F.R. § 101.62 (1993)

A *Federal Register* entry from volume 58, beginning on page 26121, from April 30, 1993 would be cited as:

58 Fed. Reg. 26121 (1993)

As you can see, the specific calendar date is not cited, just the year.

How Would You Cite to a Legal Dictionary?

The information for the correct citation format for dictionaries is found in Rule 15.7 of the Bluebook. For example:

Ballentine's Law Dictionary 1190 (3d ed. 1969)
Black's Law Dictionary 712 (6th ed. 1990)

How Are Legal Encyclopedias Cited?

Bluebook Rule 15.7 discusses legal encyclopedias. A citation to the discussion of easements would be as follows:

25 Am. Jur. 2d Easements and Licenses § 93 (1966 & Supp. 1993)
28 C.J.S. Easements § 18 (1941 & Supp. 1993)

How Do You Cite to *American Law Reports*?

This is found in Rule 16.5.5 of the Bluebook:

William B. Johnson, Annotation, Locating Easement of Way Created by Necessity, 36 A.L.R.4th 769 (1985)

How Do You Cite to a Law Review or Law Journal?

Bluebook Rule 16 indicates the citation form for a law review article as follows:

Thomas W. Merrill, Property Rules, Liability Rules, and Adverse Possession, 79 Nw. U. L. Rev. 1122 (1985)

The abbreviation for the journal name is found in Table 13 of the Bluebook. A legal newspaper is cited according to Rule 16.4:

David Bailey, Call for Video Reenactment of Jury Rejected, Chi. D. L. Bull., Nov. 1, 1993, at 1

How Are the Restatements Cited?

Bluebook Rule 12.8.5 indicates that the Restatements are cited as follows:

Restatement (Second) of Contracts § 235 (1979)

Note that the year is the year that the Restatement section was adopted. This information is given on the title page of every volume of the Restatements. When you are citing to a comment that follows the Restatement section, Rule 3.5 of the Bluebook applies. For example:

Restatement (Second) of Contracts § 235 cmt. a (1979)

How Would You Cite an Ethics Rule Found in the ABA Model Code of Professional Responsibility?

The rules for citation of ethics codes are found in Bluebook Rule 12.8.6. Rule 1.10 of the ABA Model Code would be cited as follows:

Model Code of Professional Responsibility Rule 1.10 (1992)

How Would You Cite an ABA Ethics Opinion?

The rules for citation of ethics opinions are contained in Bluebook Rule 12.8.6. For example:

ABA Comm. on Professional Ethics and Grievances, Informal Op. 88-1526 (1988)

How Would You Cite the Various Federal Rules?

Cite the federal rules in accordance with Bluebook Rule 12.8.3 as follows:

Fed. R. Civ. P. 56
Fed. R. Crim. P. 1
Fed. R. App. P. 26
Fed. R. Evid. 803

The local appellate court rules also are cited based on the same rule.

7th Cir. R. 1

Index